鳥 山 明

In this volume, Son Goku dies. I don't have that much senti-
ment for the characters I draw, but I feel a bit sad about the
death of a character that I have been drawing for almost 10
years. I tried to think of other scenarios for the story, but
Goku dying was the best one. I tried not to be too somber
about it. But still…I'm sorry, Son Goku! Forgive me!

—*Akira Toriyama, 1993*

Widely known all over the world for his playful, innovative
storytelling and humorous, distinctive art style, **Dragon Ball**
creator Akira Toriyama is also known in his native Japan for
the wildly popular **Dr. Slump**, his previous manga series
about the adventures of a mad scientist and his android
"daughter." His hit series **Dragon Ball** ran from 1984 to
1995 in Shueisha's **Weekly Shonen Jump** magazine. He is
also known for his design work on video games such as
Dragon Warrior, **Chrono Trigger** and **Tobal No. 1**. His
recent manga works include **Cowa!**, **Kajika**, **Sand Land**,
Neko Majin, and a children's book, **Toccio the Angel**. He
lives with his family in Japan.

DRAGON BALL Z VOL.19
The SHONEN JUMP Manga Edition

This graphic novel contains material that was originally published in
English in **SHONEN JUMP** #25-28.

STORY AND ART BY
AKIRA TORIYAMA

English Adaptation/Gerard Jones
Translation/Lillian Olsen
Touch-up Art & Lettering/Wayne Truman
Design/Sean Lee
Editor/Jason Thompson

Editor in Chief, Books/Alvin Lu
Editor in Chief, Magazines/Marc Weidenbaum
VP of Publishing Licensing/Rika Inouye
VP of Sales/Gonzalo Ferreyra
Sr. VP of Marketing/Liza Coppola
Publisher/Hyoe Narita

In the original Japanese edition, DRAGON BALL and DRAGON BALL Z
are known collectively as the 42-volume series DRAGON BALL. The
English DRAGON BALL Z was originally volumes 17-42 of the Japanese
DRAGON BALL.

Printed in the U.S.A.

Published by VIZ Media, LLC
P.O. Box 77010
San Francisco, CA 94107

SHONEN JUMP Manga Edition
10 9 8 7 6 5
First printing, March 2005
Fifth printing, March 2008

www.viz.com

PARENTAL ADVISORY
DRAGON BALL Z is rated A for All Ages.
Contains fantasy violence. Recommended
for any age group.
ratings.viz.com

THE WORLD'S
MOST POPULAR MANGA
www.shonenjump.com

SHONEN JUMP MANGA

Vol. 19

DB: 35 of 42

STORY AND ART BY
AKIRA TORIYAMA

THE MAIN CHARACTERS

BULMA

Goku's oldest friend, Bulma is a scientific genius.

KAIÔ-SAMA

Also known as the "Lord of Worlds", Kaiô-sama is one of the deities of the Dragon Ball universe. He lives on a private planet in the Other World.

SON GOHAN

Goku's young son, a half-human, half-Saiyan. Is he truly more powerful than his father?

SON GOKU

The greatest martial artist on Earth, he is one of the last of the Saiyans, an almost extinct alien race. Like Trunks and Vegeta, he can power-up by transforming into a "Super Saiyan." He also has the power to teleport.

KURIRIN

Goku's former martial arts schoolmate.

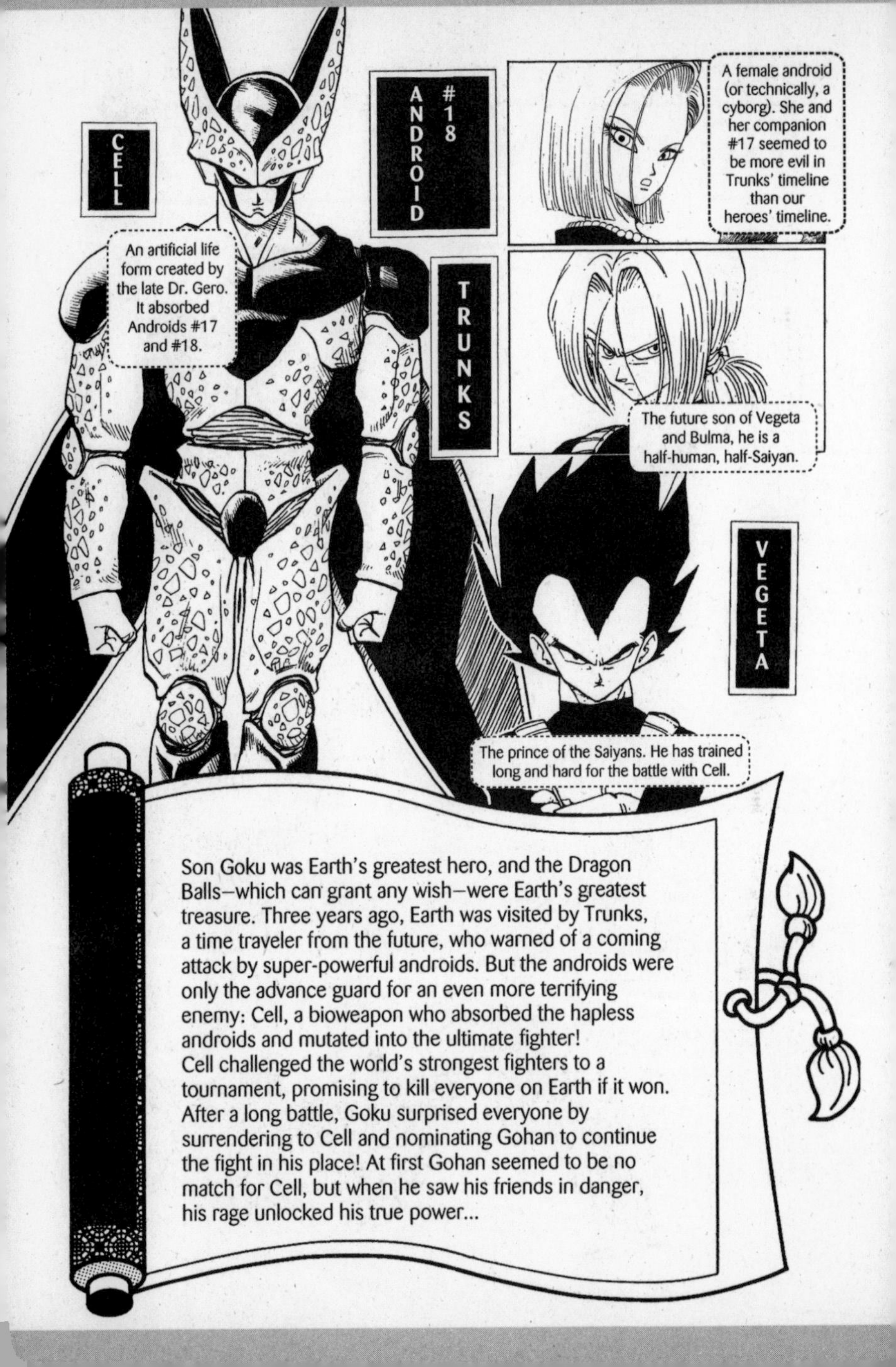

ANDROID #18
A female android (or technically, a cyborg). She and her companion #17 seemed to be more evil in Trunks' timeline than our heroes' timeline.
TRUNKS
The future son of Vegeta and Bulma, he is a half-human, half-Saiyan.
VEGETA
The prince of the Saiyans. He has trained long and hard for the battle with Cell.
CELL
An artificial life form created by the late Dr. Gero. It absorbed Androids #17 and #18.

Son Goku was Earth's greatest hero, and the Dragon Balls—which can grant any wish—were Earth's greatest treasure. Three years ago, Earth was visited by Trunks, a time traveler from the future, who warned of a coming attack by super-powerful androids. But the androids were only the advance guard for an even more terrifying enemy: Cell, a bioweapon who absorbed the hapless androids and mutated into the ultimate fighter!

Cell challenged the world's strongest fighters to a tournament, promising to kill everyone on Earth if it won. After a long battle, Goku surprised everyone by surrendering to Cell and nominating Gohan to continue the fight in his place! At first Gohan seemed to be no match for Cell, but when he saw his friends in danger, his rage unlocked his true power...

DRAGON BALL Z 19

IT'S THE CONTENTS!

DRAGON BALL

DBZ:215 • Cell vs. Gohan

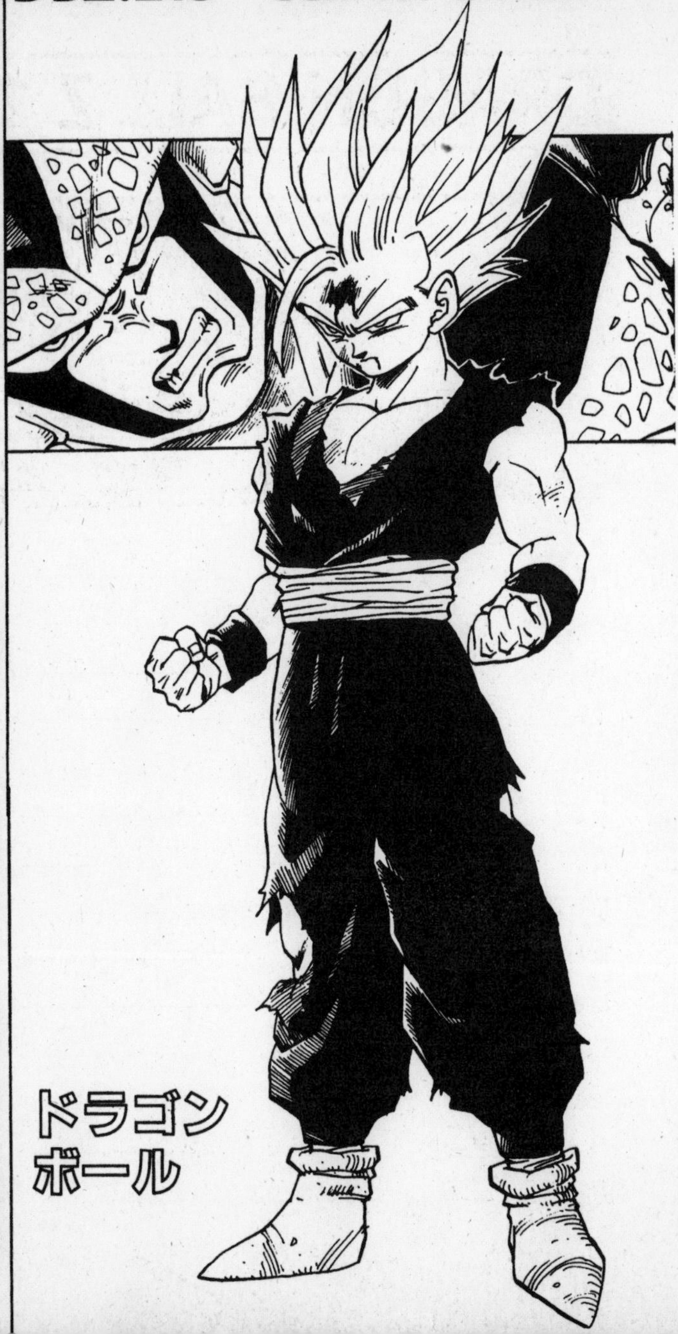

ドラゴン
ボール

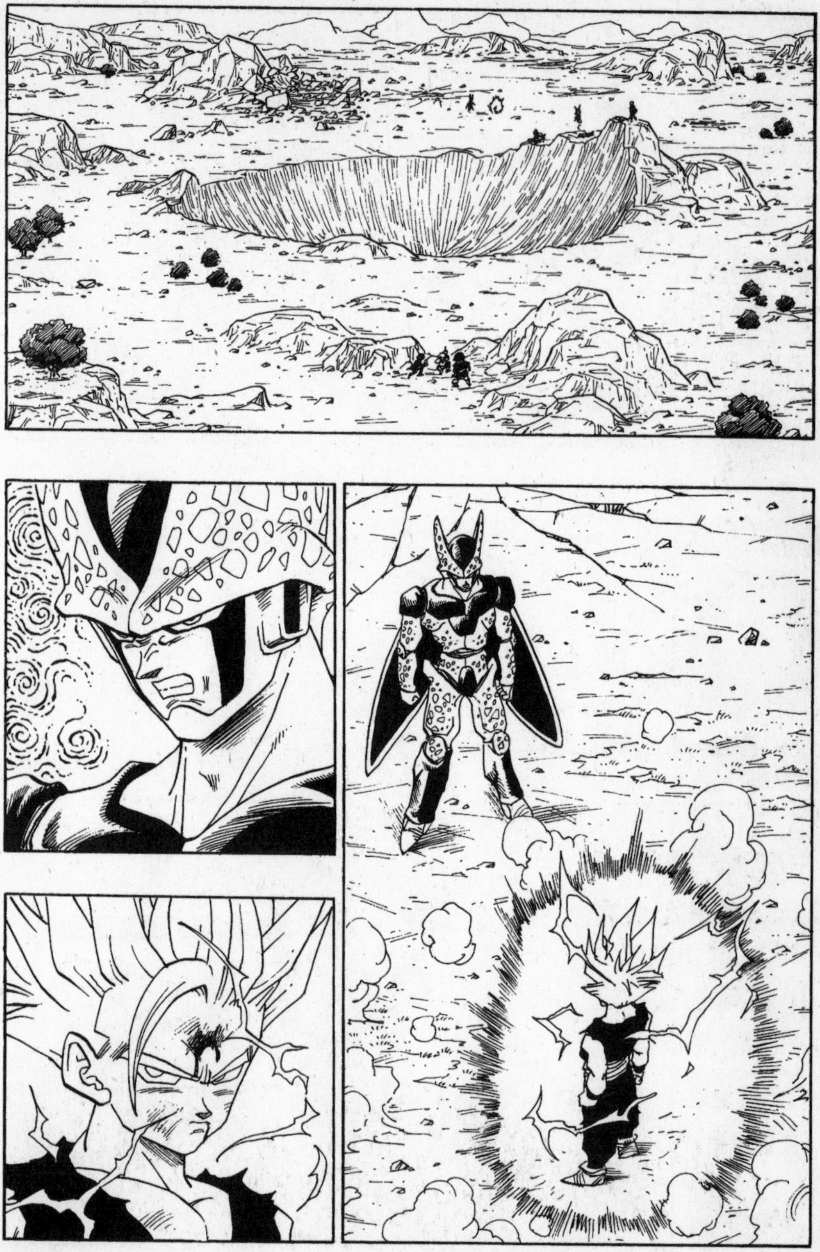

READ THIS WAY

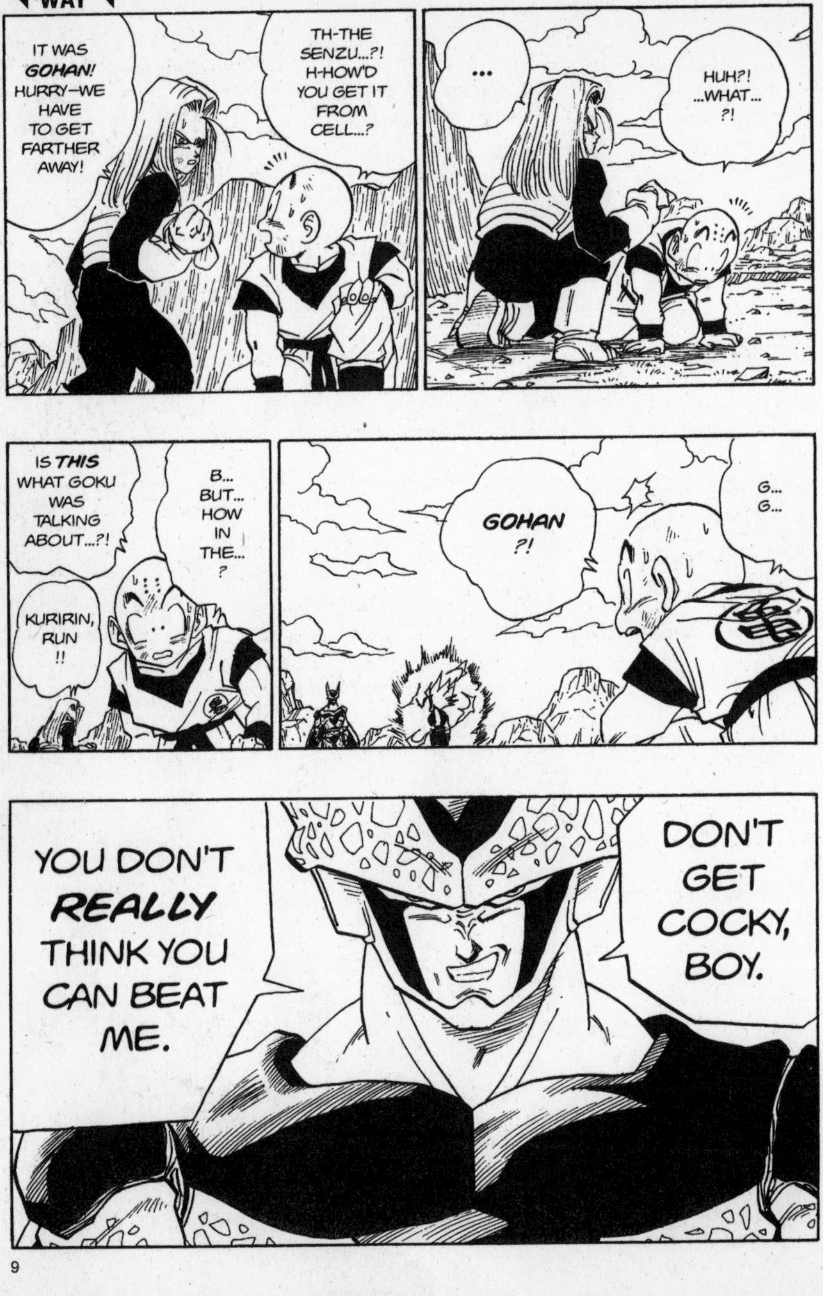
HUH?! ...WHAT... ?!
...
TH-THE SENZU...?! H-HOW'D YOU GET IT FROM CELL...?
IT WAS GOHAN! HURRY—WE HAVE TO GET FARTHER AWAY!
G... G...
GOHAN ?!
B... BUT... HOW IN THE...?
IS THIS WHAT GOKU WAS TALKING ABOUT...?!
KURIRIN, RUN !!
DON'T GET COCKY, BOY.
YOU DON'T REALLY THINK YOU CAN BEAT ME.

READ THIS WAY

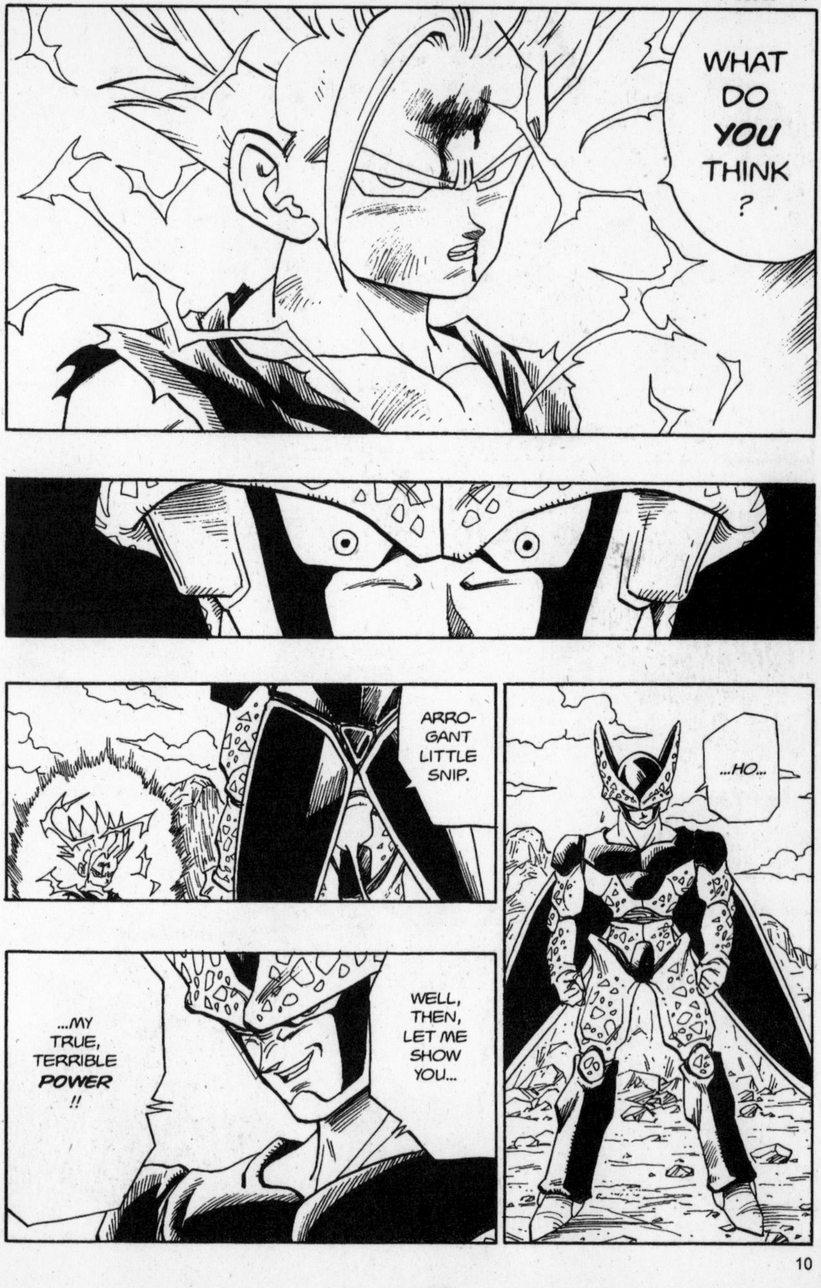
WHAT DO *YOU* THINK ?
...HO...
ARRO- GANT LITTLE SNIP.
WELL, THEN, LET ME SHOW YOU...
...MY TRUE, TERRIBLE ***POWER*** !!

« READ THIS WAY «

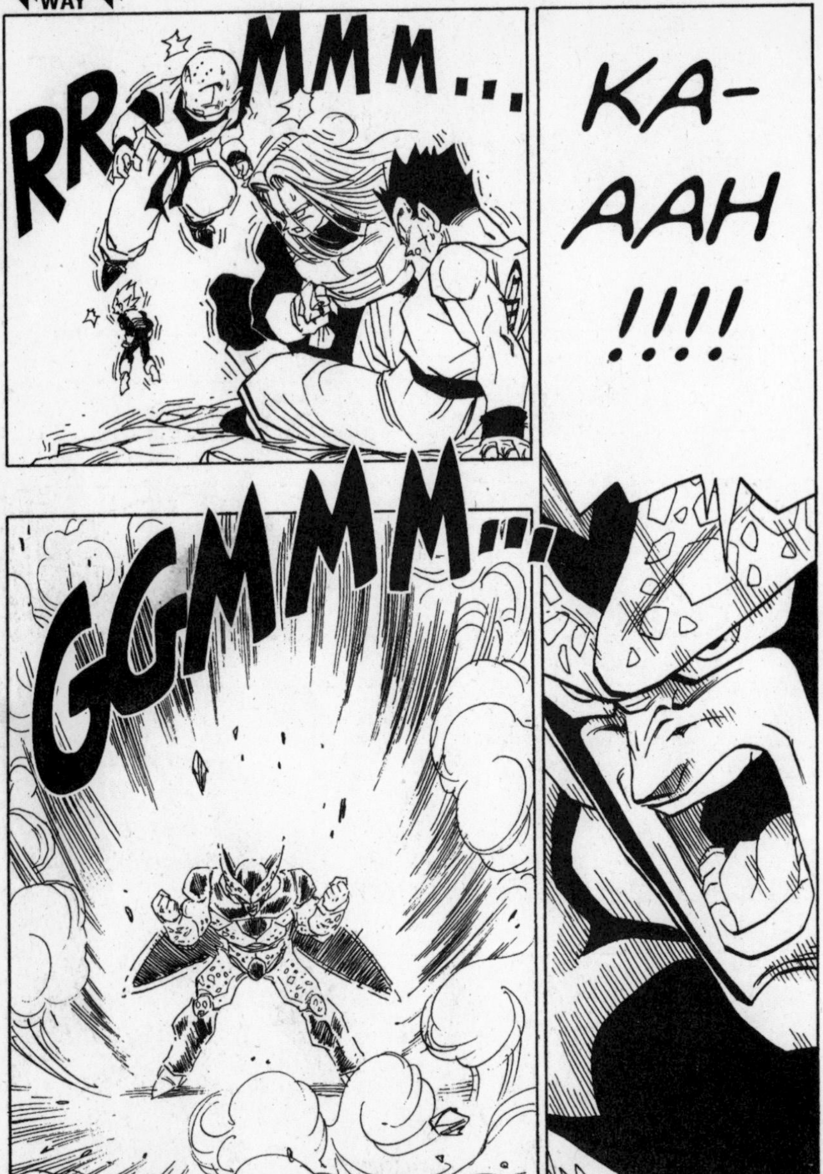
KA-
AAH
!!!!
RRMMMM...
GGMMMM...

READ THIS WAY

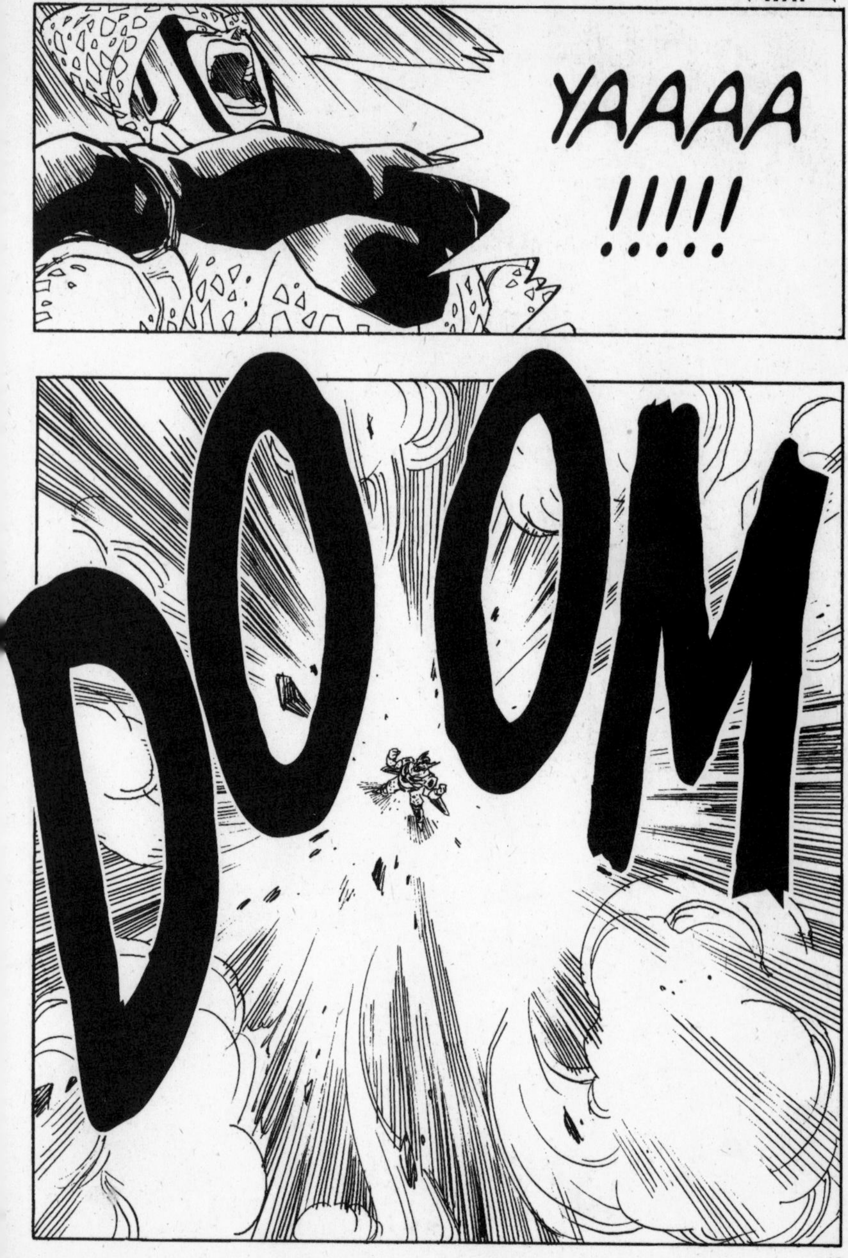
YAAAA!!!!!
DOOM

READ THIS WAY

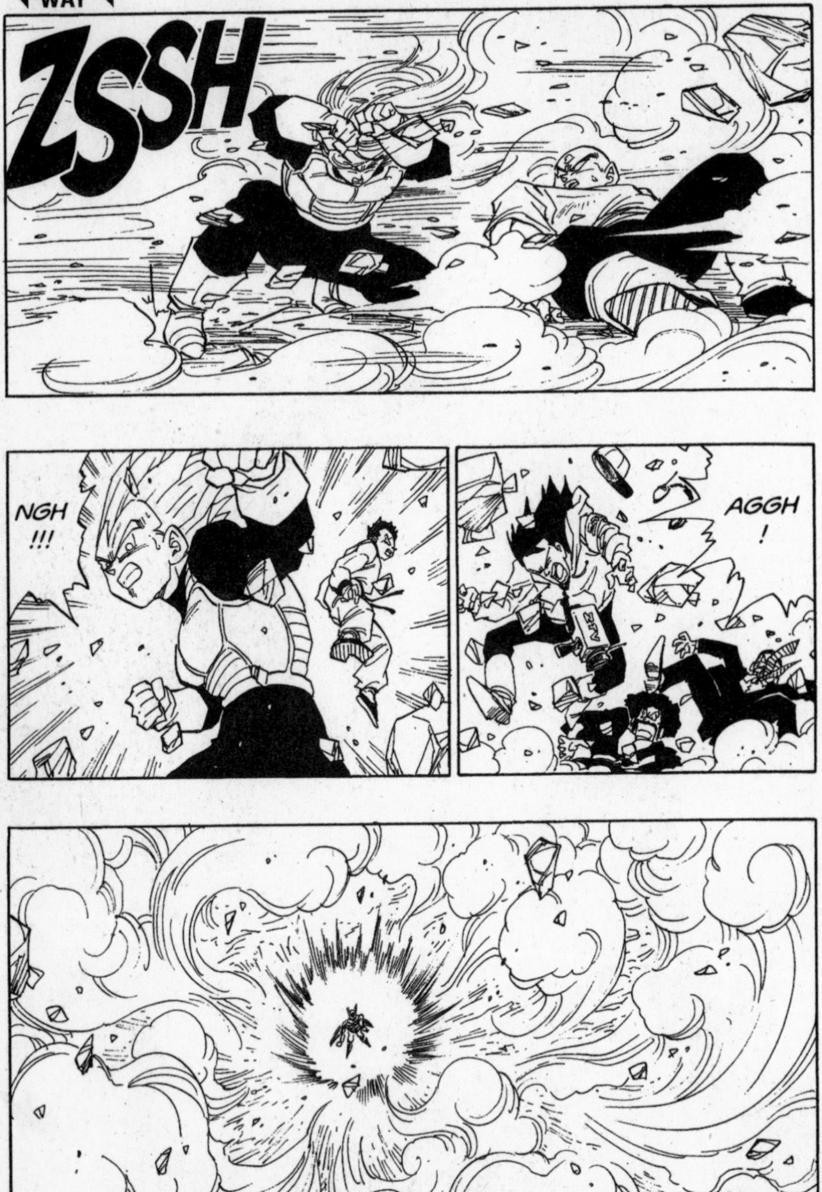
ZSSH
AGGH !
NGH !!!

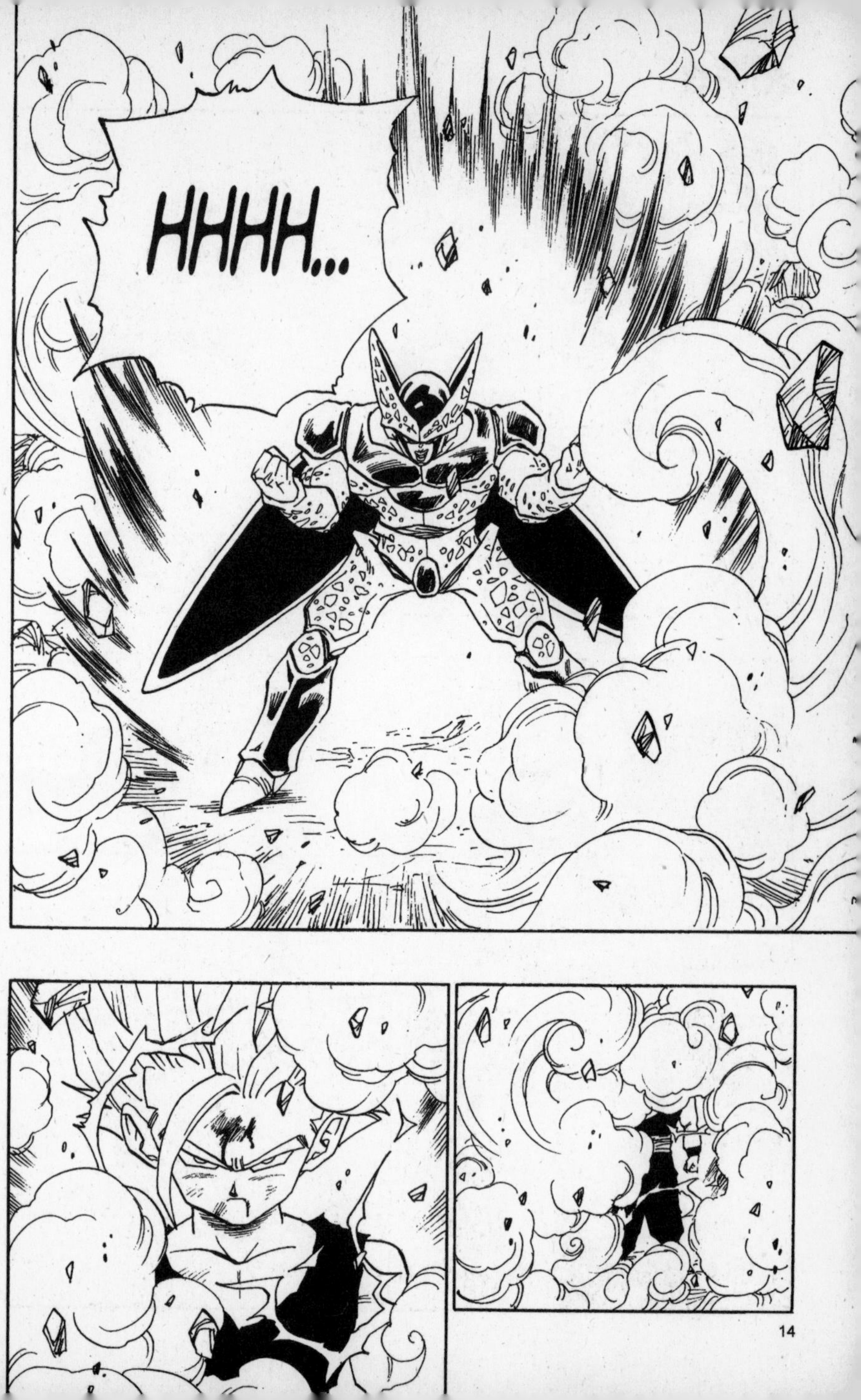
HHHH...

THIS...IS CELL'S FULL POWER AT LAST...

I FEEL THE WHOLE PLANET TREMBLING...

WHOOPEE.

WELL? NOW YOU KNOW!

...HEH HEH HEH.

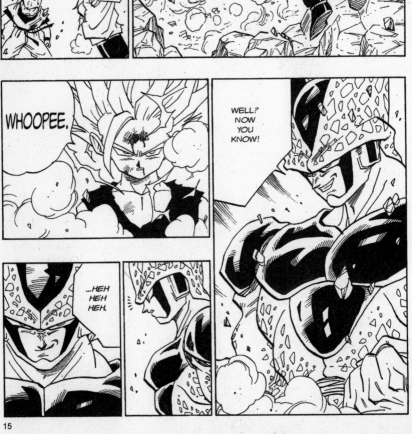

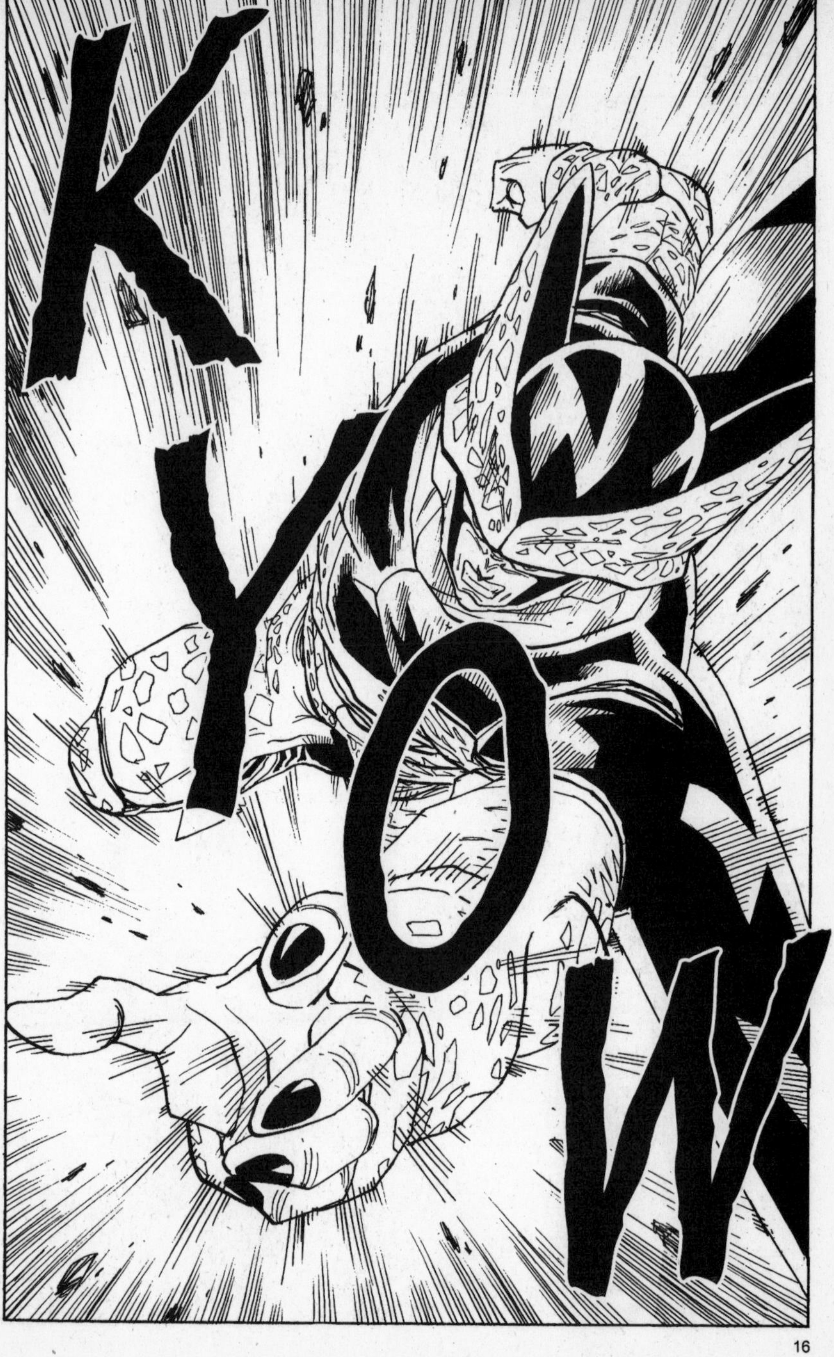
KYOOW

READ THIS WAY

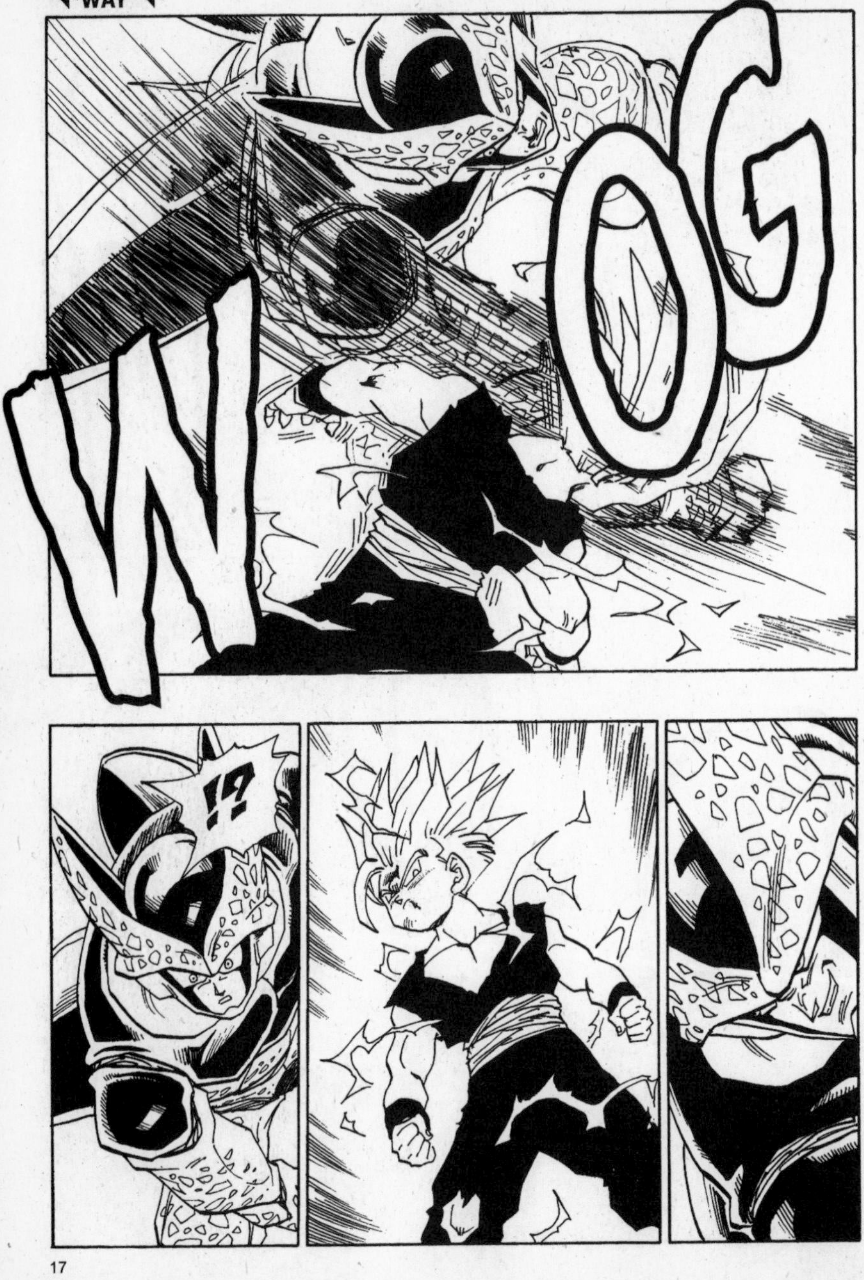
WOOG
!?

READ THIS WAY

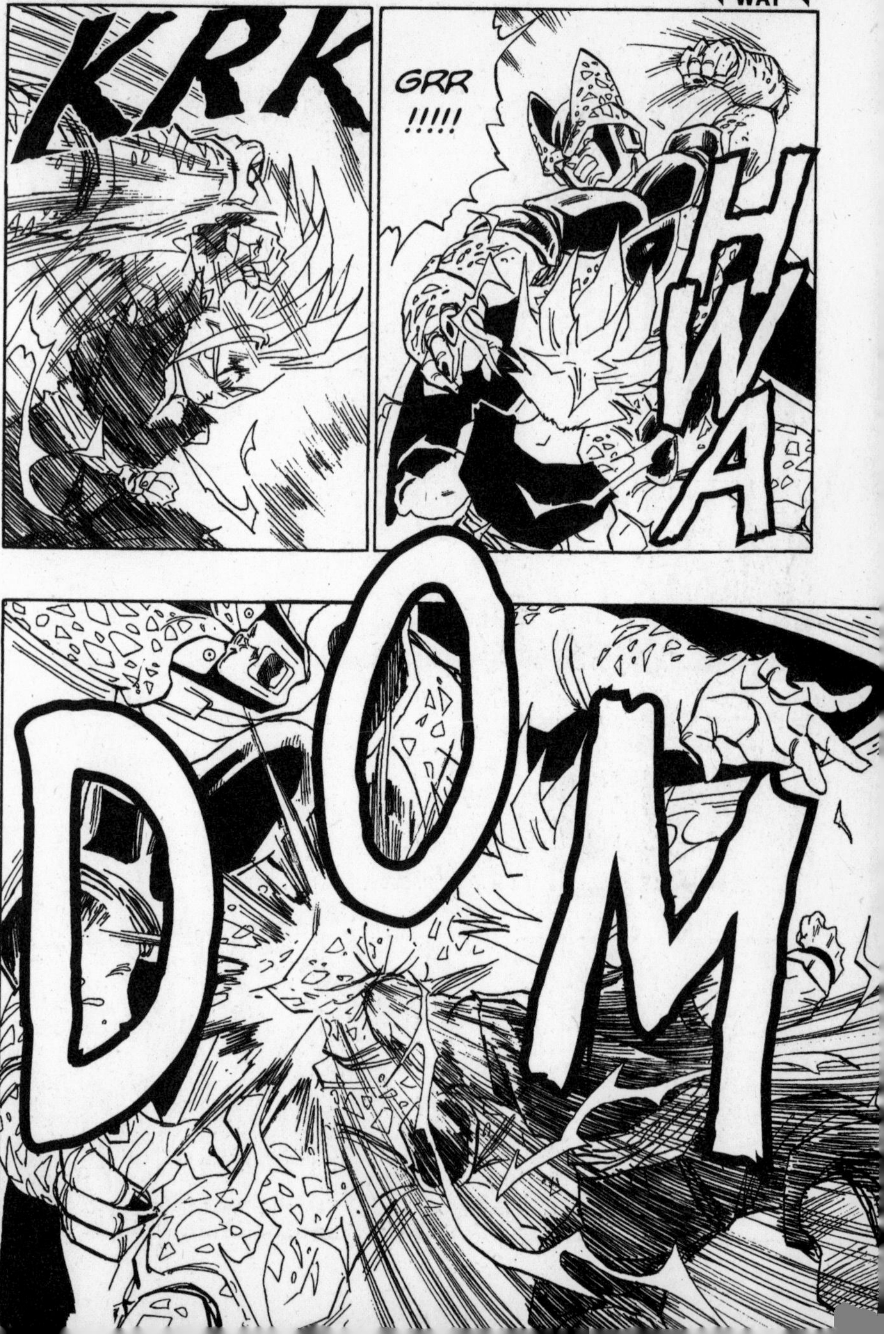
GRR !!!!!
HWA
KRK
DOM

READ THIS WAY

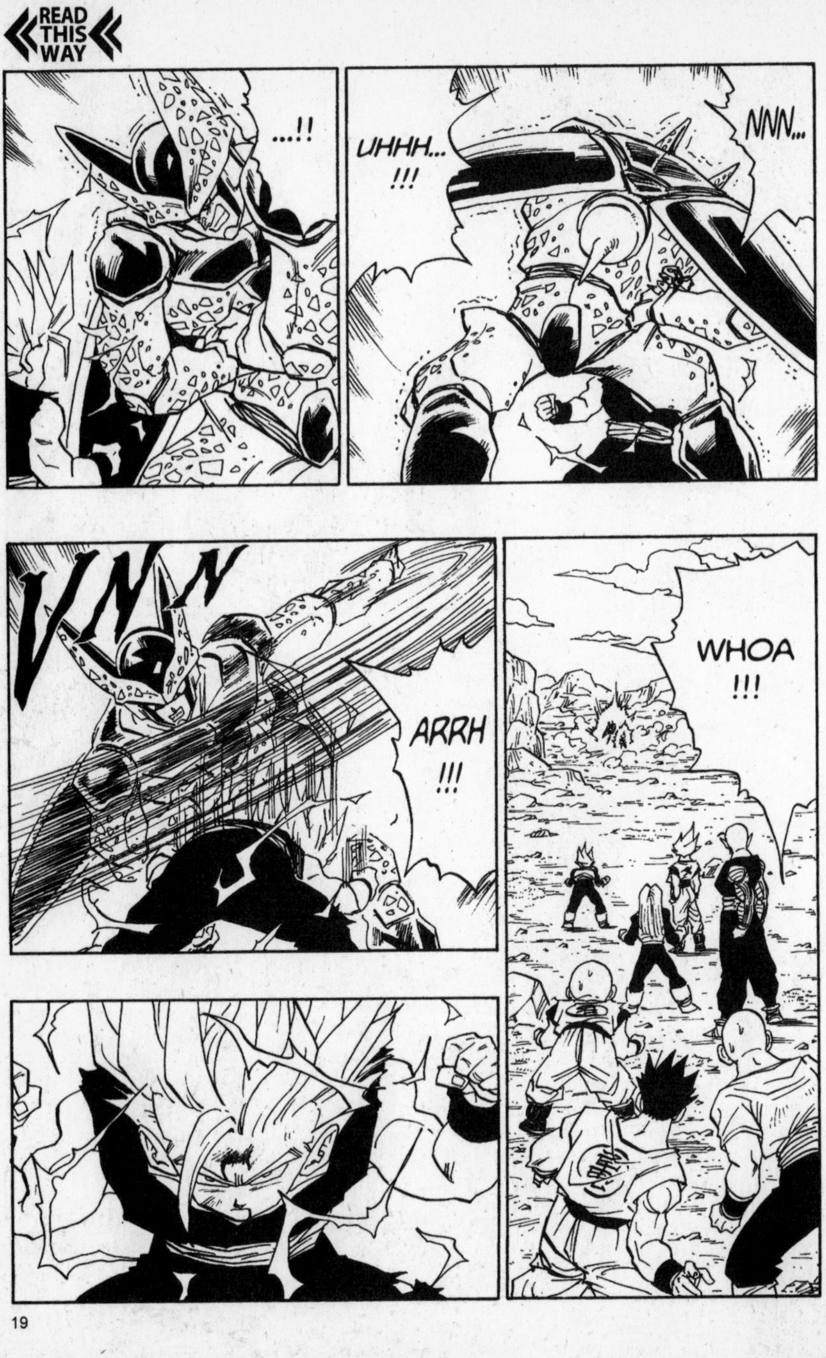
NNN...
UHHH... !!!
...!!
WHOA !!!
ARRH !!!
VNN

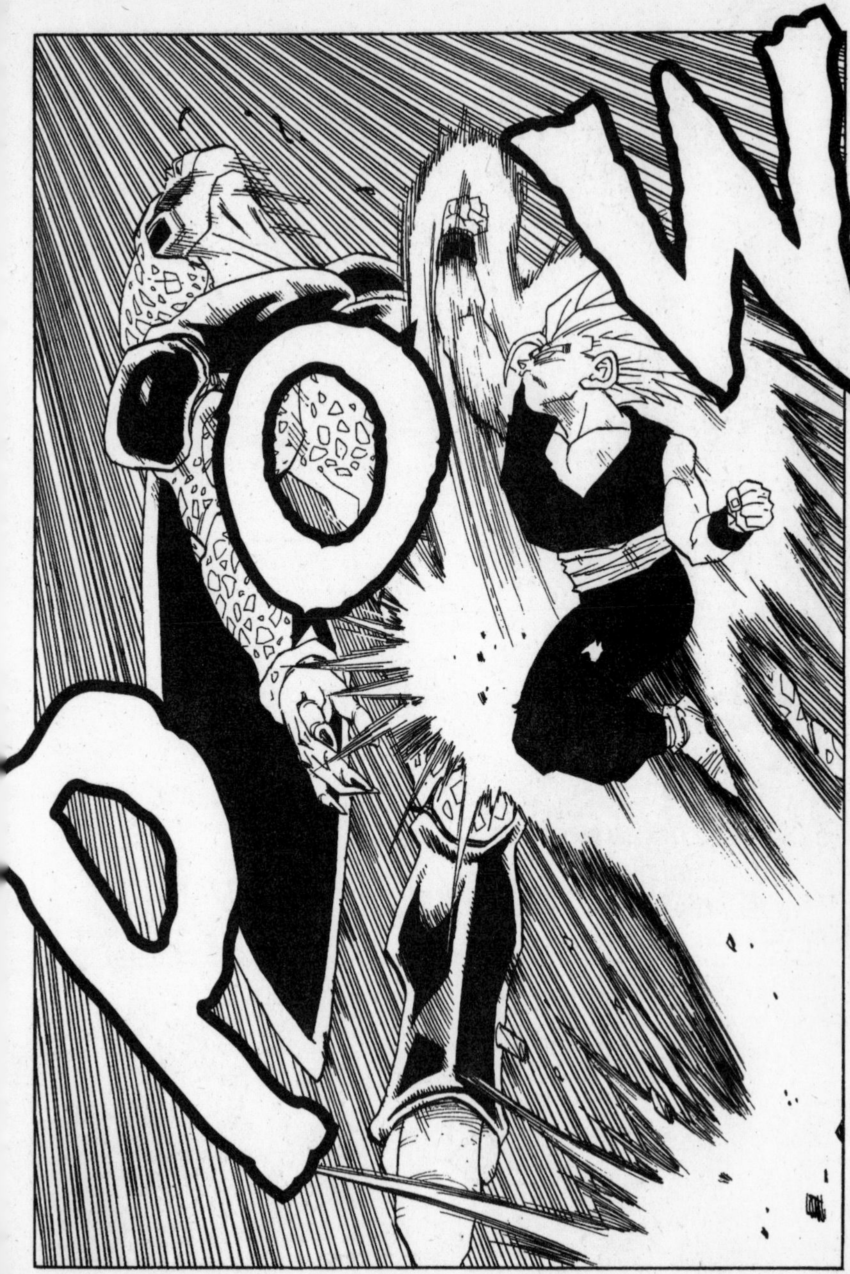

READ THIS WAY

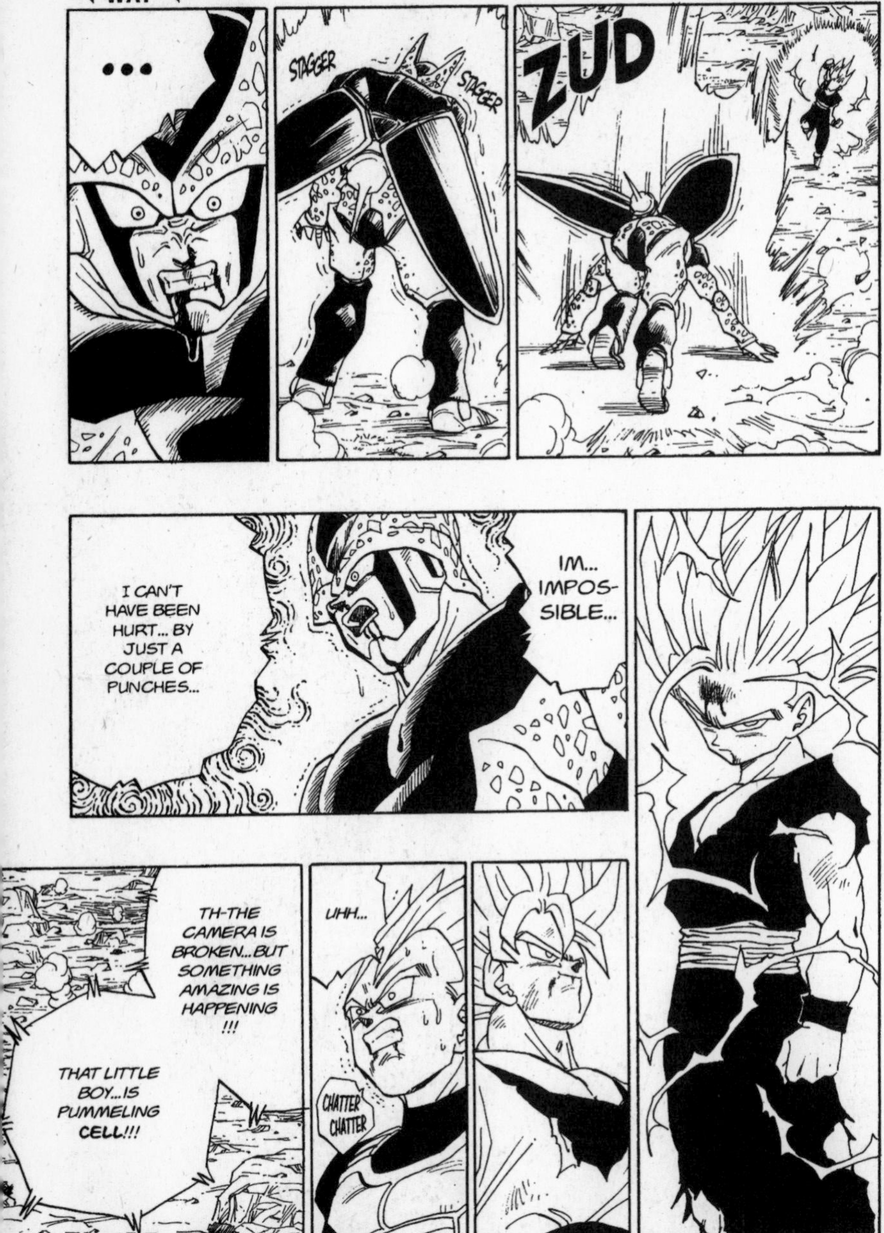
ZUD
STAGGER
STAGGER
...
IM... IMPOSSIBLE...
I CAN'T HAVE BEEN HURT... BY JUST A COUPLE OF PUNCHES...
UHH...
CHATTER CHATTER
TH-THE CAMERA IS BROKEN...BUT SOMETHING AMAZING IS HAPPENING!!!
THAT LITTLE BOY...IS PUMMELING CELL!!!

NEXT: Target: Earth!

DBZ: 216
The Ultimate Kamehameha

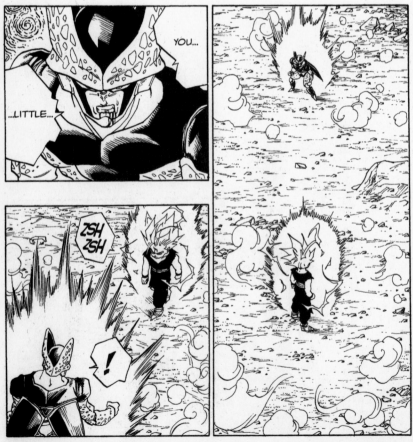

READ THIS WAY

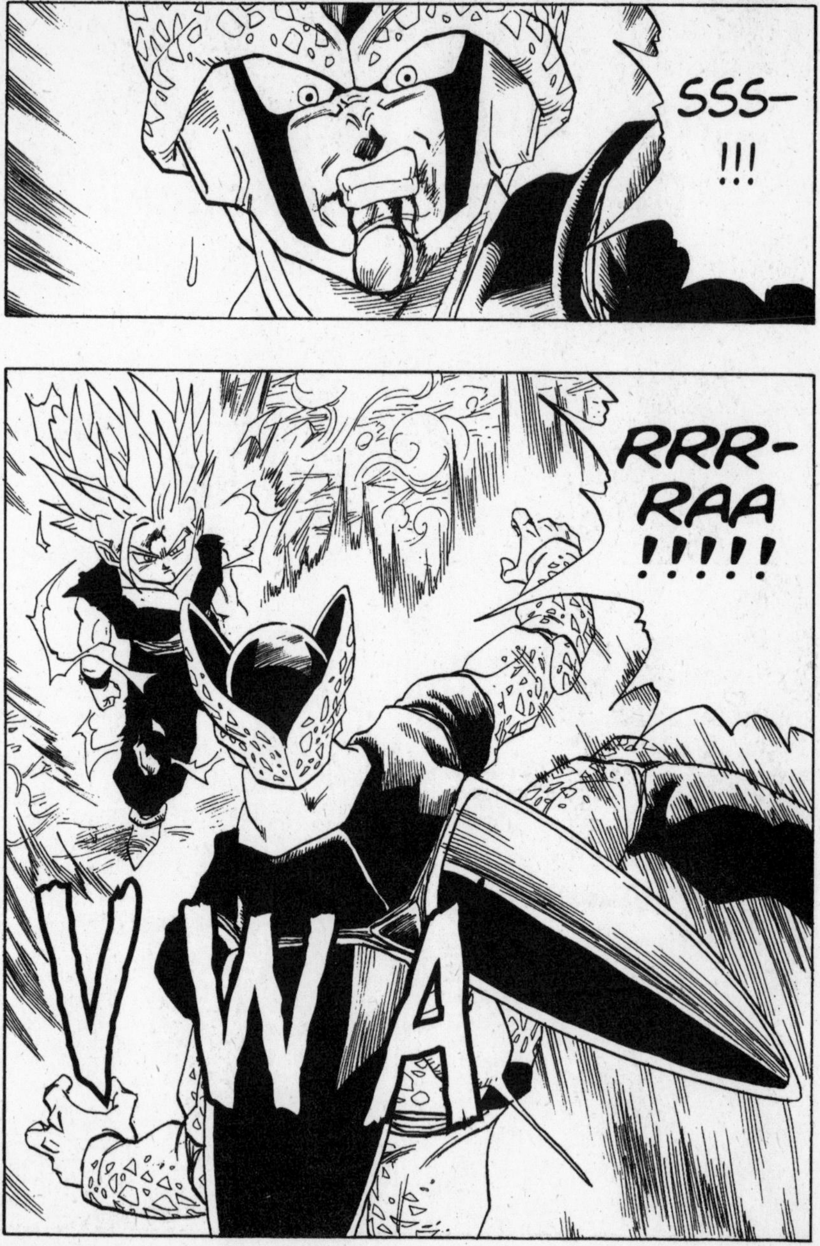
SSS-
!!!
RRR-
RAA
!!!!!
VWA

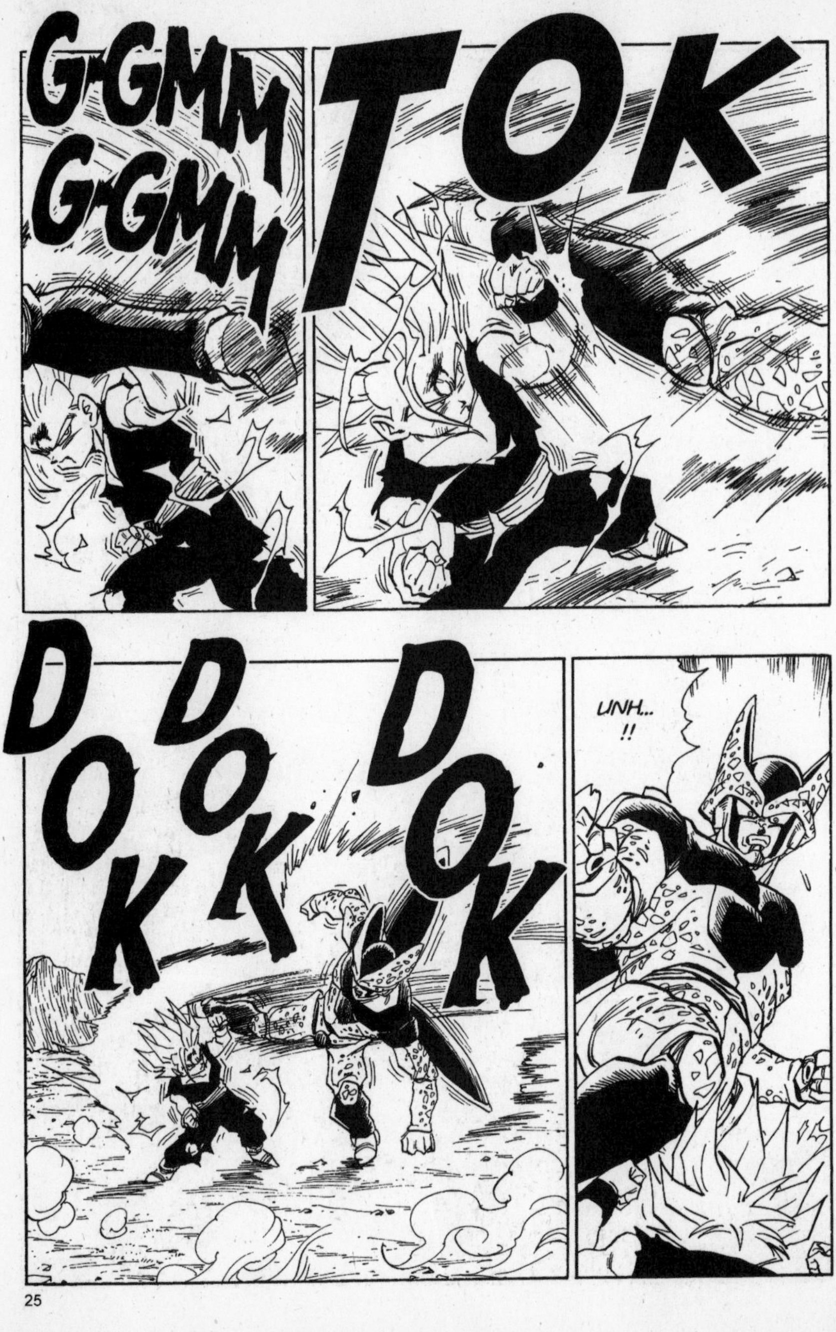
TOK
G-GMM G-GMM
UNH... !!
DOK DOK DOK

READ THIS WAY

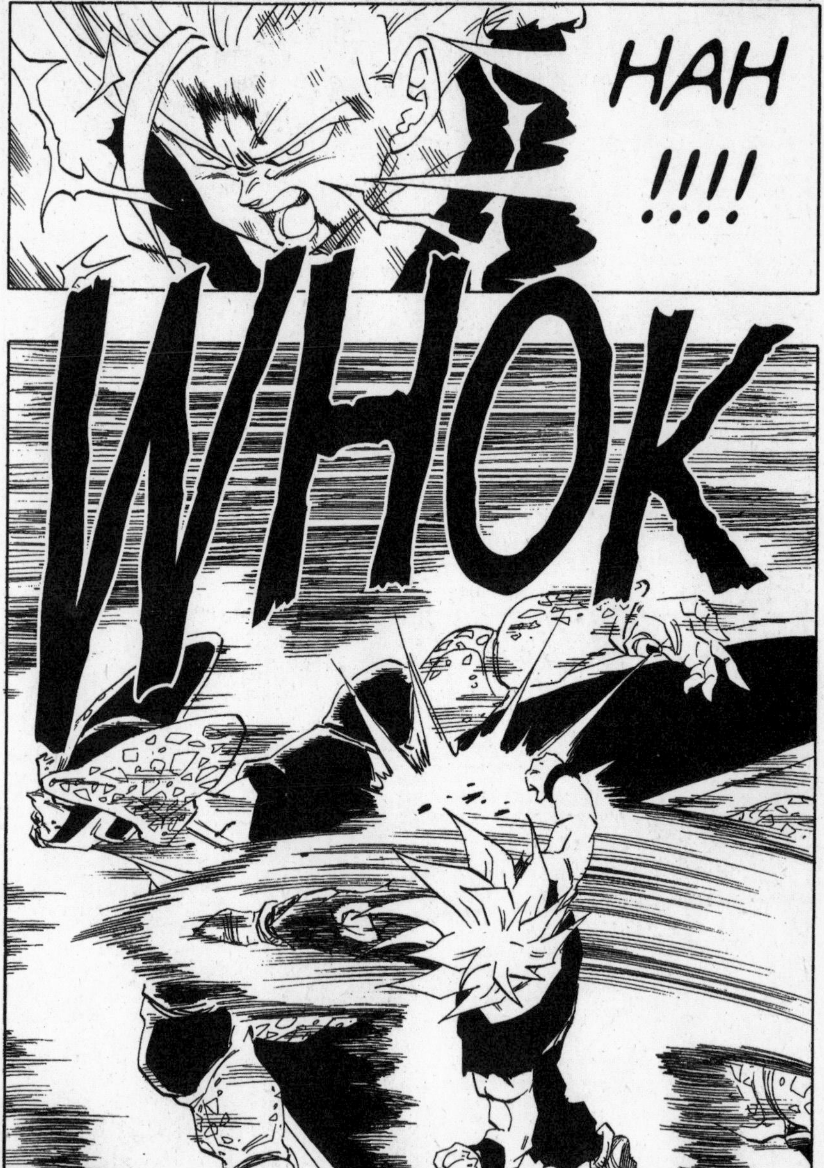
HAH !!!!
WHOK

READ THIS WAY

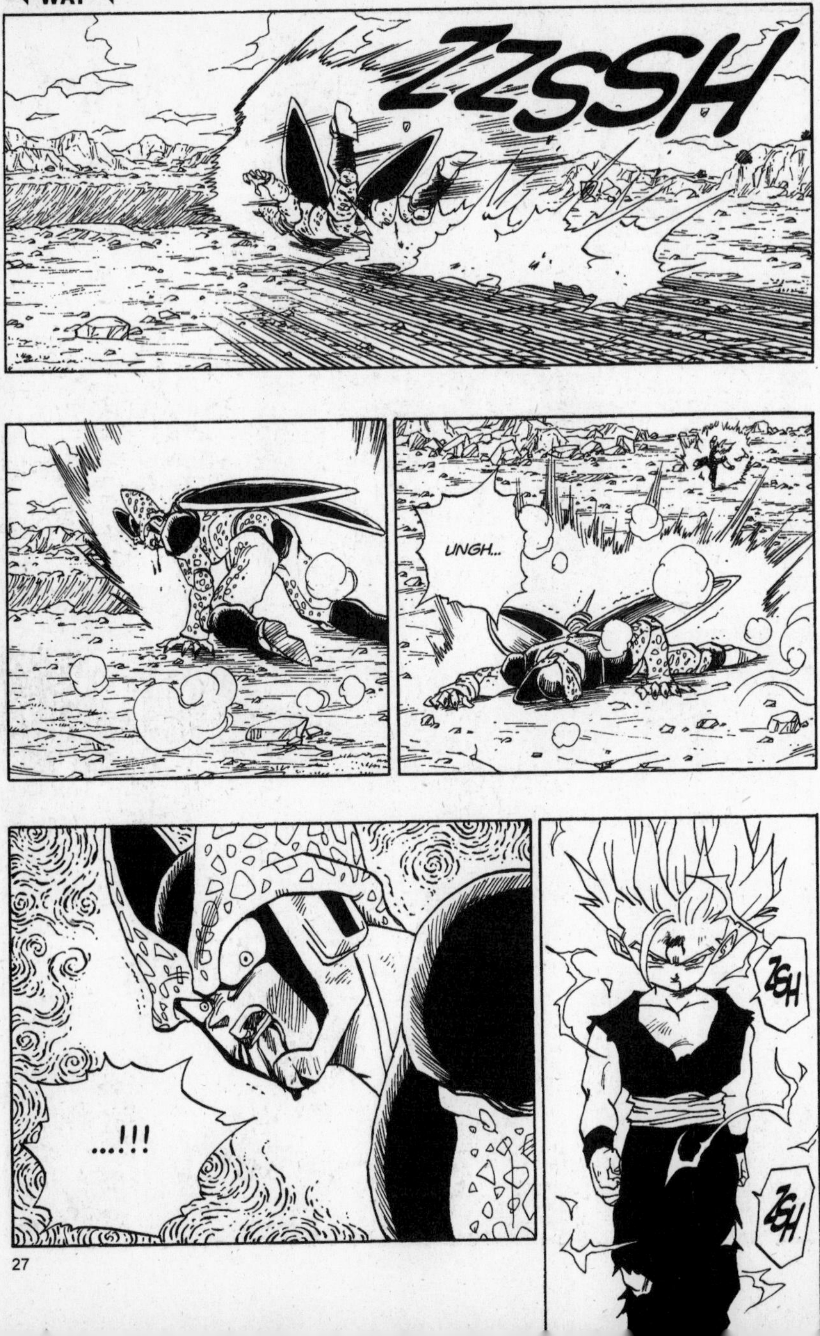
ZZSSH
UNGH...
ZSH
ZSH
...!!!

READ THIS WAY

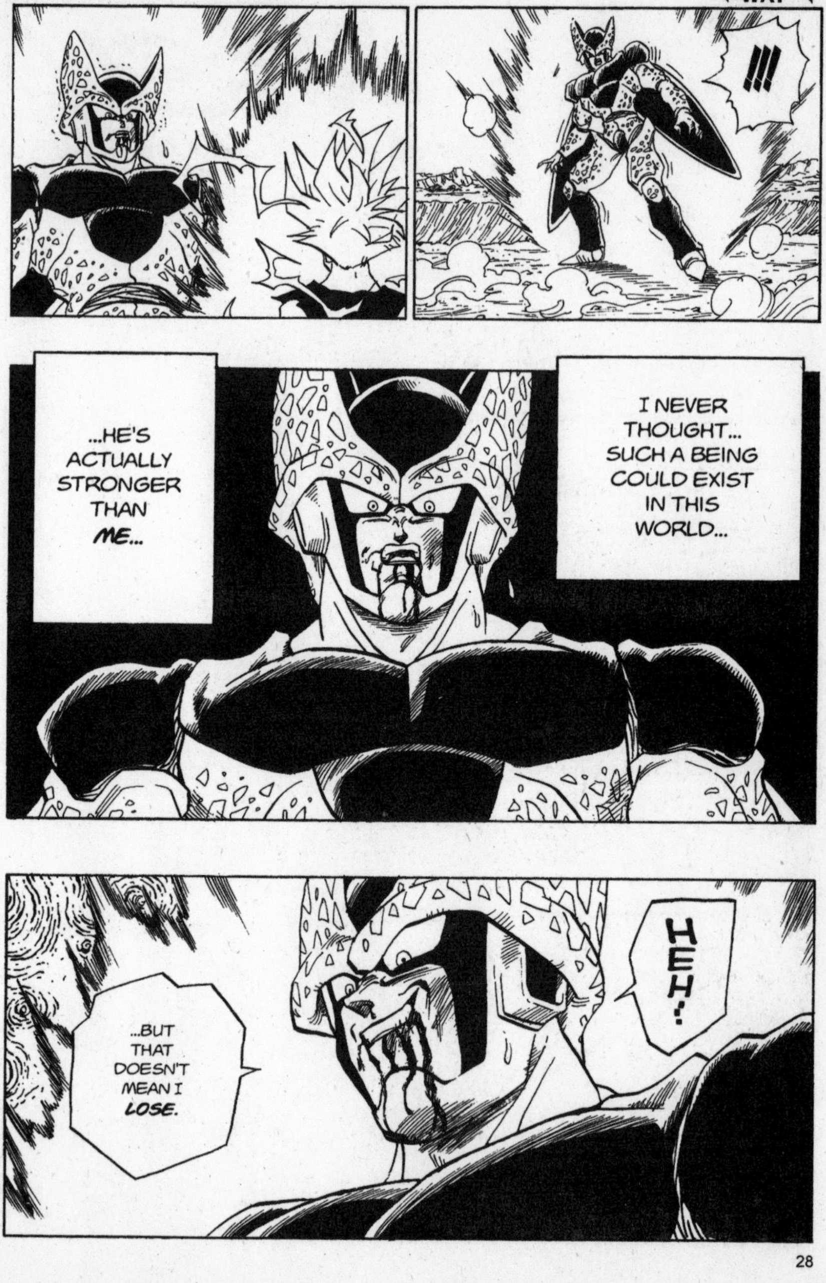
!!!
I NEVER THOUGHT... SUCH A BEING COULD EXIST IN THIS WORLD...
...HE'S ACTUALLY STRONGER THAN *ME*...
HEH!
...BUT THAT DOESN'T MEAN I *LOSE*.

READ THIS WAY

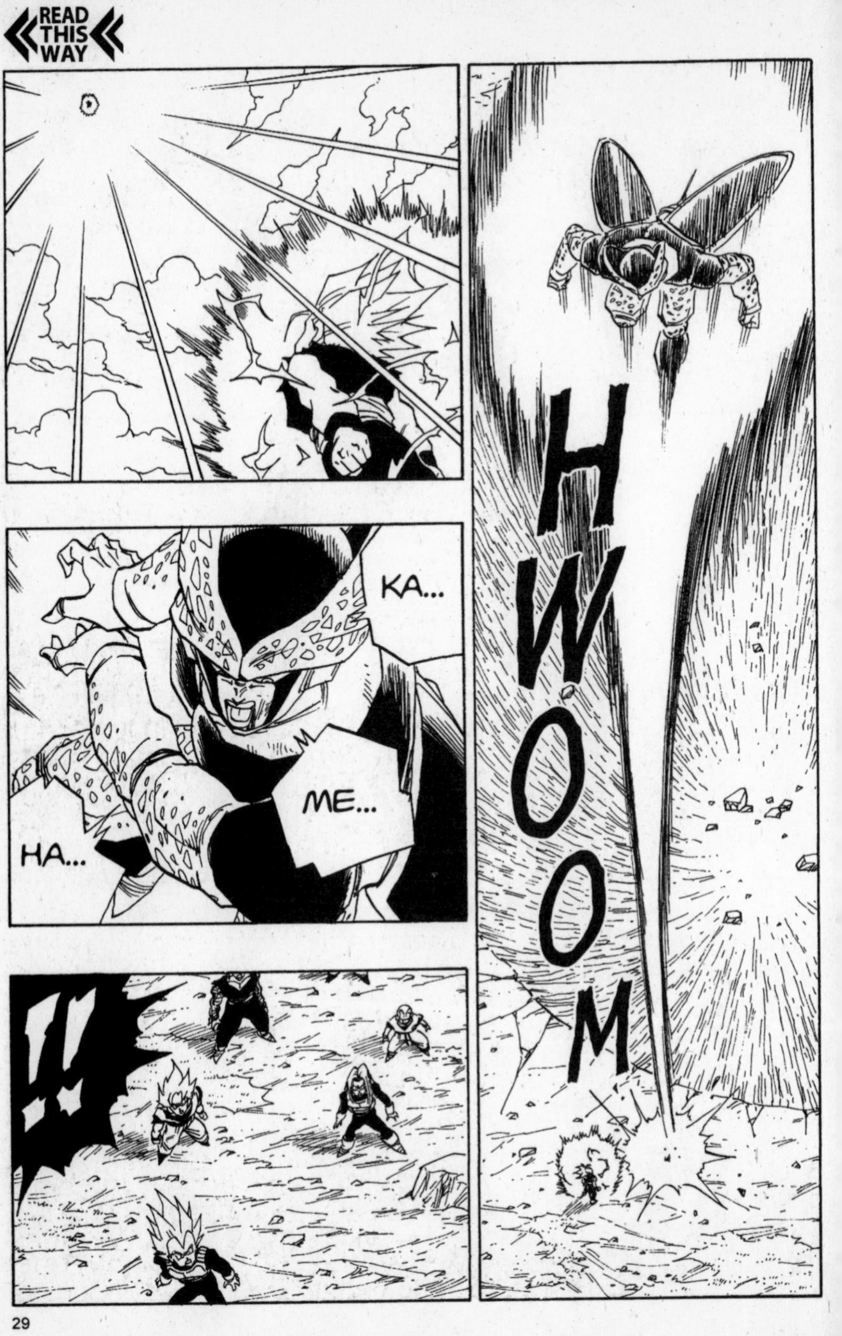
HWOOM
KA...
ME...
HA...
!!

READ THIS WAY

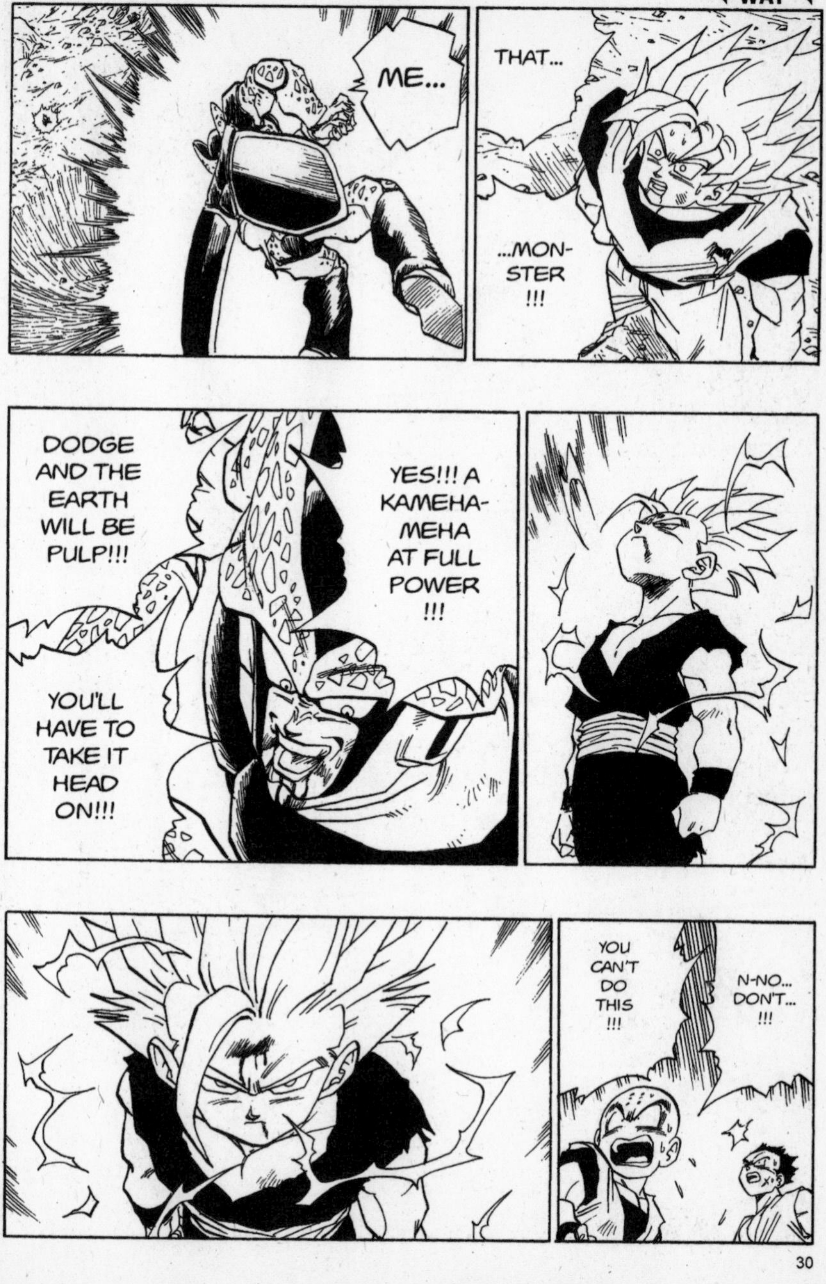
THAT...
...MON-STER!!!
ME...
YES!!! A KAMEHA-MEHA AT FULL POWER!!!
DODGE AND THE EARTH WILL BE PULP!!!
YOU'LL HAVE TO TAKE IT HEAD ON!!!
N-NO... DON'T...!!!
YOU CAN'T DO THIS!!!

READ THIS WAY

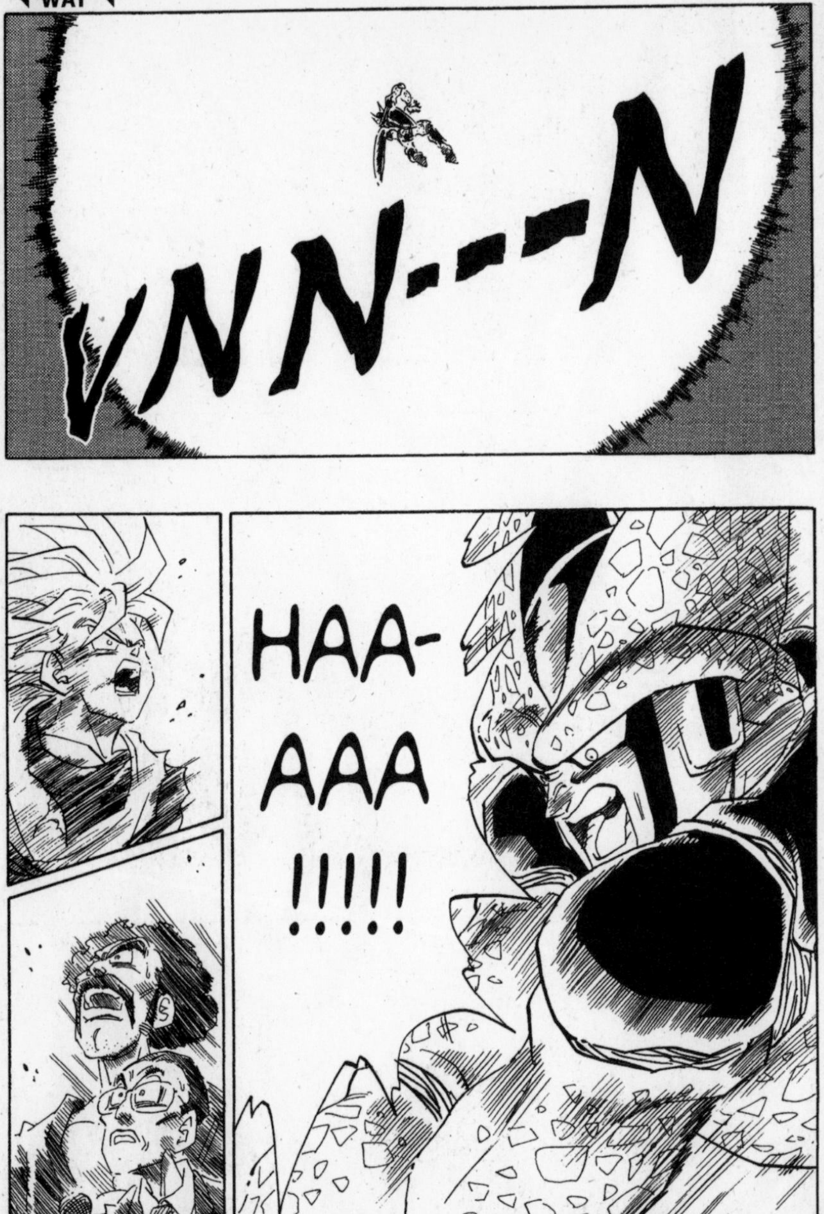
VNN--N
HAA-AAA!!!!!

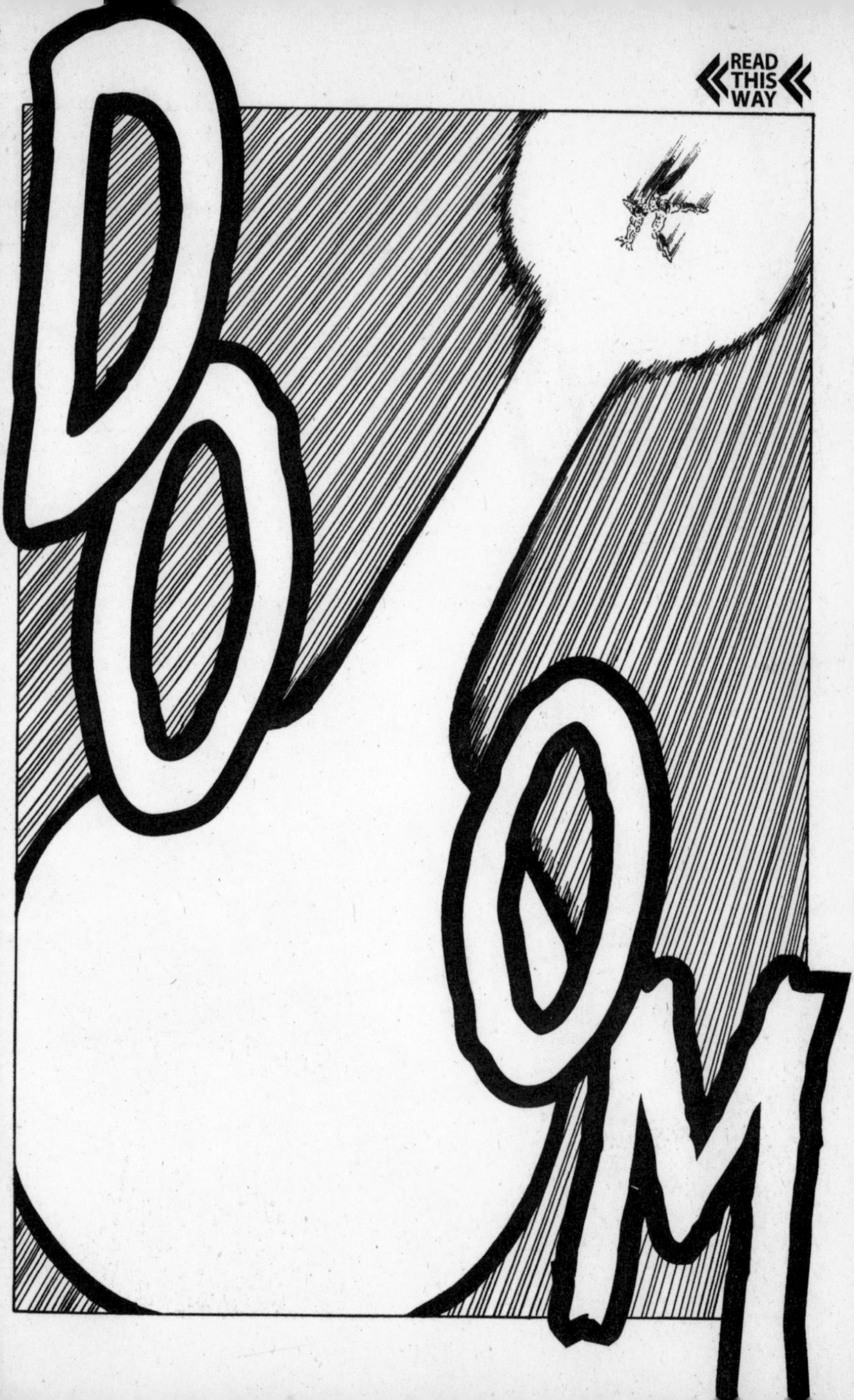
READ THIS WAY
DOOM

READ THIS WAY

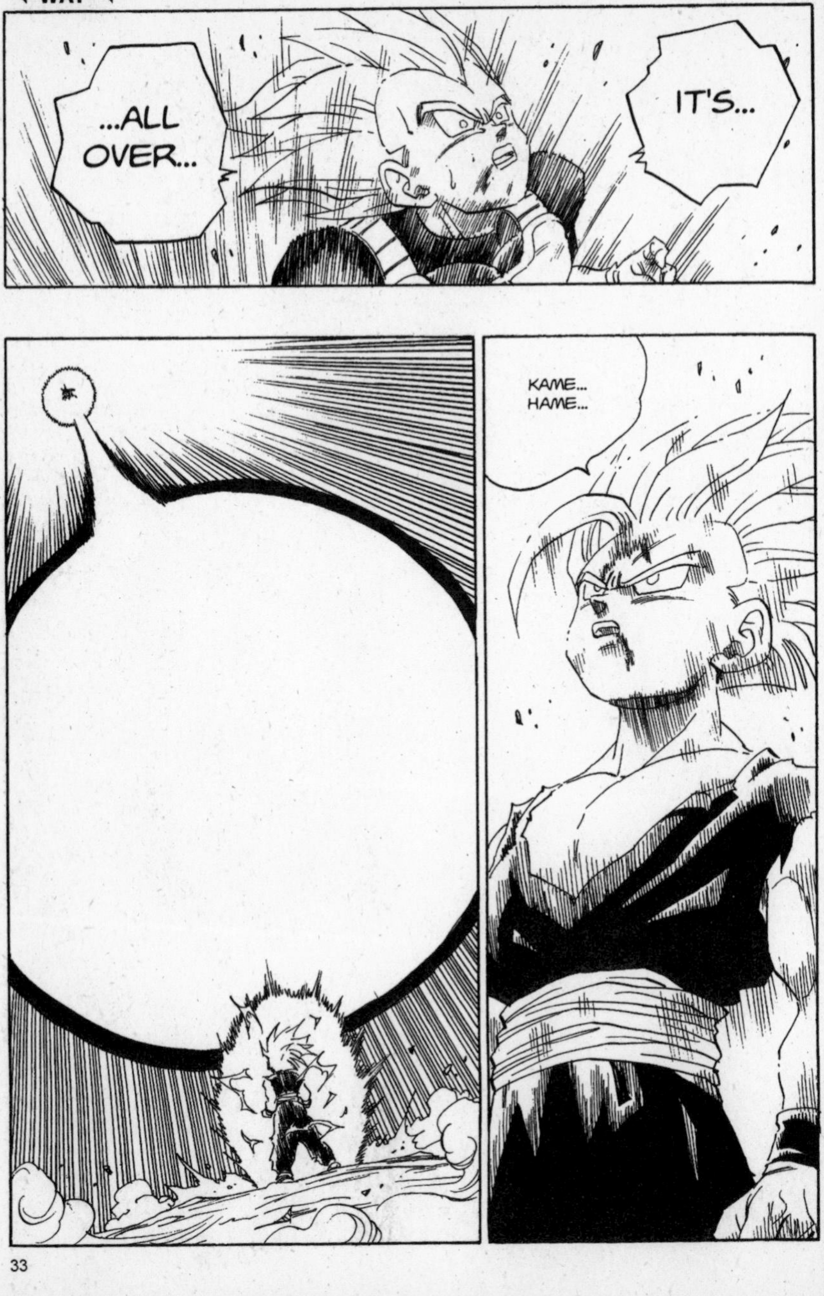

IT'S...
...ALL OVER...
KAME... HAME...

READ THIS WAY

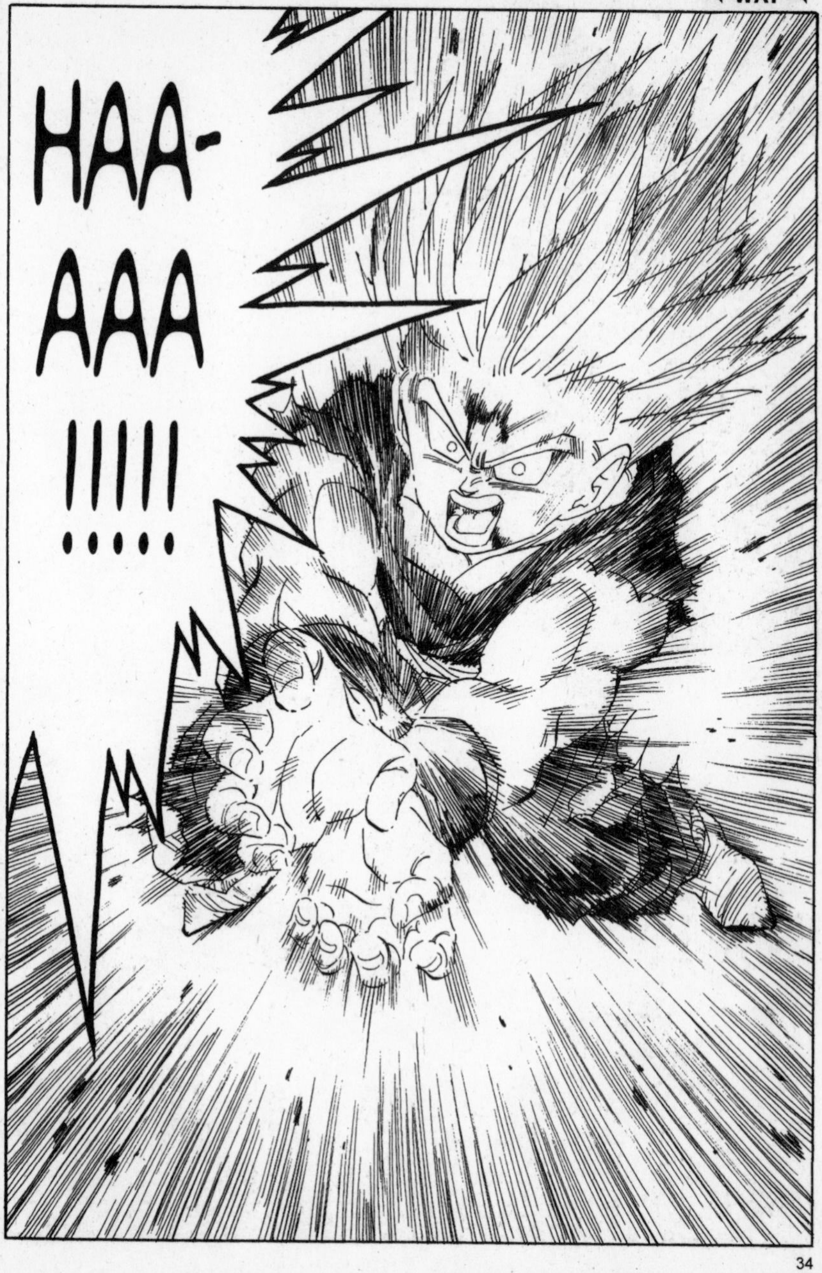
HAA-AAA!!!!!.....

READ THIS WAY

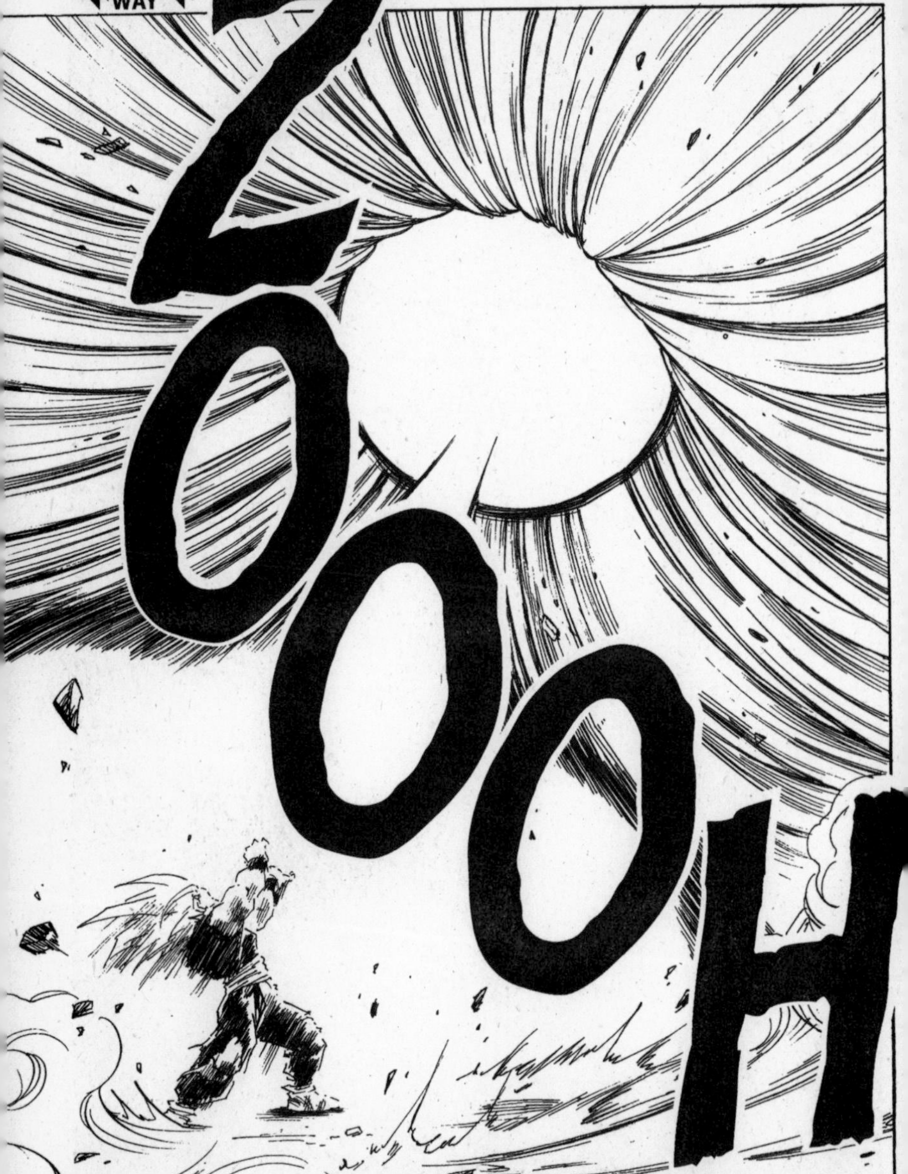
ZOOOOH

READ THIS WAY

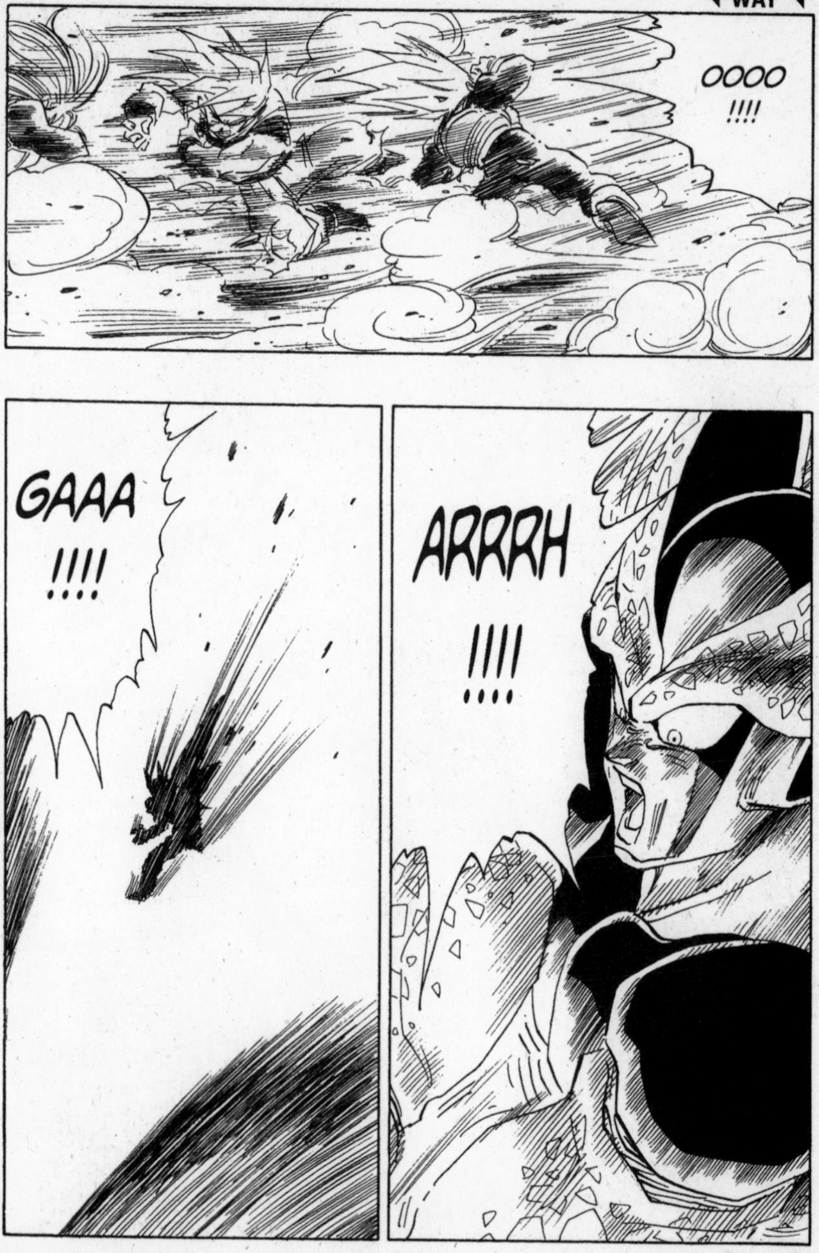
OOOO !!!!
ARRRH !!!!
GAAA !!!!

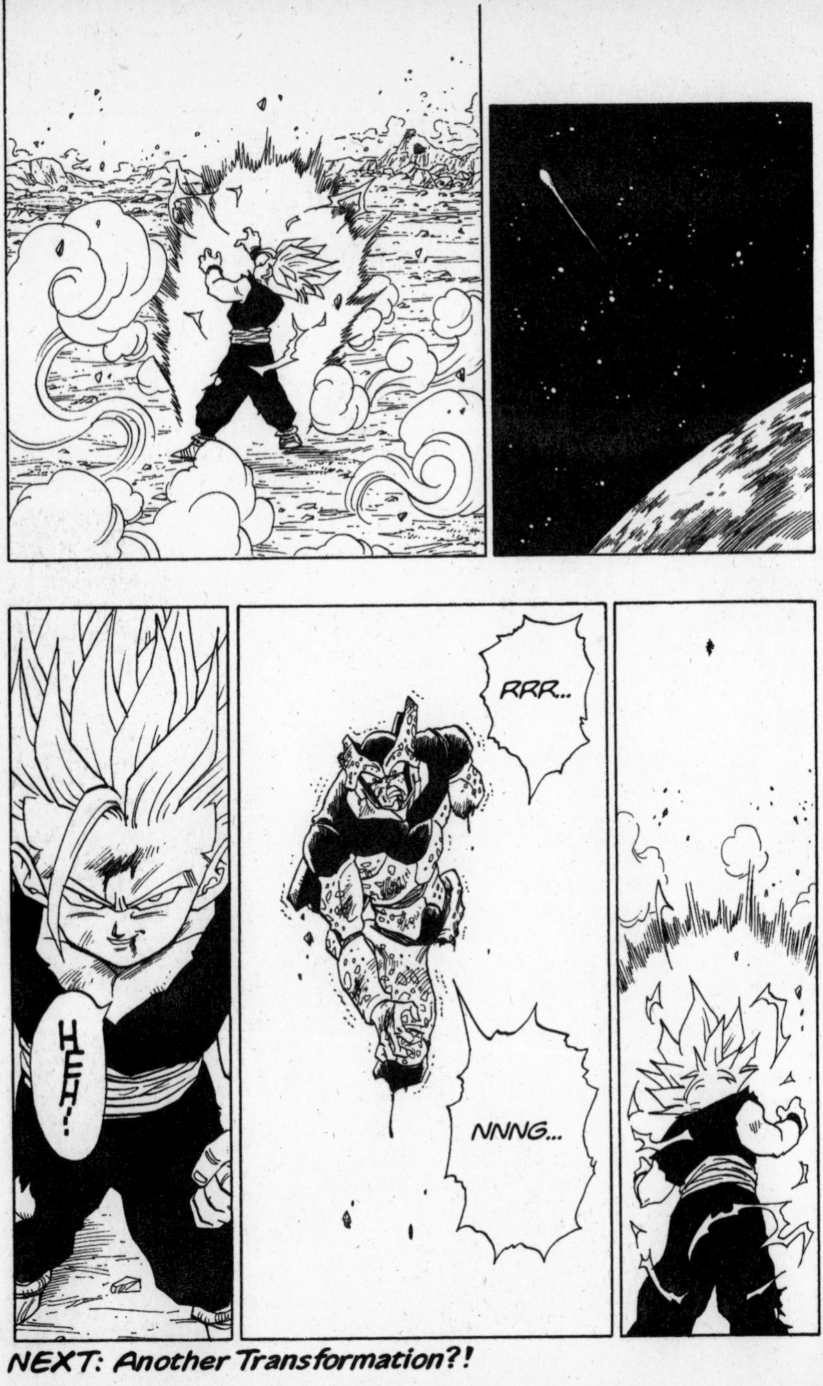
RRR...
NNNG...
HEH!!

NEXT: Another Transformation?!

DBZ:217
Cell, Brought to Bay

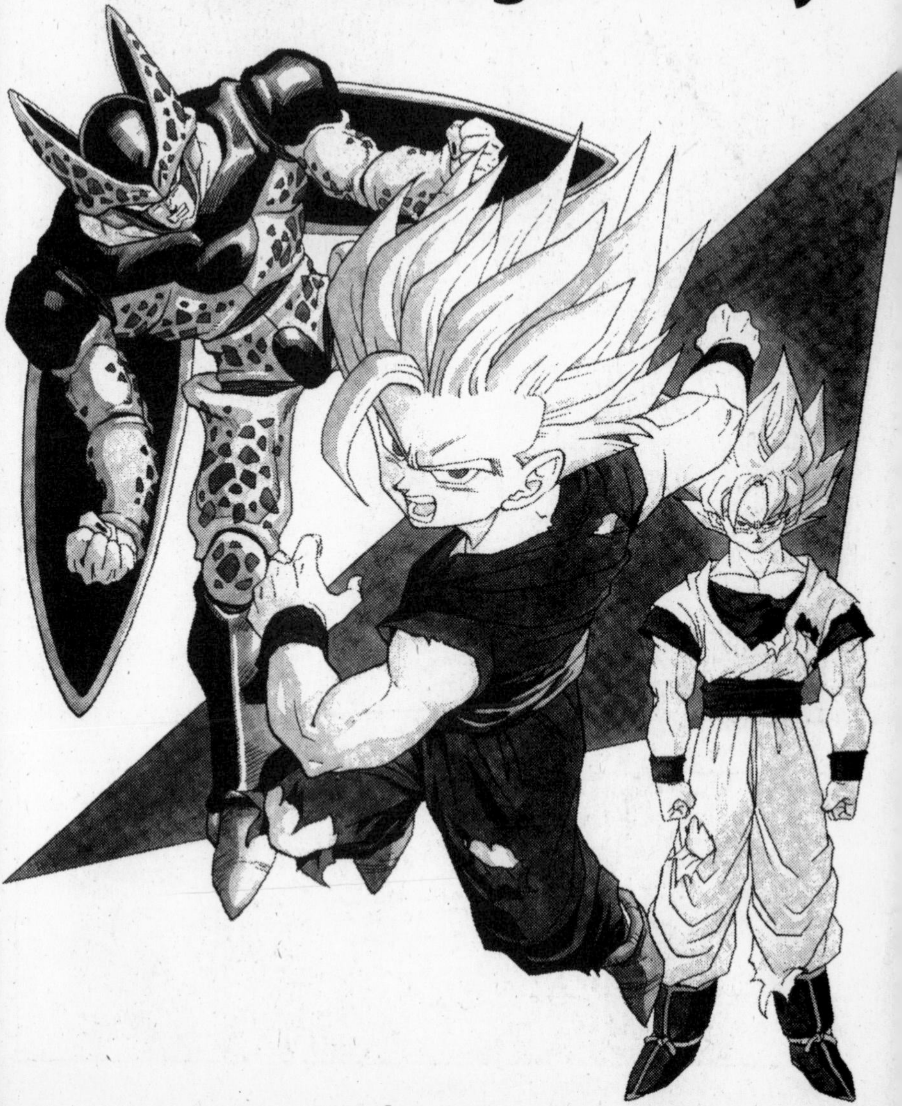

READ THIS WAY

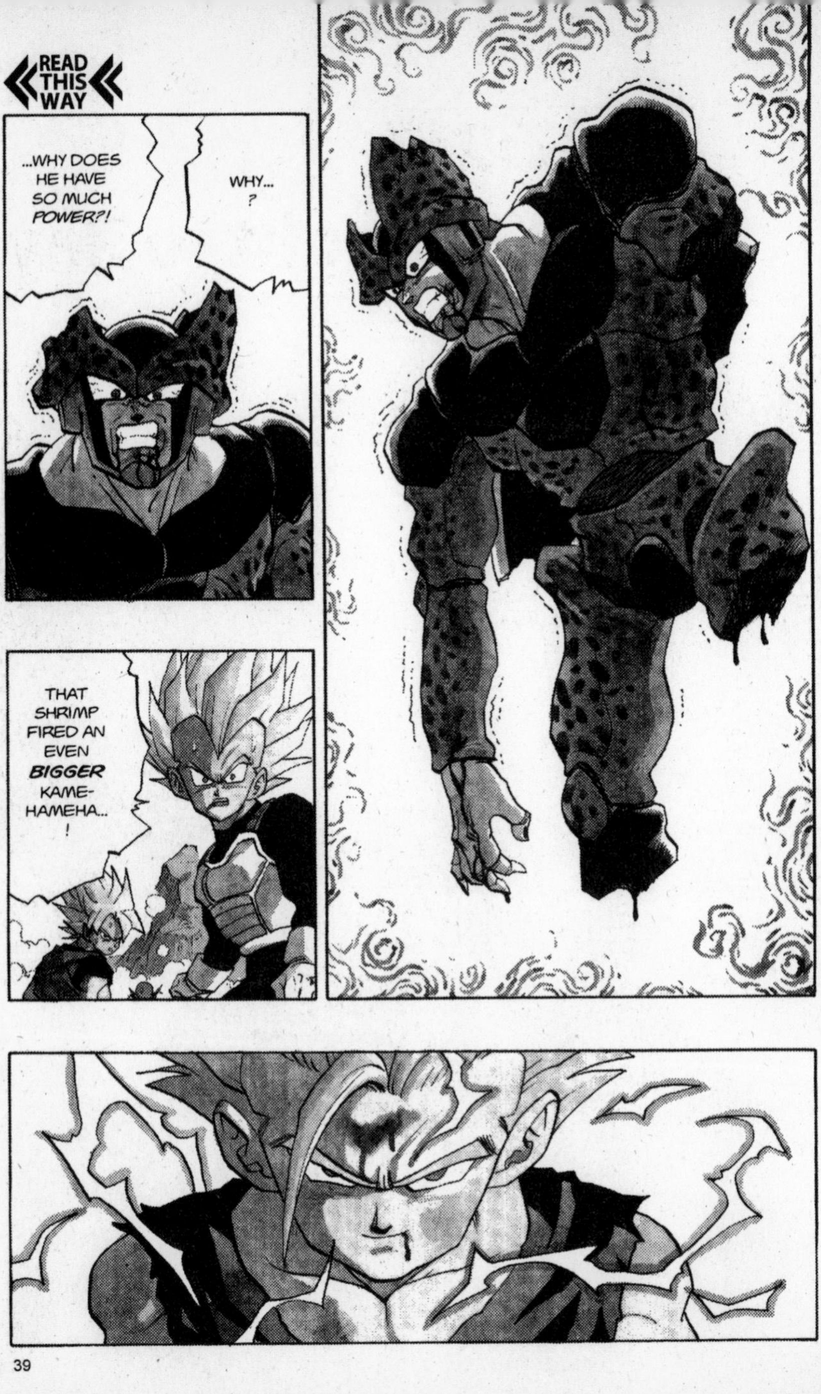
WHY... ?
...WHY DOES HE HAVE SO MUCH *POWER?!*
THAT SHRIMP FIRED AN EVEN ***BIGGER*** KAME-HAMEHA... !

READ THIS WAY

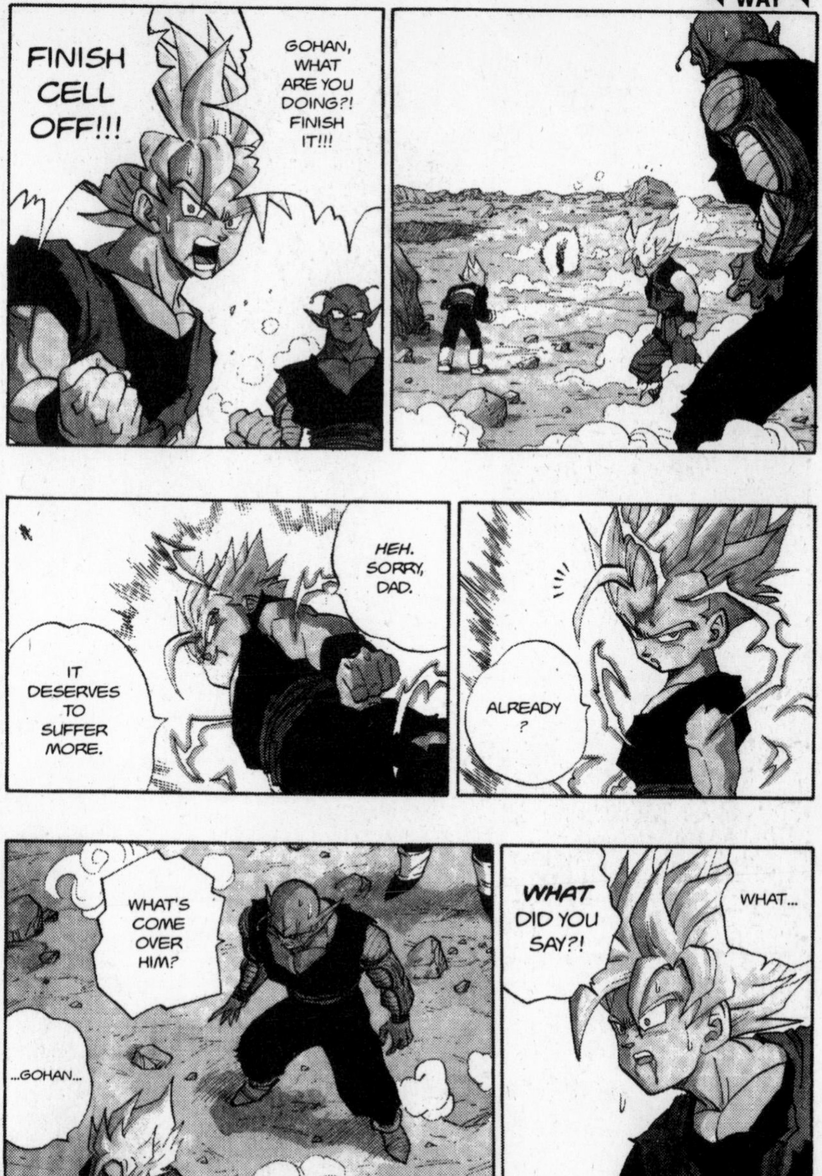
GOHAN, WHAT ARE YOU DOING?! FINISH IT!!!
FINISH CELL OFF!!!
ALREADY?
HEH. SORRY, DAD.
IT DESERVES TO SUFFER MORE.
WHAT...
WHAT DID YOU SAY?!
WHAT'S COME OVER HIM?
...GOHAN...

READ THIS WAY

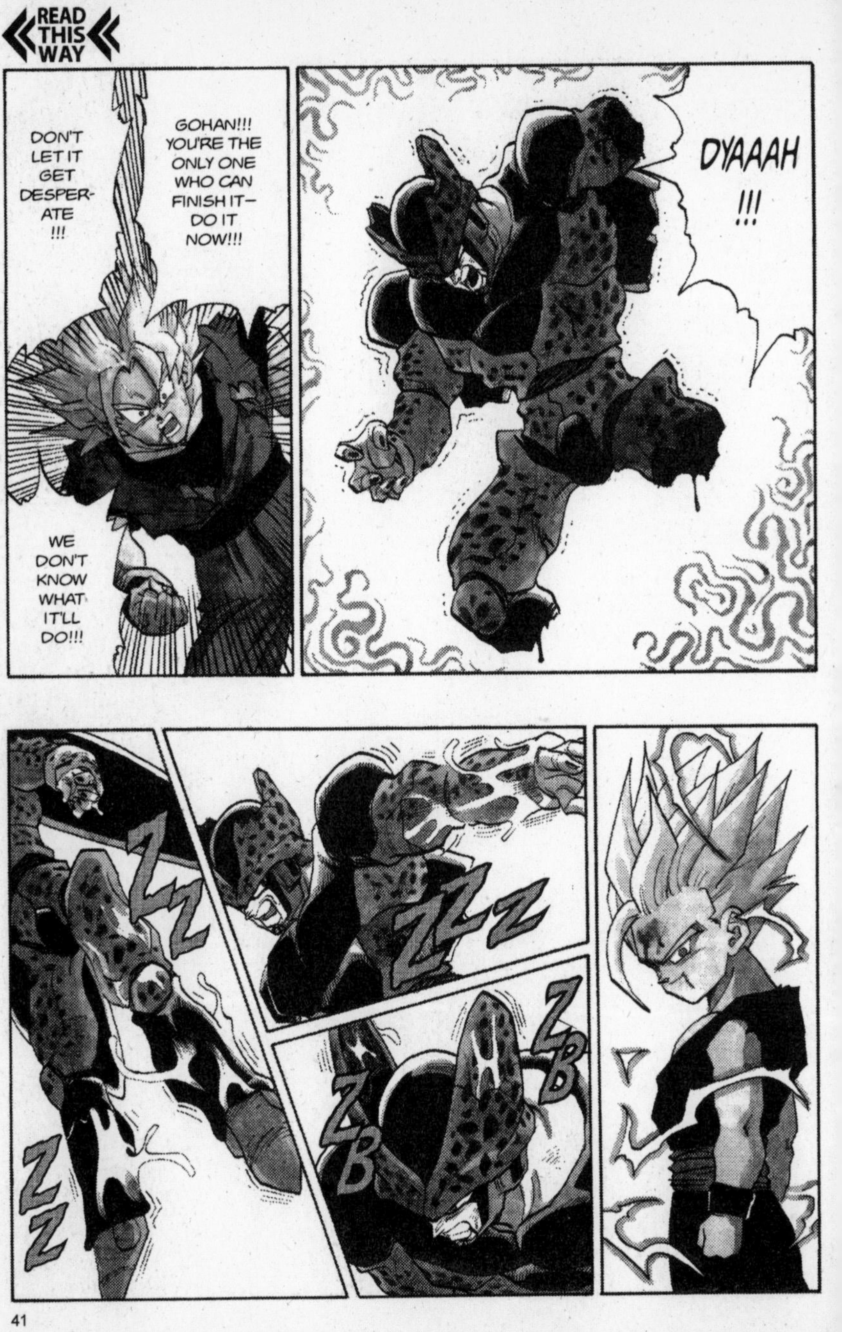

DYAAAH!!!
GOHAN!!! YOU'RE THE ONLY ONE WHO CAN FINISH IT— DO IT NOW!!!
DON'T LET IT GET DESPER-ATE!!!
WE DON'T KNOW WHAT IT'LL DO!!!
ZZZ
ZB
ZB
ZZ
ZZ

Y...

YOU... ARE...

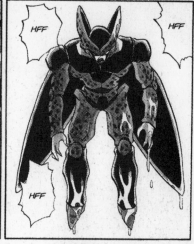

HFF

HFF

HFF

NRR AUGH !!!!!

...GONNA PAY !!!!

READ THIS WAY

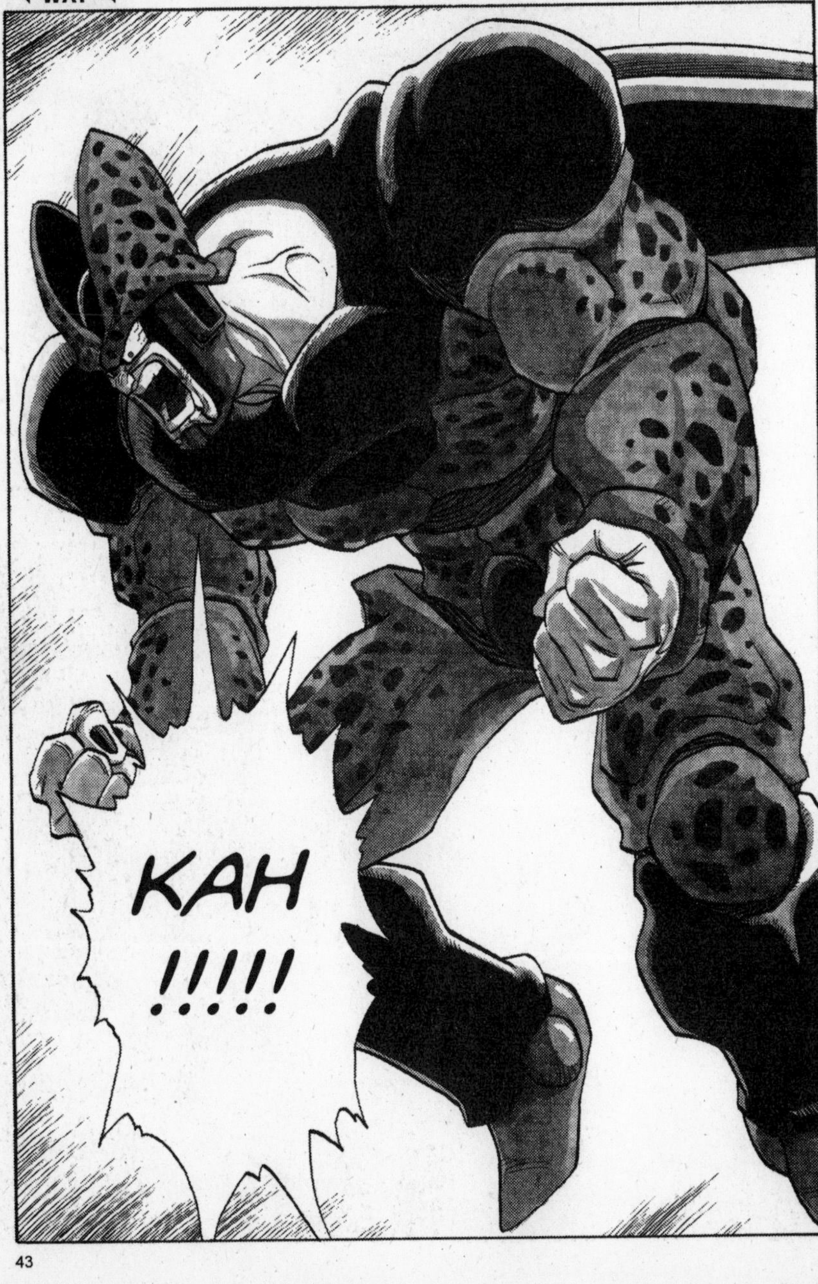
KAH
!!!!!

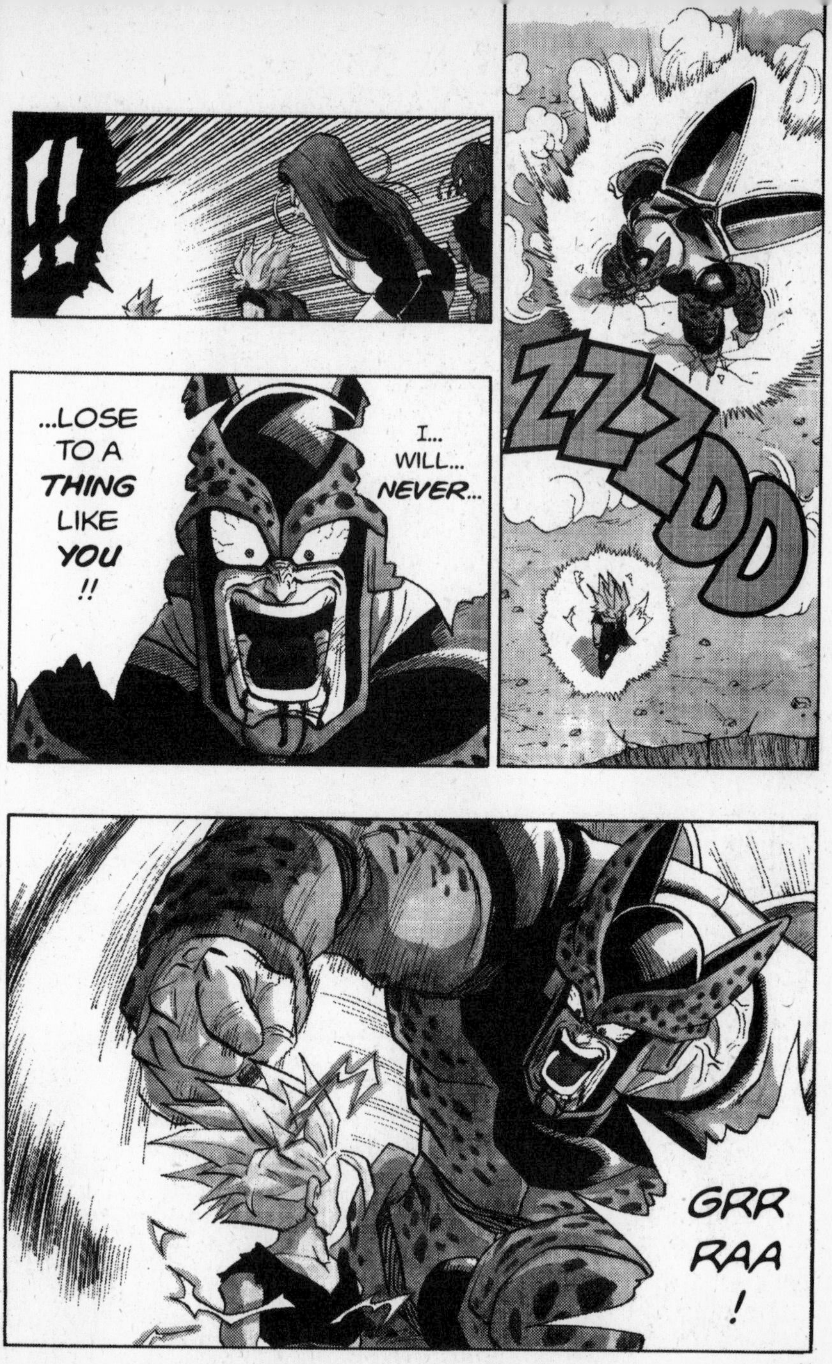
ZZZDD
!!
I... WILL... NEVER...
...LOSE TO A THING LIKE YOU !!
GRR RAA !

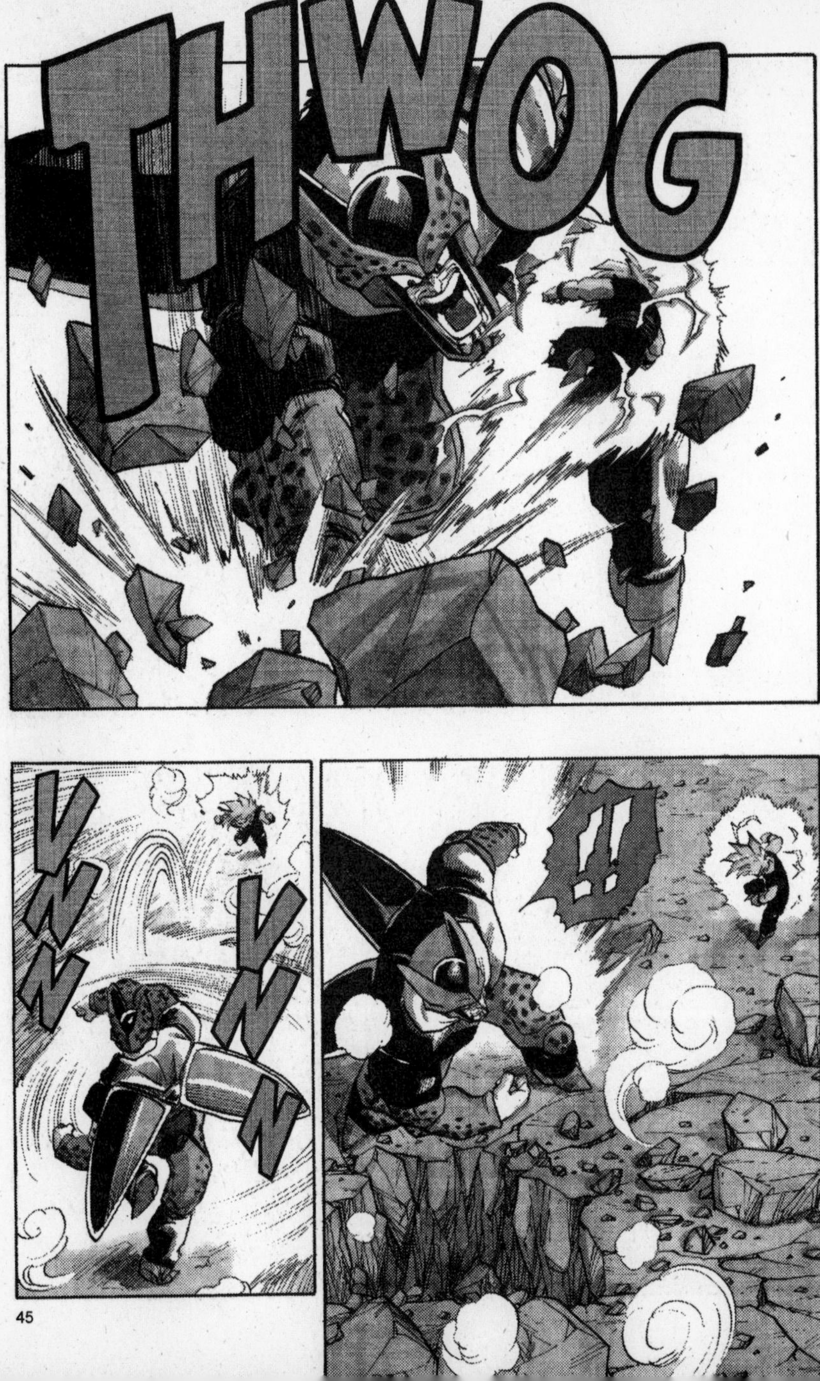
THWOG
!!
VNN
VNN

READ THIS WAY

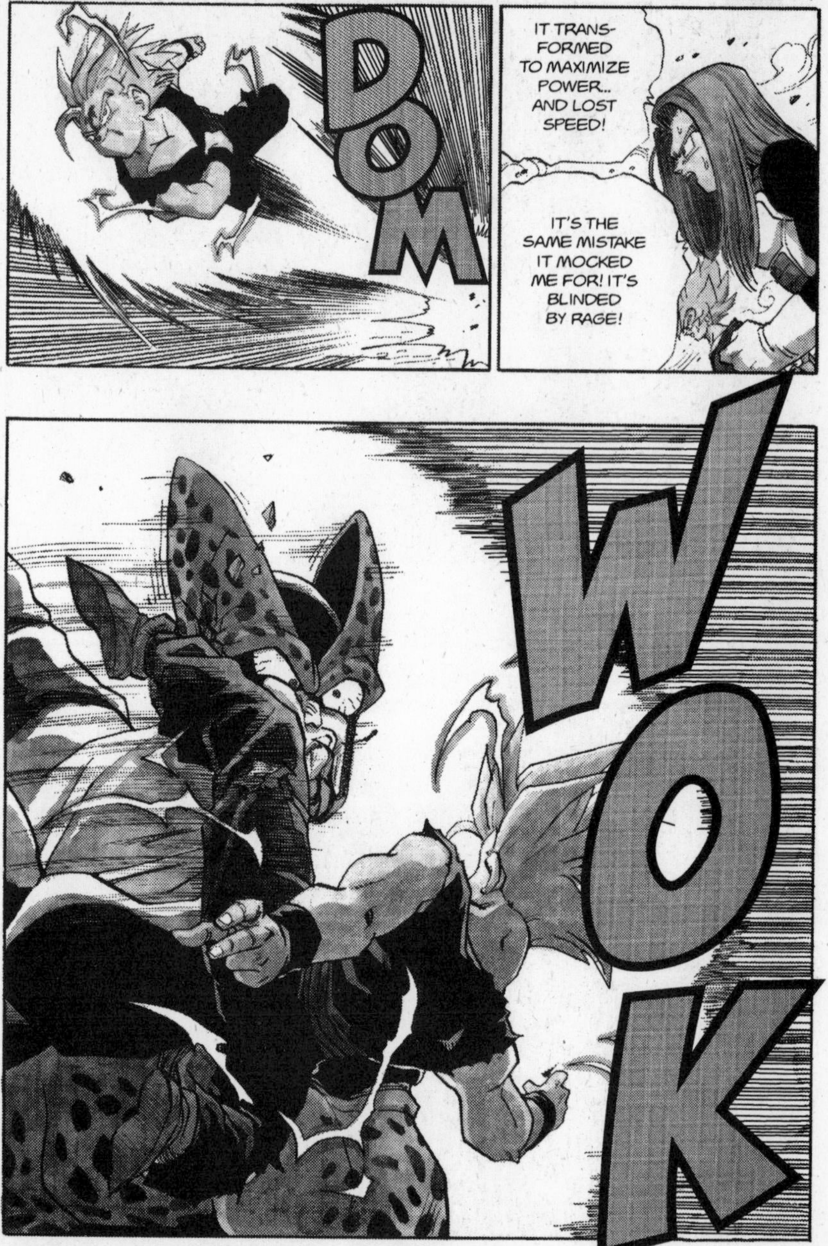
IT TRANS-FORMED TO MAXIMIZE POWER... AND LOST SPEED!
IT'S THE SAME MISTAKE IT MOCKED ME FOR! IT'S BLINDED BY RAGE!
DOM
WOK

READ THIS WAY

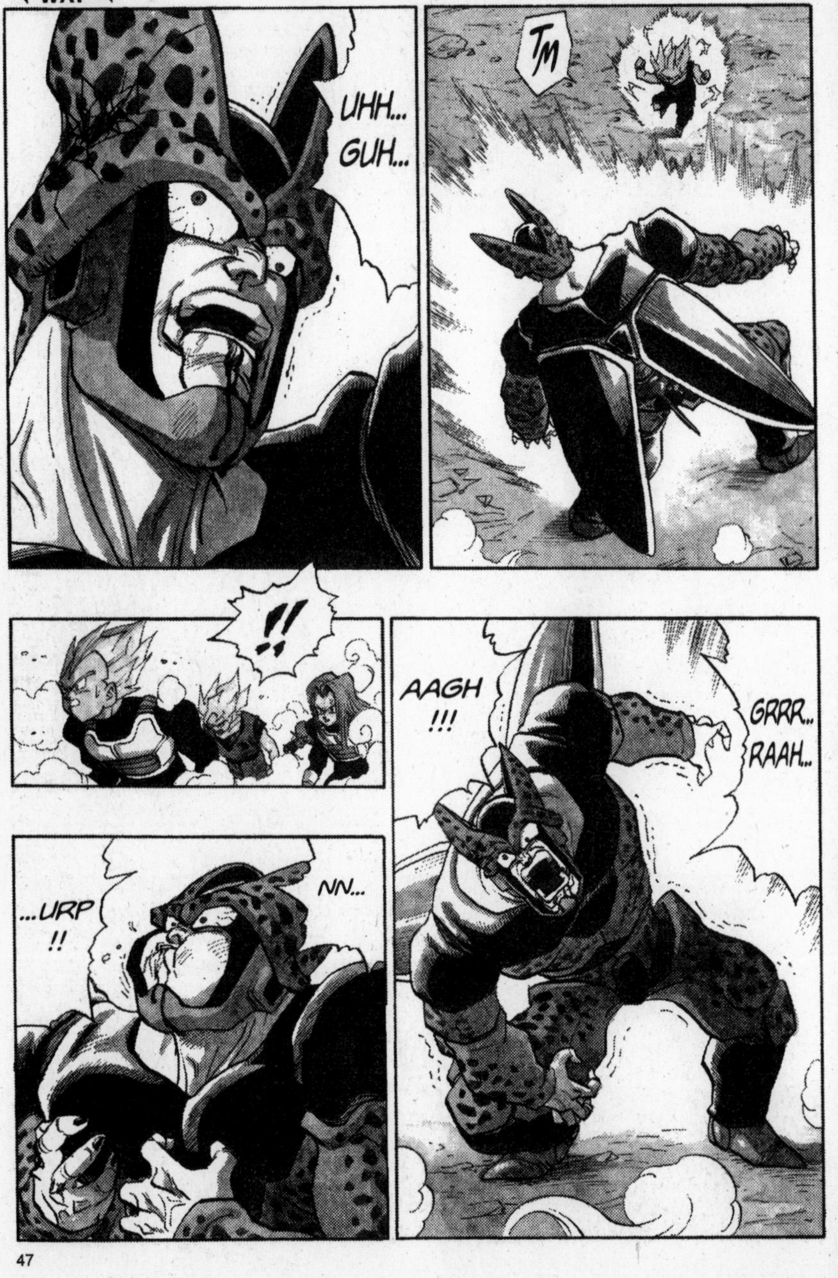
TM
UHH... GUH...
GRRR.. RAAH..
AAGH !!!
!!
NN...
...URP !!

READ THIS WAY

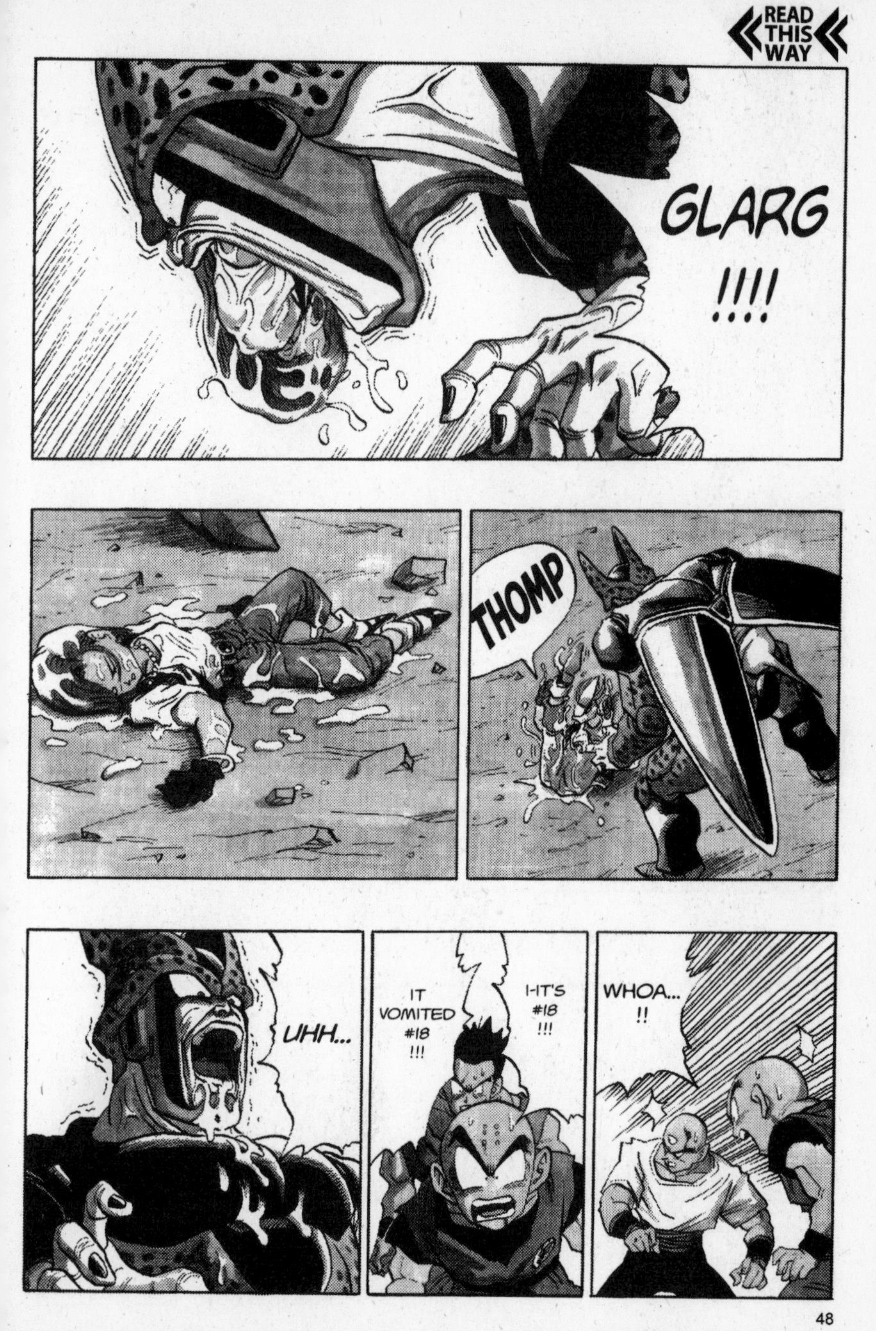

GLARG
!!!!
THOMP
WHOA...
!!
I-IT'S
#18
!!!
IT
VOMITED
#18
!!!
UHH...

READ THIS WAY

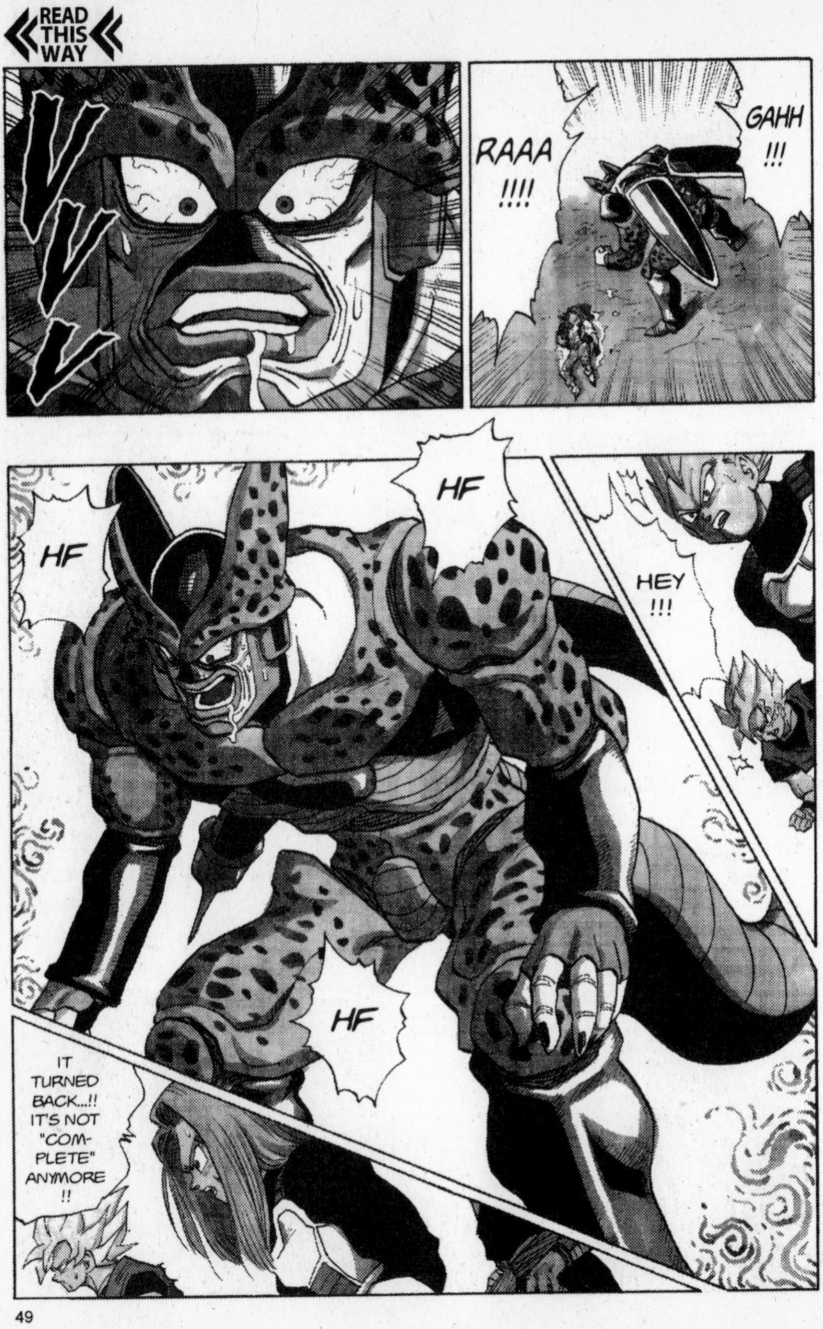
GAHH !!!
RAAA !!!!
VVV
HEY !!!
HF
HF
HF
IT TURNED BACK...!! IT'S NOT "COMPLETE" ANYMORE !!

READ THIS WAY

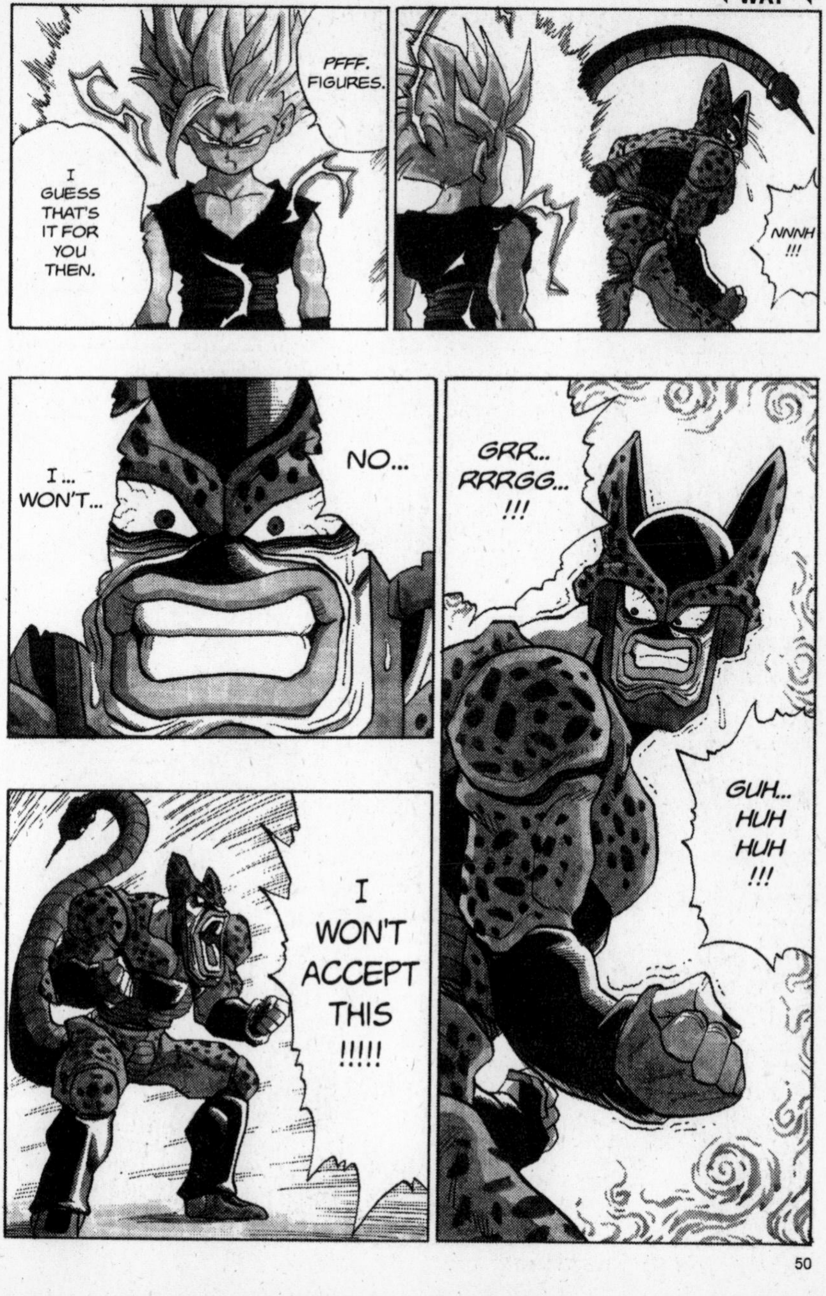
PFFF. FIGURES.
NNNH !!!
I GUESS THAT'S IT FOR YOU THEN.
GRR... RRRGG... !!!
NO...
I... WON'T...
GUH... HUH HUH !!!
I WON'T ACCEPT THIS !!!!!

READ THIS WAY

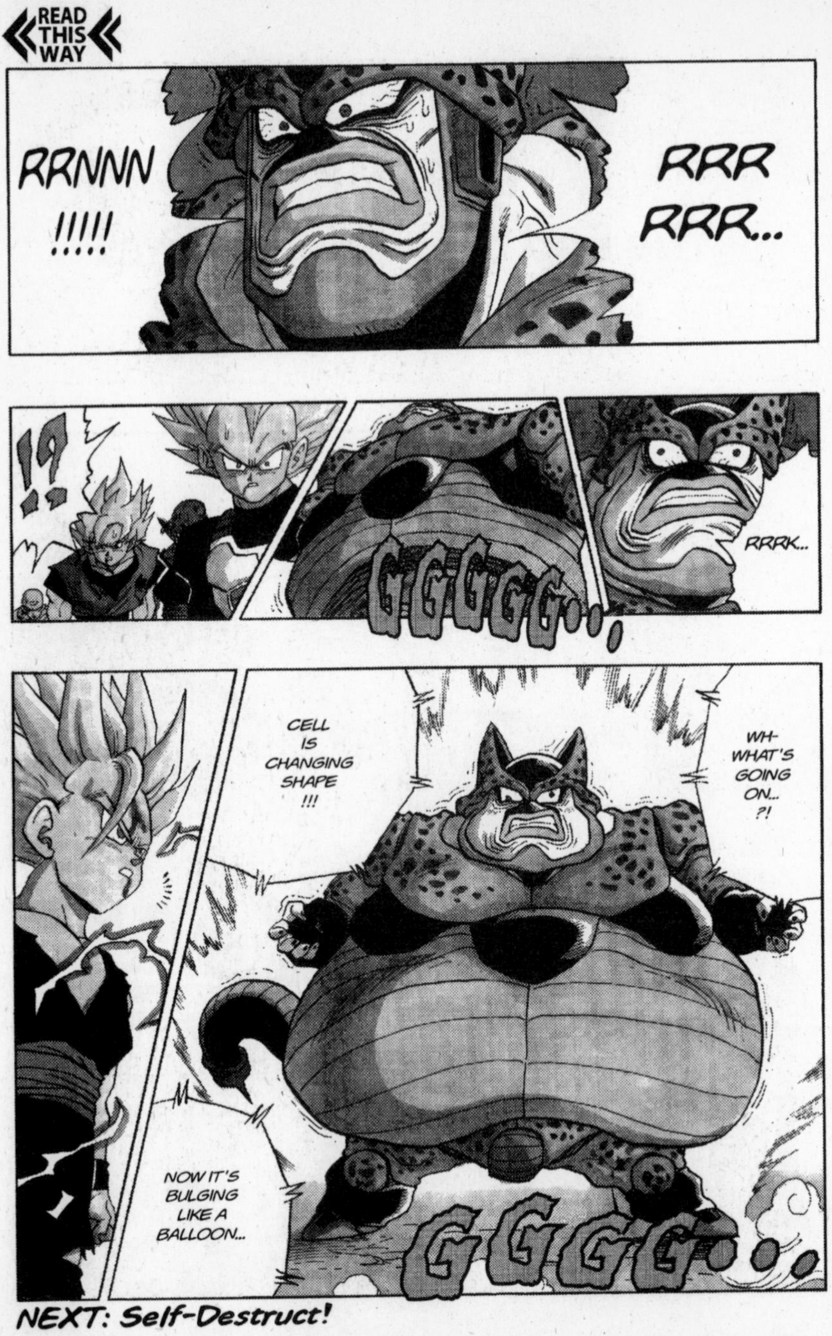

RRR RRR...
RRNNN !!!!!
RRRK...
GGGGG...
!?
WH- WHAT'S GOING ON...?!
CELL IS CHANGING SHAPE!!!
NOW IT'S BULGING LIKE A BALLOON...
GGGG...

NEXT: Self-Destruct!

DBZ:218
The End of the Cell Game

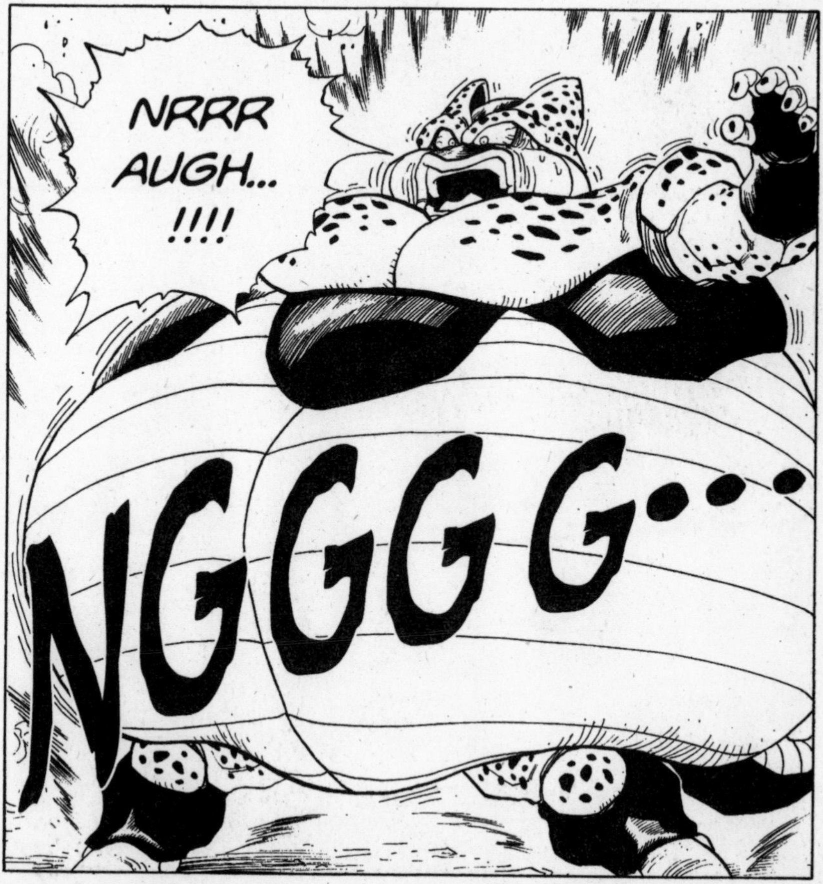
NRRR AUGH... !!!!
NGGGG...

READ THIS WAY

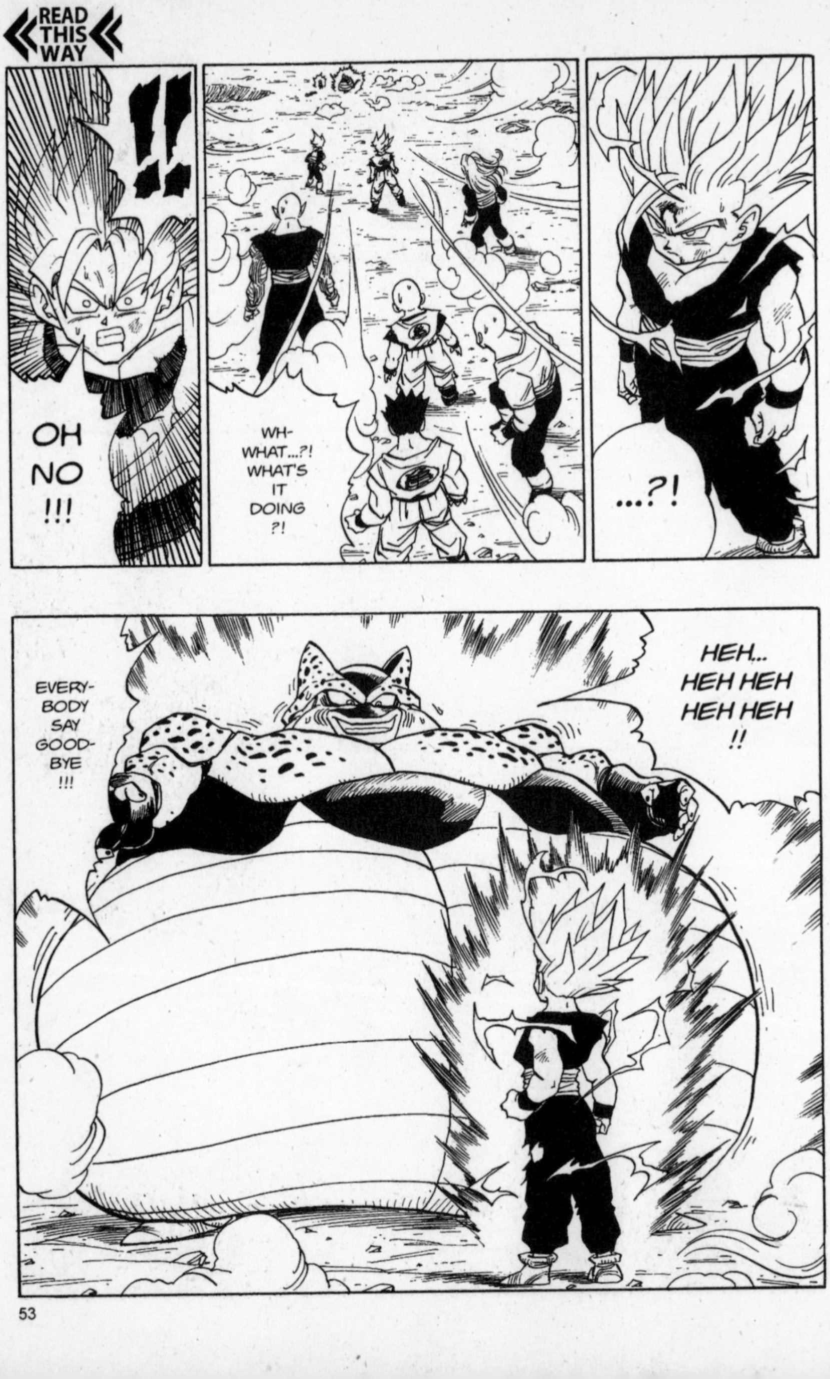
...?!
WH-WHAT...?! WHAT'S IT DOING ?!
!!
OH NO !!!
HEH... HEH HEH HEH HEH !!
EVERY-BODY SAY GOOD-BYE !!!

READ THIS WAY

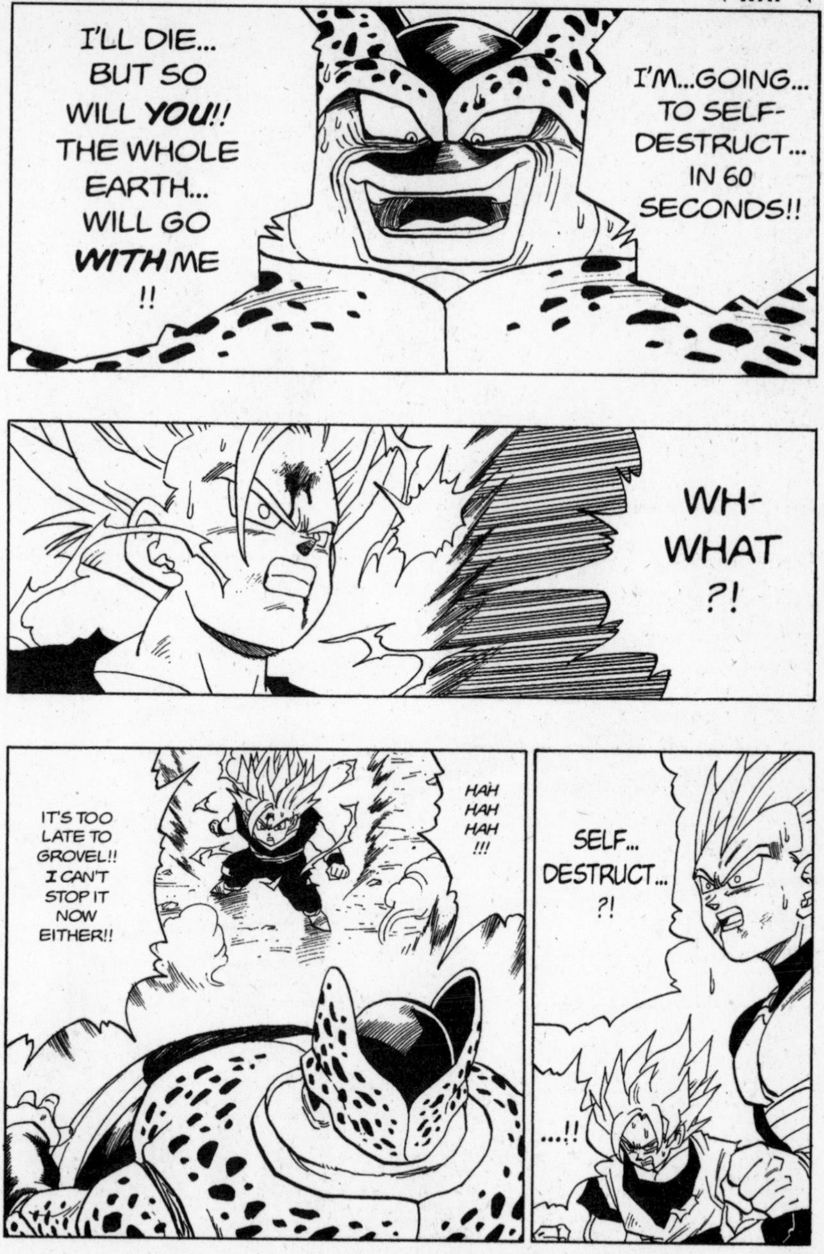

I'M...GOING... TO SELF-DESTRUCT... IN 60 SECONDS!!
I'LL DIE... BUT SO WILL **YOU**!! THE WHOLE EARTH... WILL GO **WITH** ME!!
WH-WHAT?!
SELF... DESTRUCT...?!
...!!
HAH HAH HAH!!!
IT'S TOO LATE TO GROVEL!! I CAN'T STOP IT NOW EITHER!!

READ THIS WAY

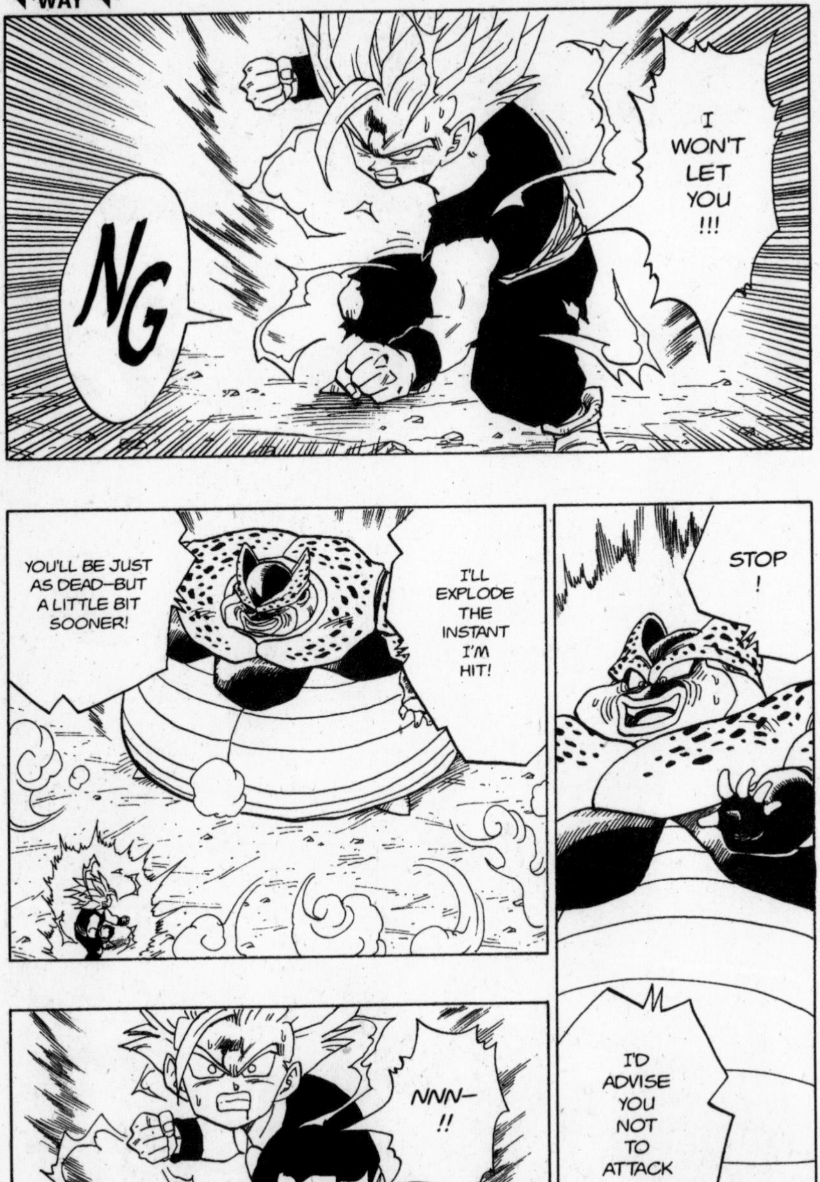
I WON'T LET YOU!!!
NG
STOP!
I'D ADVISE YOU NOT TO ATTACK!
I'LL EXPLODE THE INSTANT I'M HIT!
YOU'LL BE JUST AS DEAD—BUT A LITTLE BIT SOONER!
NNN-!!

READ THIS WAY

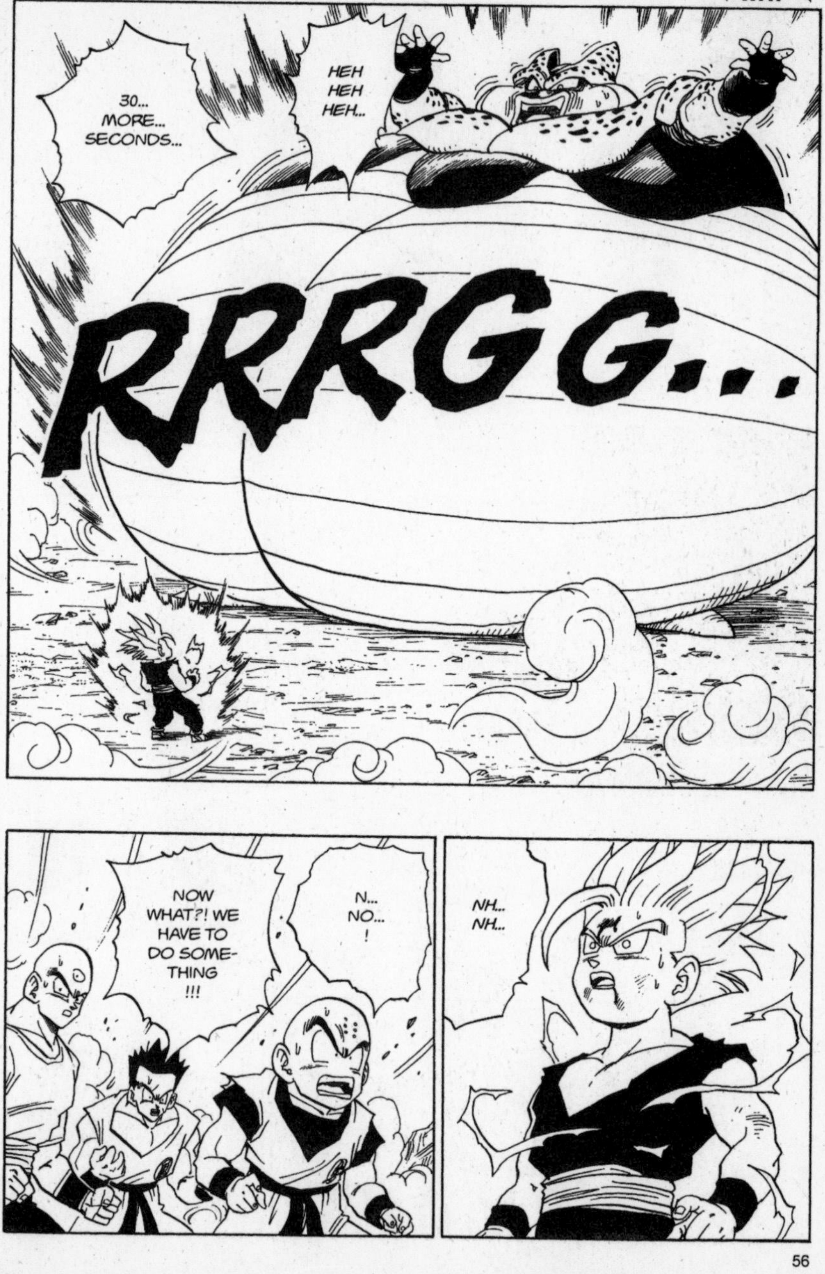

HEH HEH HEH...
30... MORE... SECONDS...
RRRGG...
NH... NH...
N... NO... !
NOW WHAT?! WE HAVE TO DO SOMETHING !!!

READ THIS WAY

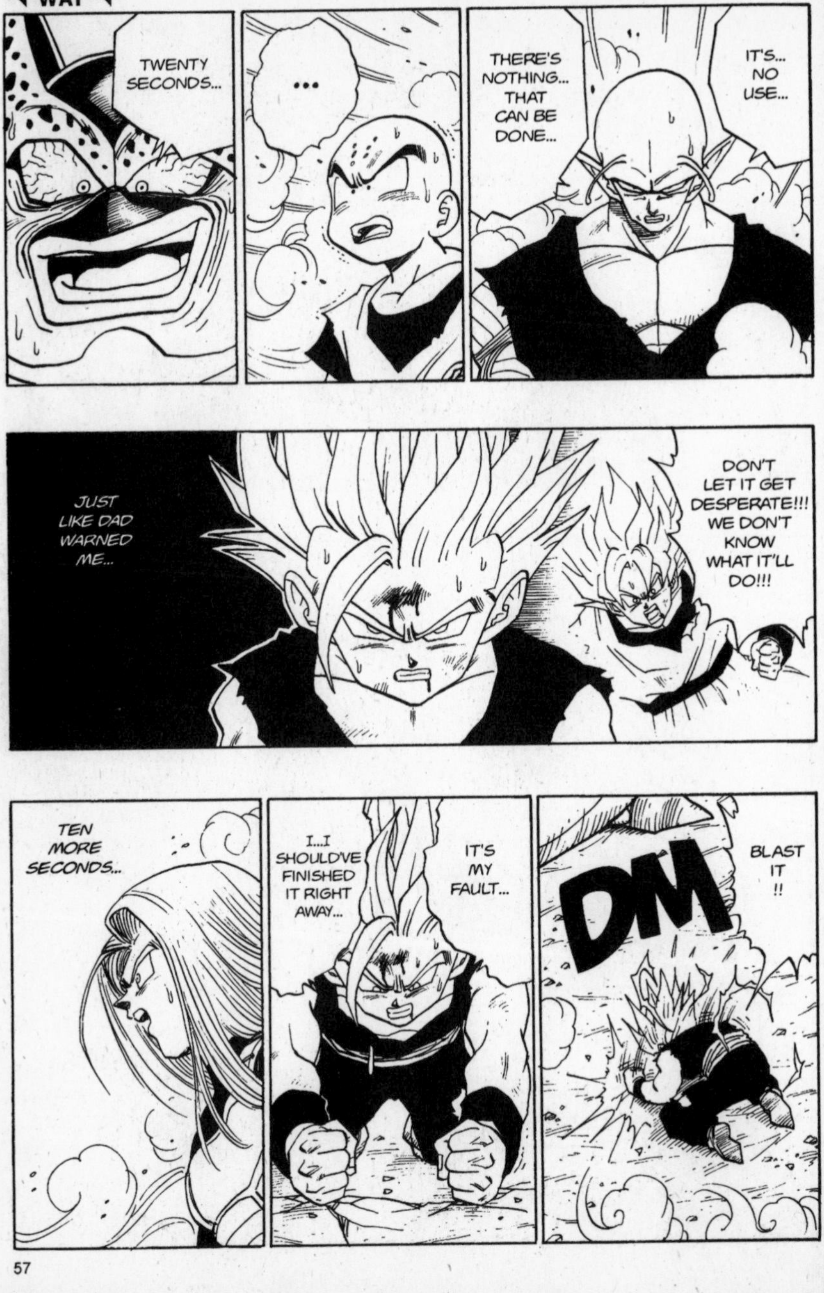
IT'S... NO USE...
THERE'S NOTHING... THAT CAN BE DONE...
...
TWENTY SECONDS...
DON'T LET IT GET DESPERATE!!! WE DON'T KNOW WHAT IT'LL DO!!!
JUST LIKE DAD WARNED ME...
BLAST IT !!
DM
IT'S MY FAULT...
I...I SHOULD'VE FINISHED IT RIGHT AWAY...
TEN MORE SECONDS...

READ THIS WAY

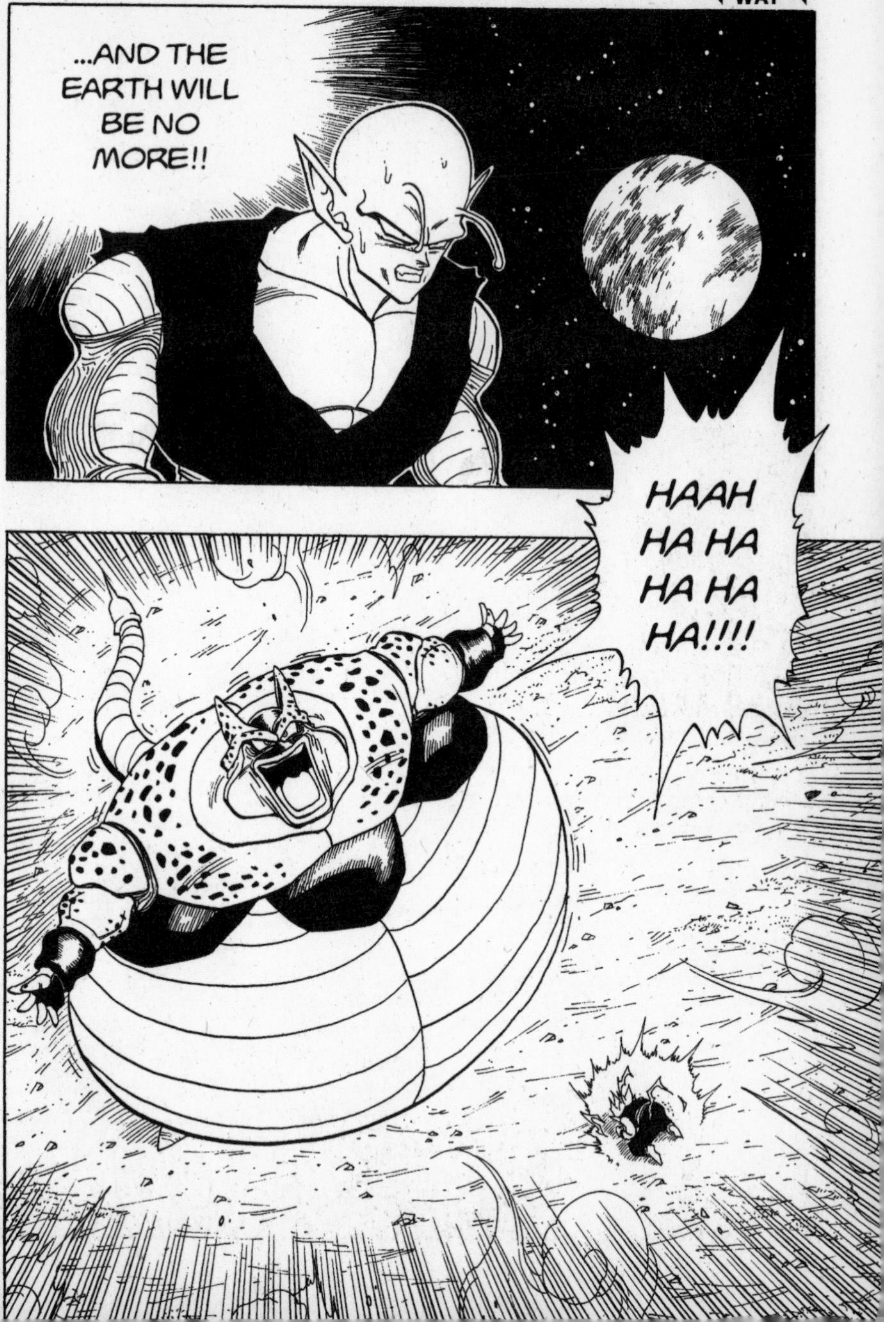
...AND THE EARTH WILL BE NO MORE!!
HAAH HA HA HA HA HA!!!!

READ THIS WAY

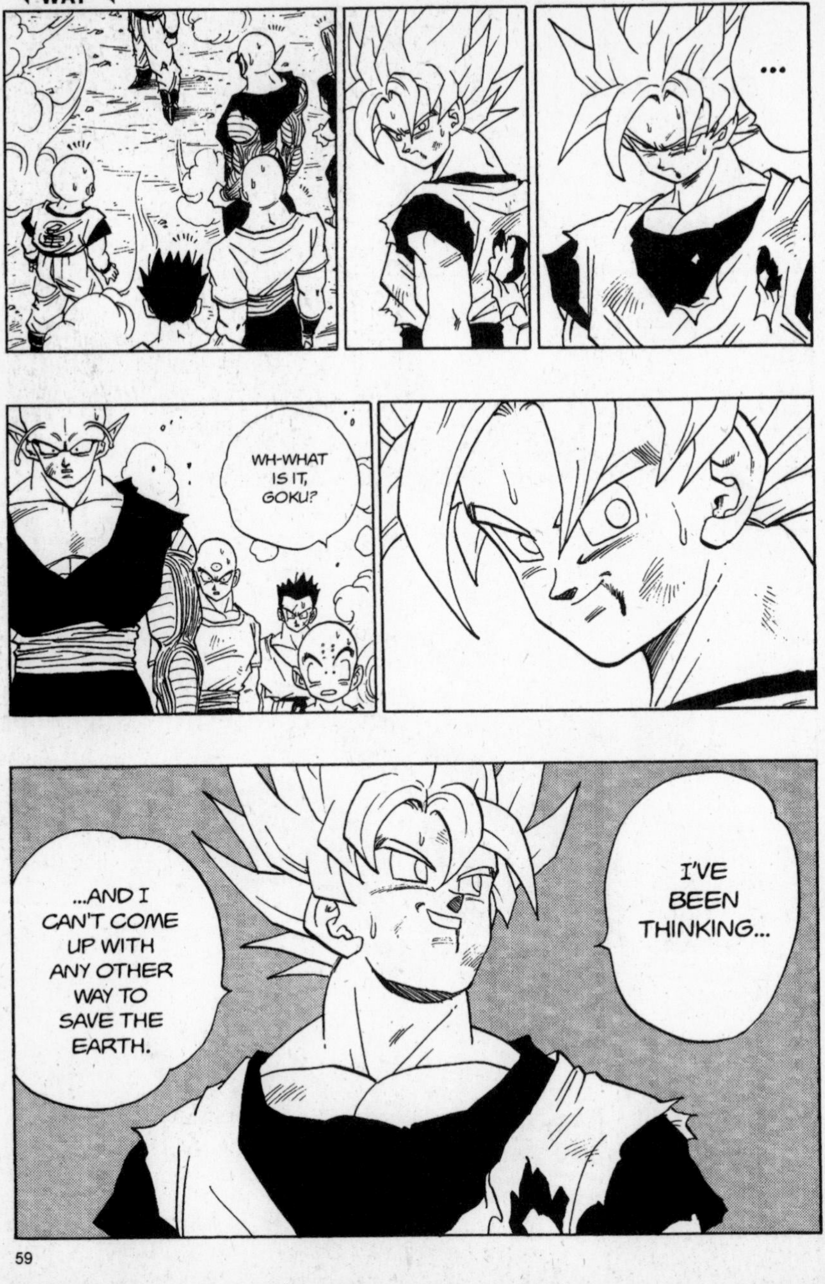
...
WH-WHAT IS IT, GOKU?
I'VE BEEN THINKING...
...AND I CAN'T COME UP WITH ANY OTHER WAY TO SAVE THE EARTH.

READ THIS WAY

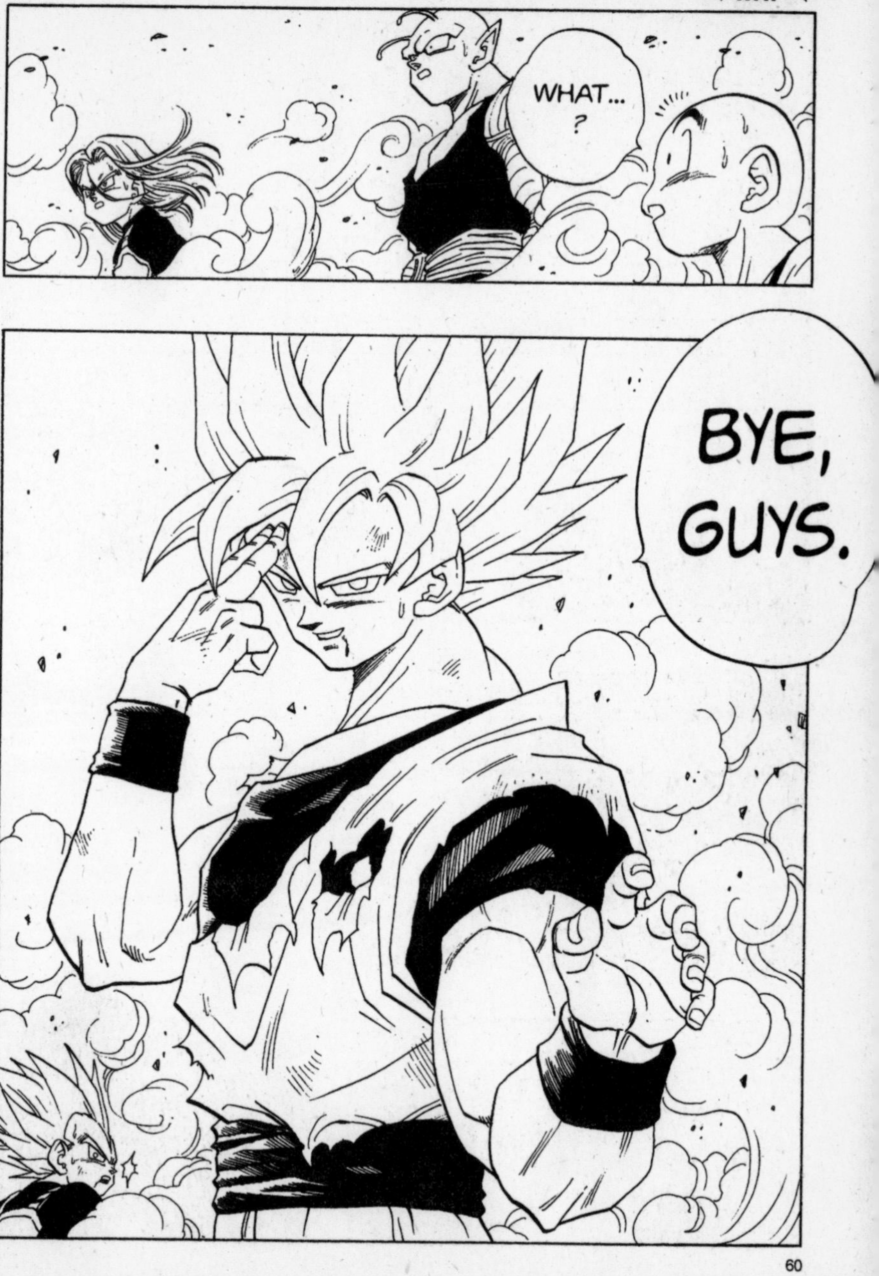
WHAT... ?
BYE, GUYS.

READ THIS WAY

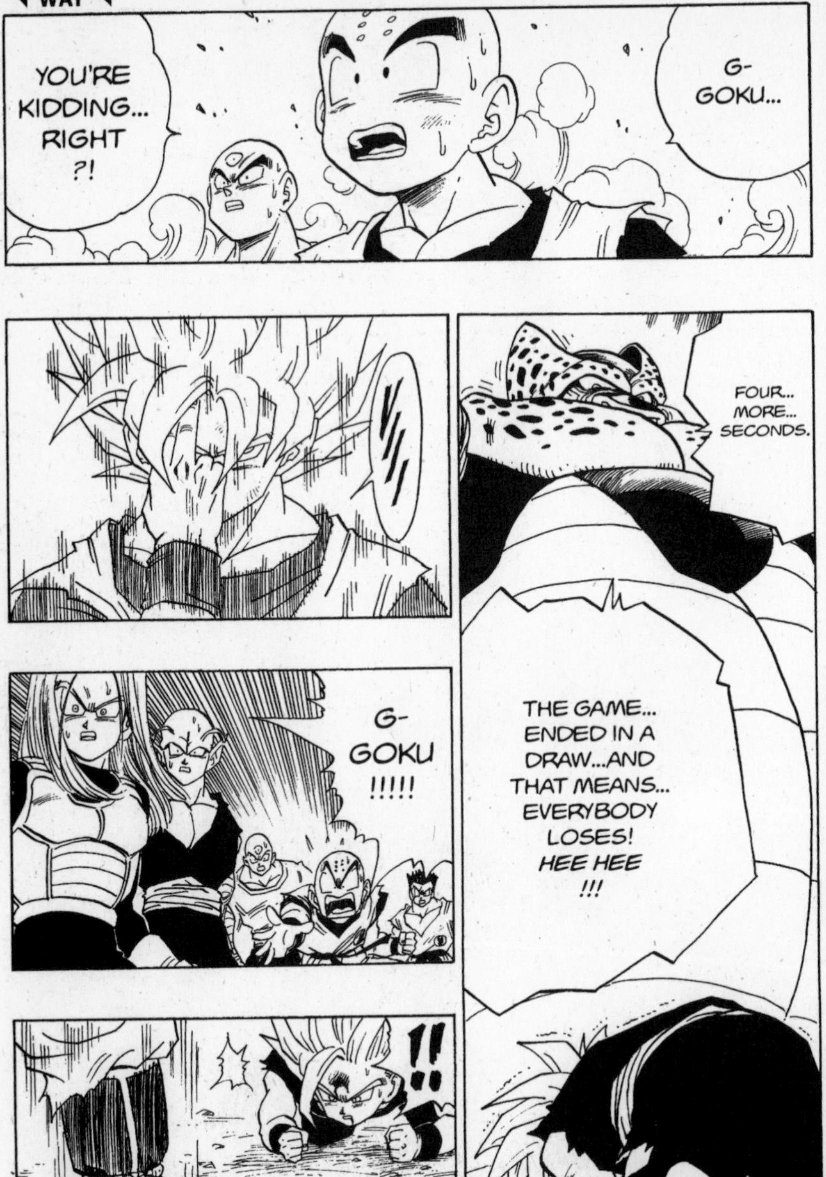

G- GOKU...
YOU'RE KIDDING... RIGHT ?!
FOUR... MORE... SECONDS.
THE GAME... ENDED IN A DRAW...AND THAT MEANS... EVERYBODY LOSES! HEE HEE !!!
G- GOKU !!!!!
!!

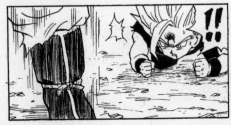

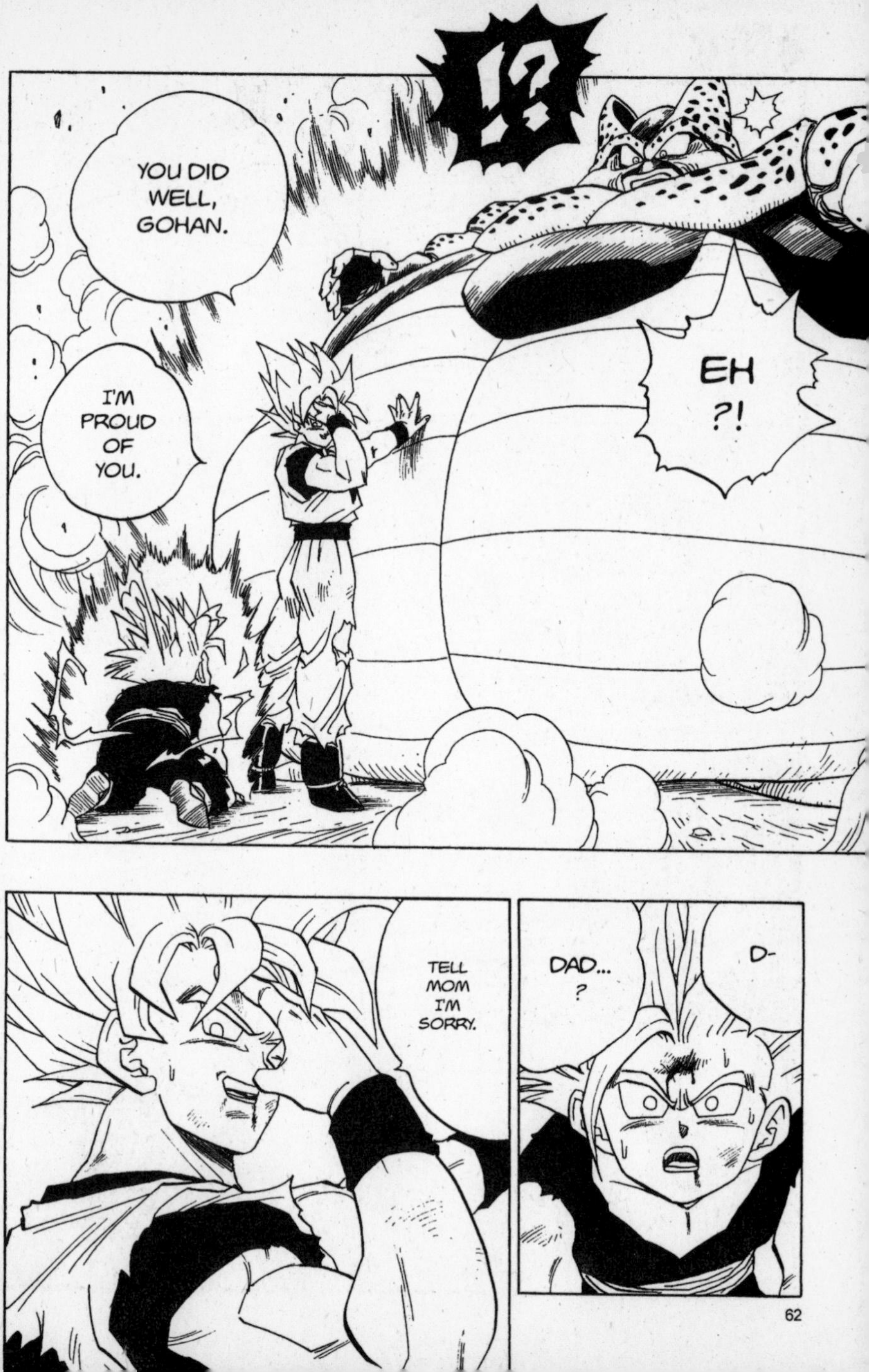
!?
EH ?!
YOU DID WELL, GOHAN.
I'M PROUD OF YOU.
D-
DAD... ?
TELL MOM I'M SORRY.

READ THIS WAY

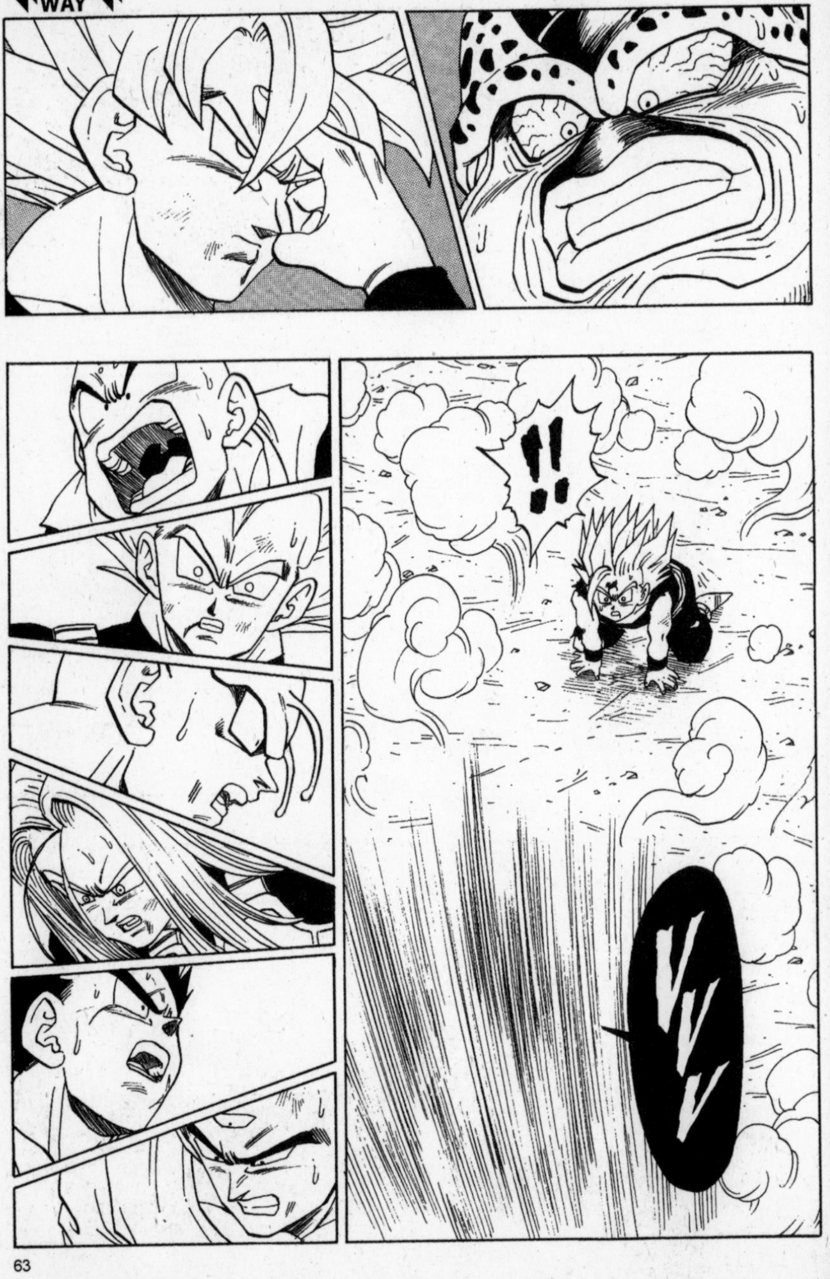
!!

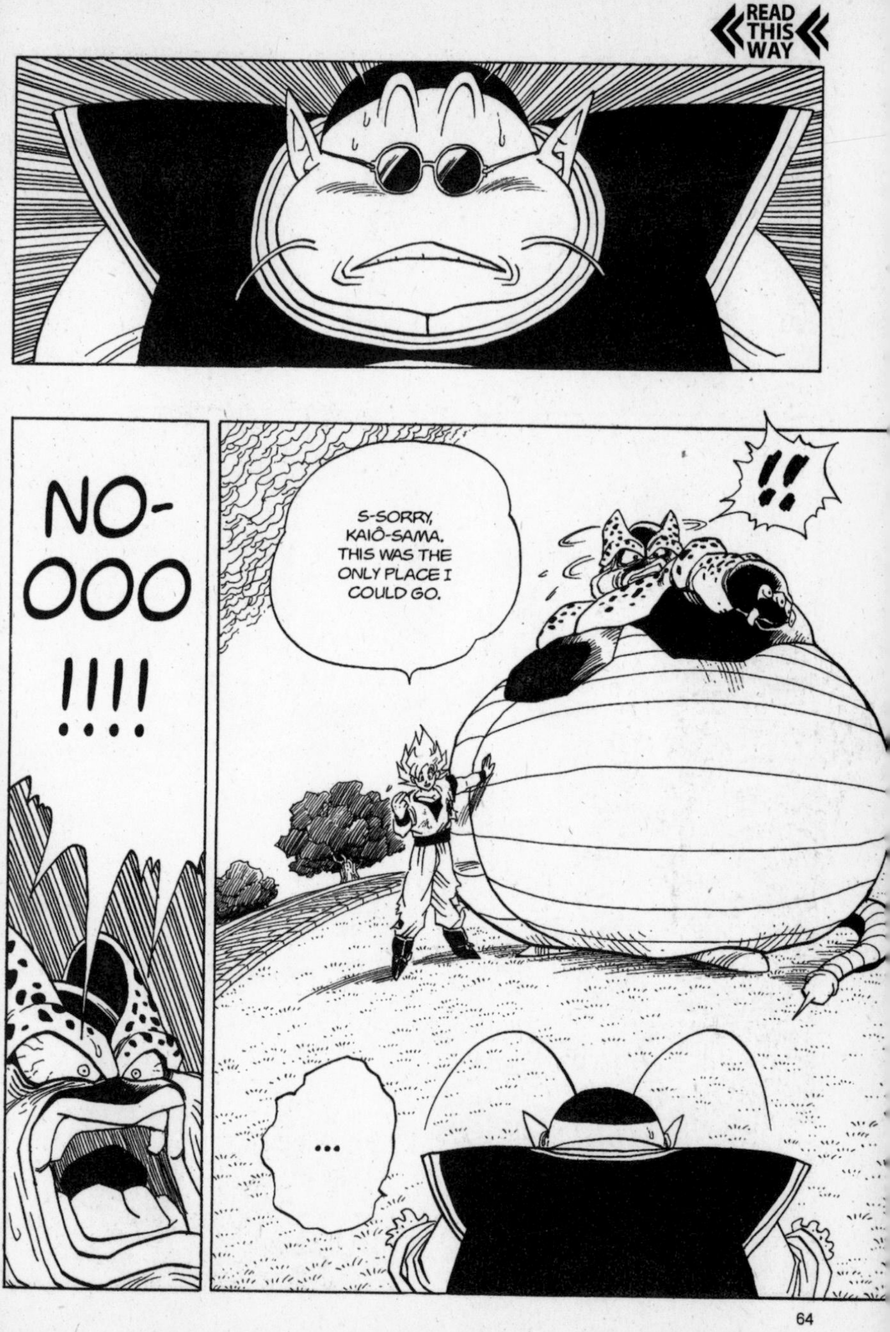
READ THIS WAY
!!
S-SORRY, KAIÔ-SAMA. THIS WAS THE ONLY PLACE I COULD GO.
...
NO-OOO !!!!

READ THIS WAY

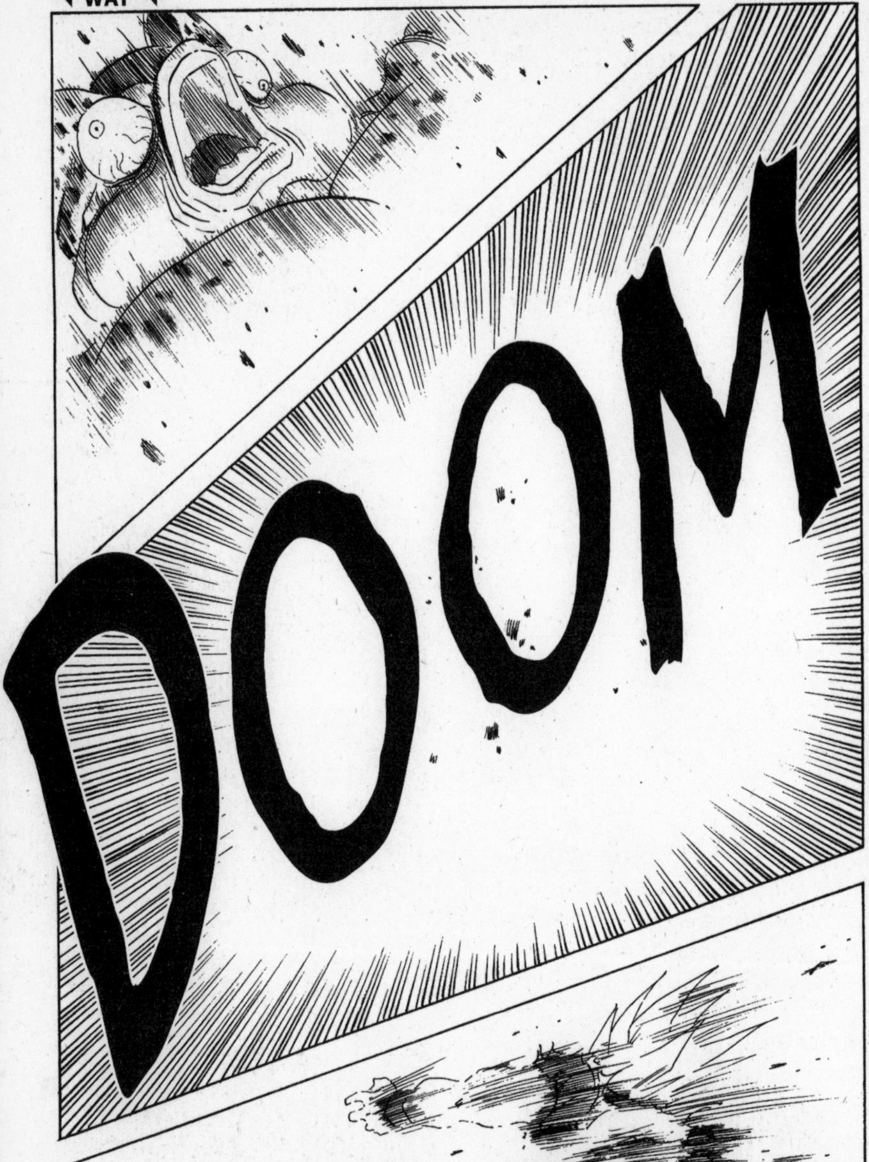
DOOM

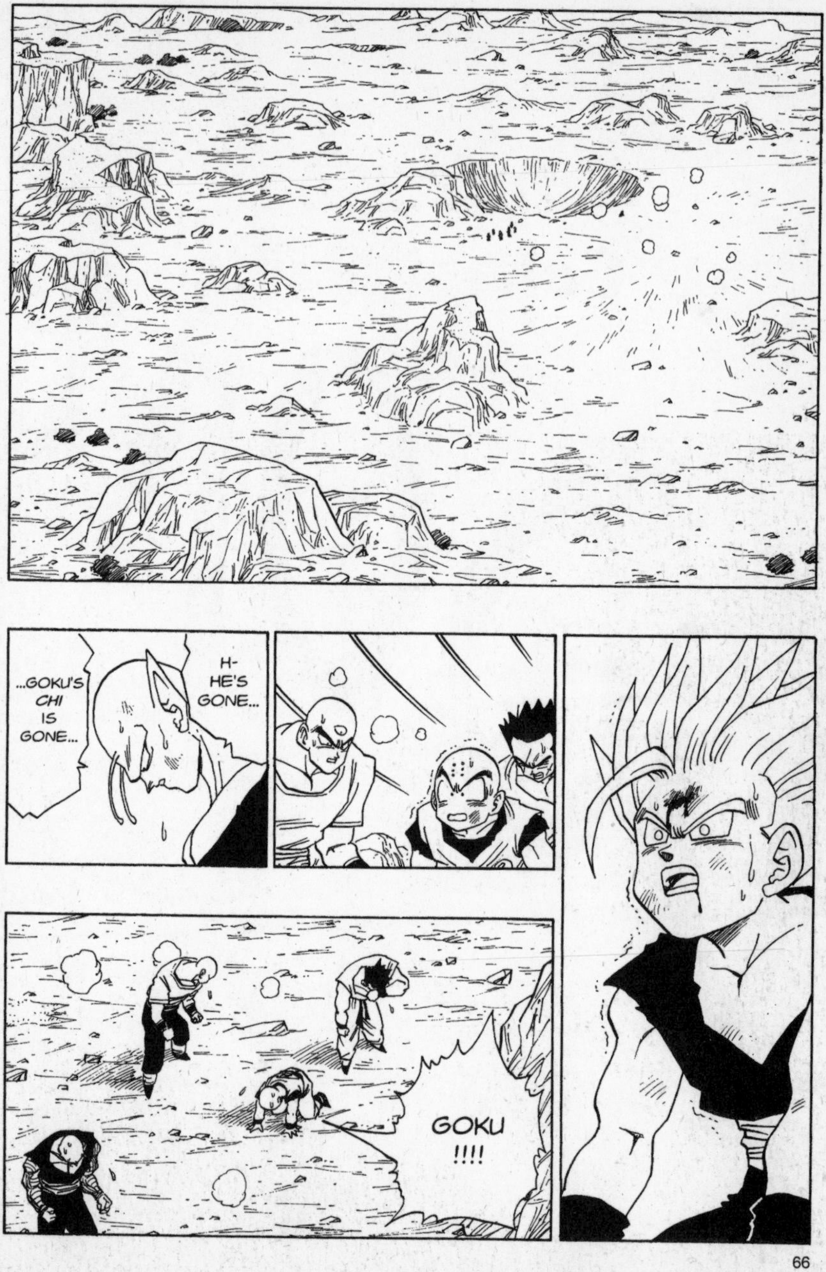

H- HE'S GONE...
...GOKU'S CHI IS GONE...
GOKU !!!!

DBZ:219
Gohan's Pain

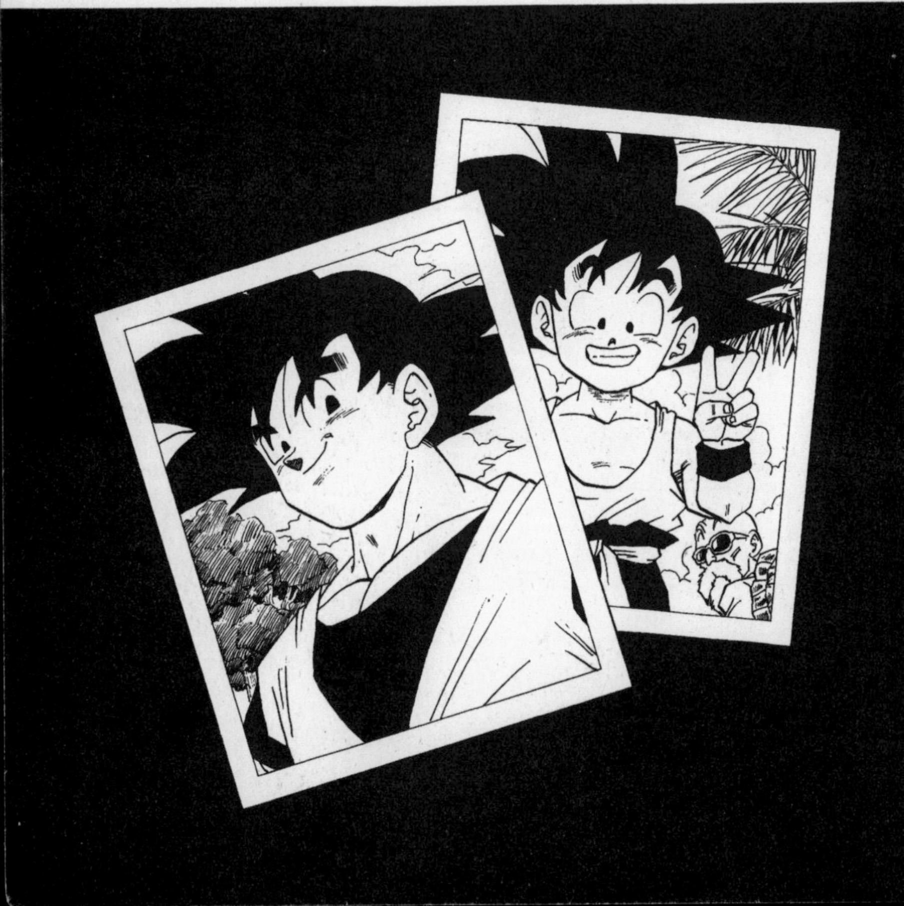

READ THIS WAY

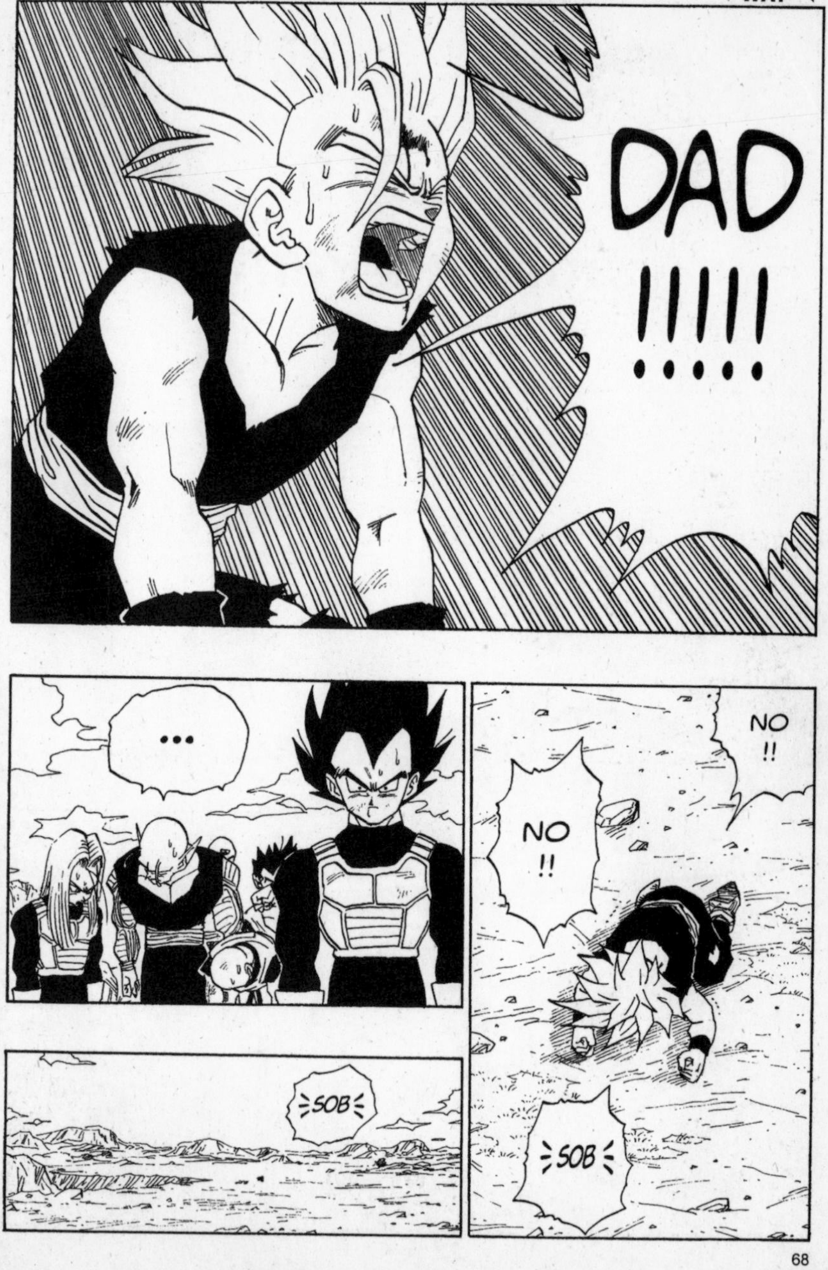
DAD !!!!!
NO !!
NO !!
SOB
...
SOB

READ THIS WAY

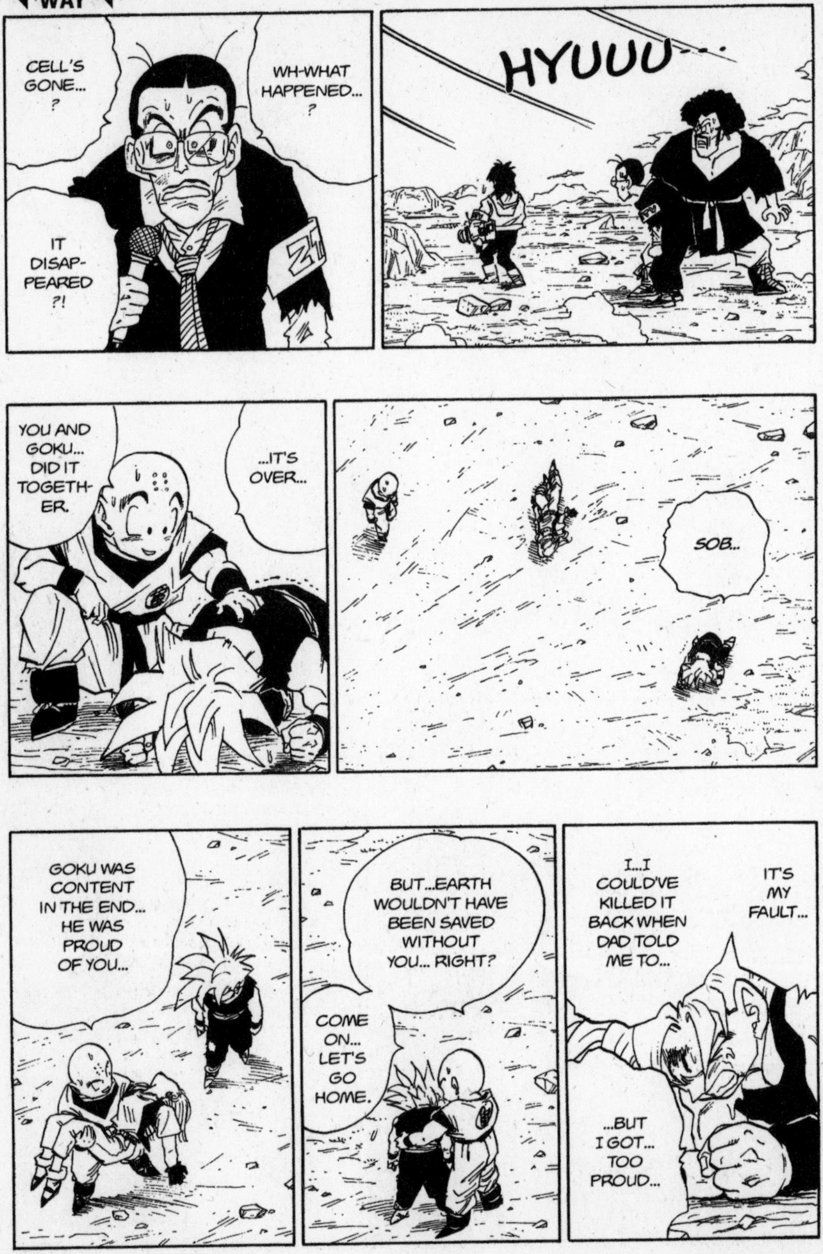
HYUUU
WH-WHAT HAPPENED...?
CELL'S GONE...?
IT DISAPPEARED?!
SOB...
...IT'S OVER...
YOU AND GOKU... DID IT TOGETHER.
IT'S MY FAULT...
I...I COULD'VE KILLED IT BACK WHEN DAD TOLD ME TO...
...BUT I GOT... TOO PROUD...
BUT...EARTH WOULDN'T HAVE BEEN SAVED WITHOUT YOU... RIGHT?
COME ON... LET'S GO HOME.
GOKU WAS CONTENT IN THE END... HE WAS PROUD OF YOU...

READ THIS WAY

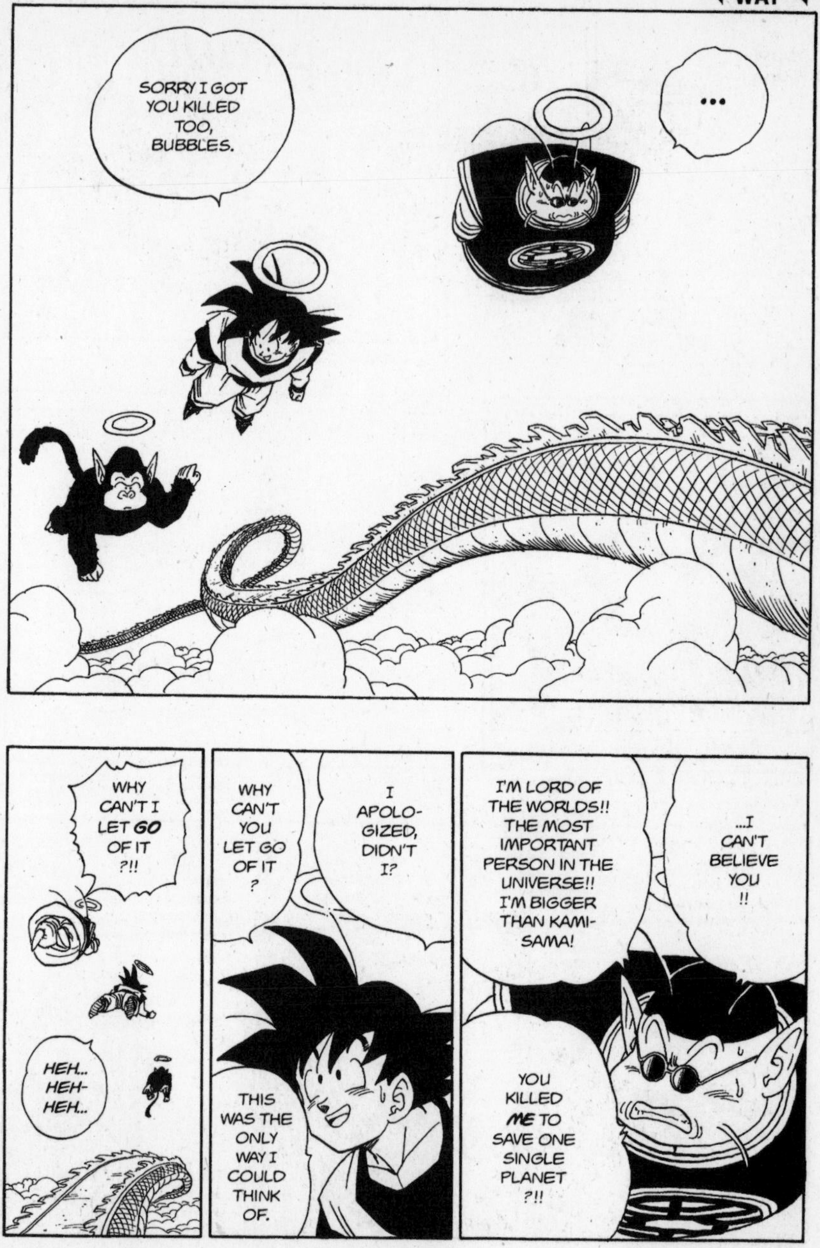
...
SORRY I GOT YOU KILLED TOO, BUBBLES.
...I CAN'T BELIEVE YOU !!
I'M LORD OF THE WORLDS!! THE MOST IMPORTANT PERSON IN THE UNIVERSE!! I'M BIGGER THAN KAMI-SAMA!
YOU KILLED ME TO SAVE ONE SINGLE PLANET ?!!
I APOLO-GIZED, DIDN'T I?
WHY CAN'T YOU LET GO OF IT ?
THIS WAS THE ONLY WAY I COULD THINK OF.
WHY CAN'T I LET GO OF IT ?!!
HEH... HEH-HEH...

READ THIS WAY

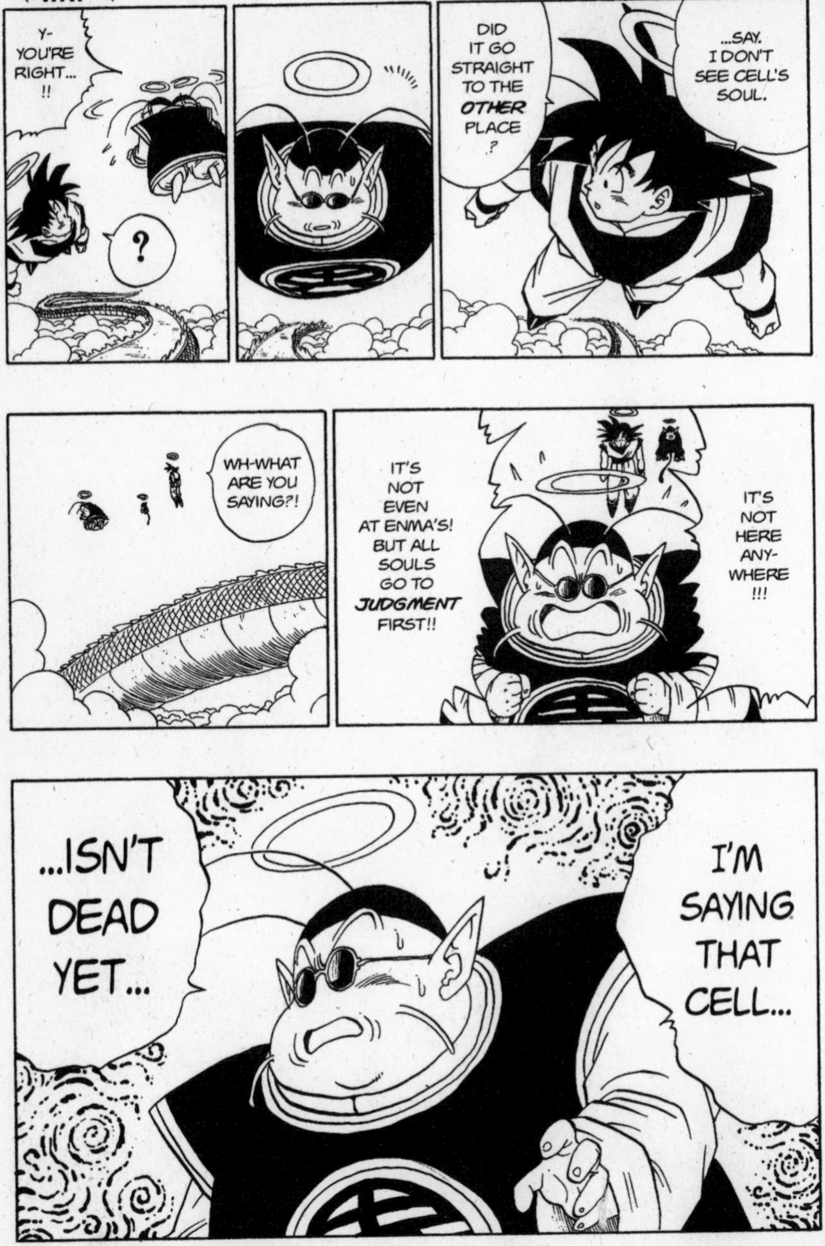
...SAY. I DON'T SEE CELL'S SOUL.
DID IT GO STRAIGHT TO THE *OTHER* PLACE?
Y- YOU'RE RIGHT... !!
?
IT'S NOT HERE ANYWHERE!!!
IT'S NOT EVEN AT ENMA'S! BUT ALL SOULS GO TO *JUDGMENT* FIRST!!
WH-WHAT ARE YOU SAYING?!
I'M SAYING THAT CELL...
...ISN'T DEAD YET...

READ THIS WAY

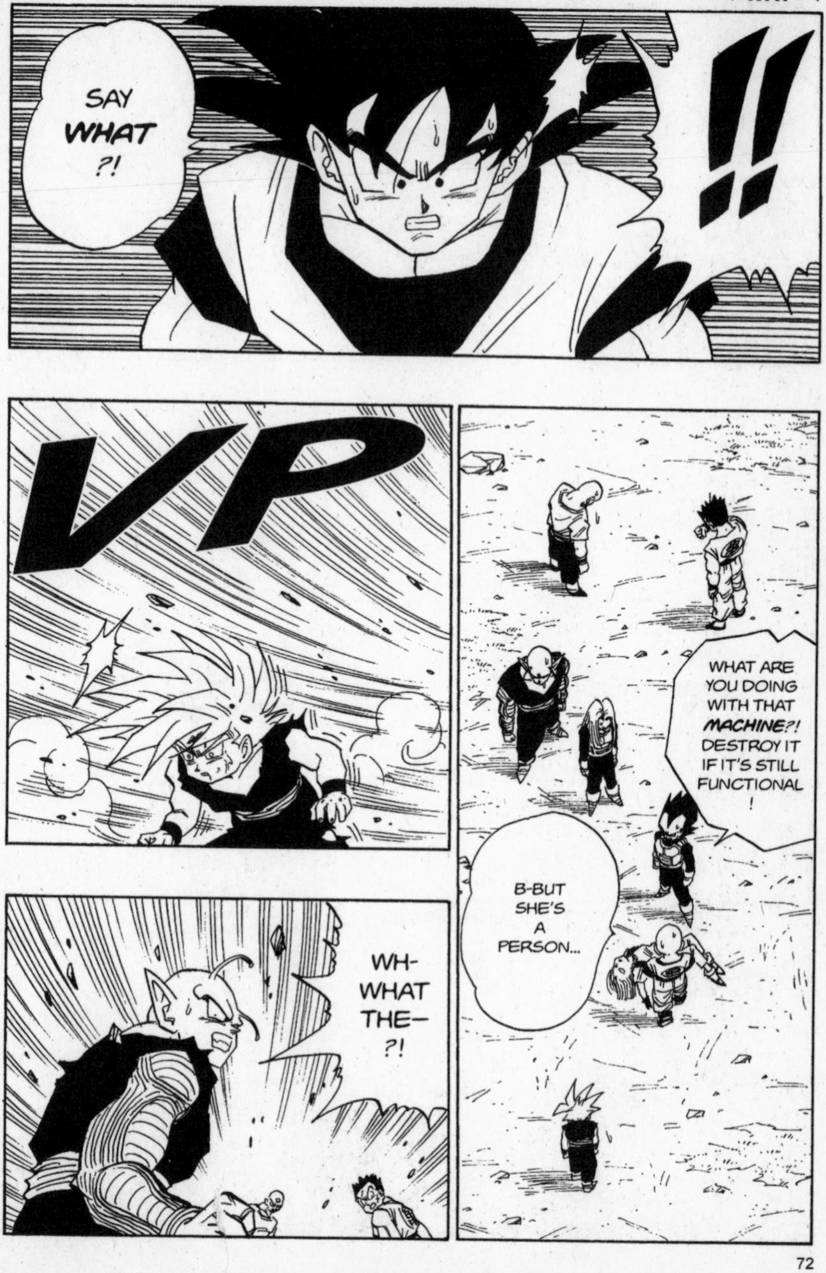

!!
SAY WHAT ?!
WHAT ARE YOU DOING WITH THAT MACHINE?! DESTROY IT IF IT'S STILL FUNCTIONAL !
B-BUT SHE'S A PERSON...
VP
WH-WHAT THE-?!

READ THIS WAY

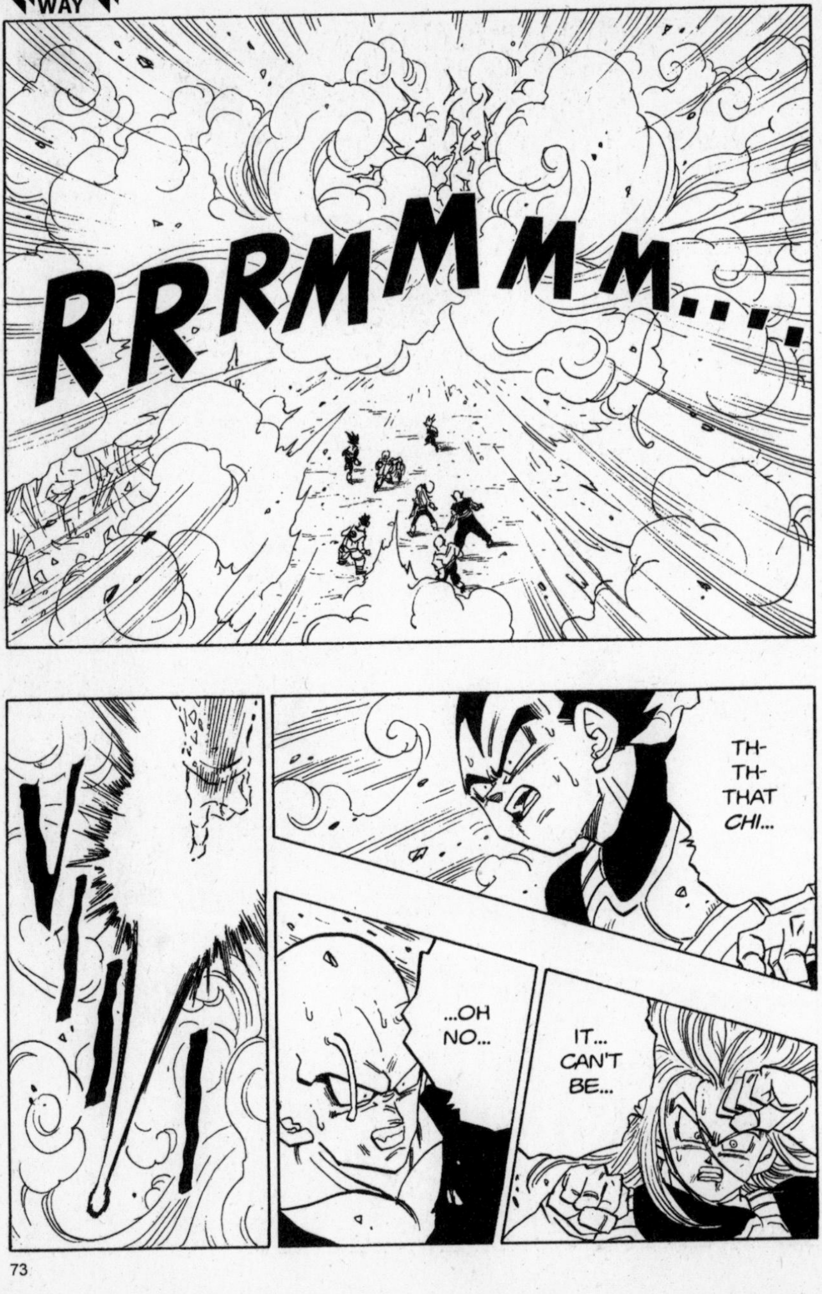
RRRMMMM....
TH- TH- THAT CHI...
IT... CAN'T BE...
...OH NO...

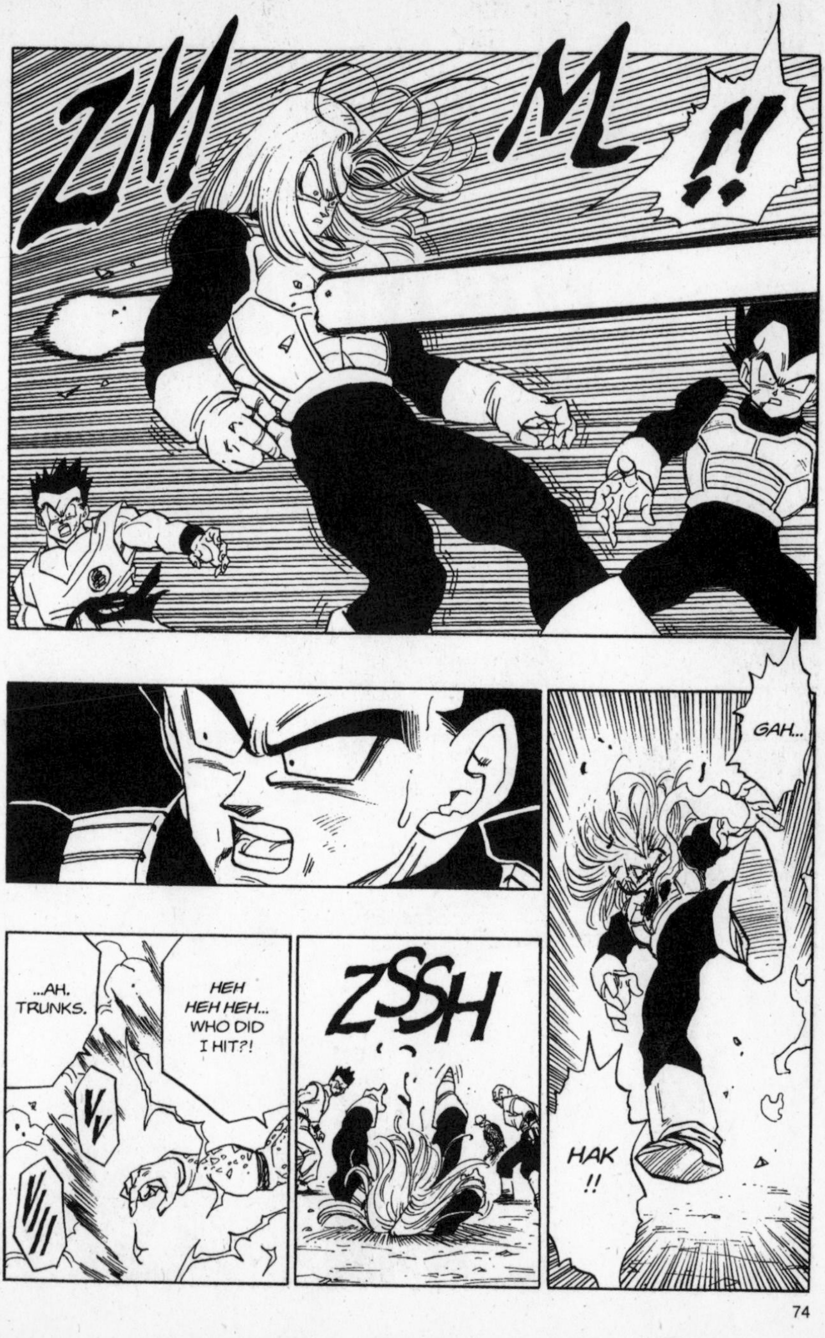
ZMMM!!
GAH...
HAK !!
ZSSH
HEH HEH HEH... WHO DID I HIT?!
...AH. TRUNKS.

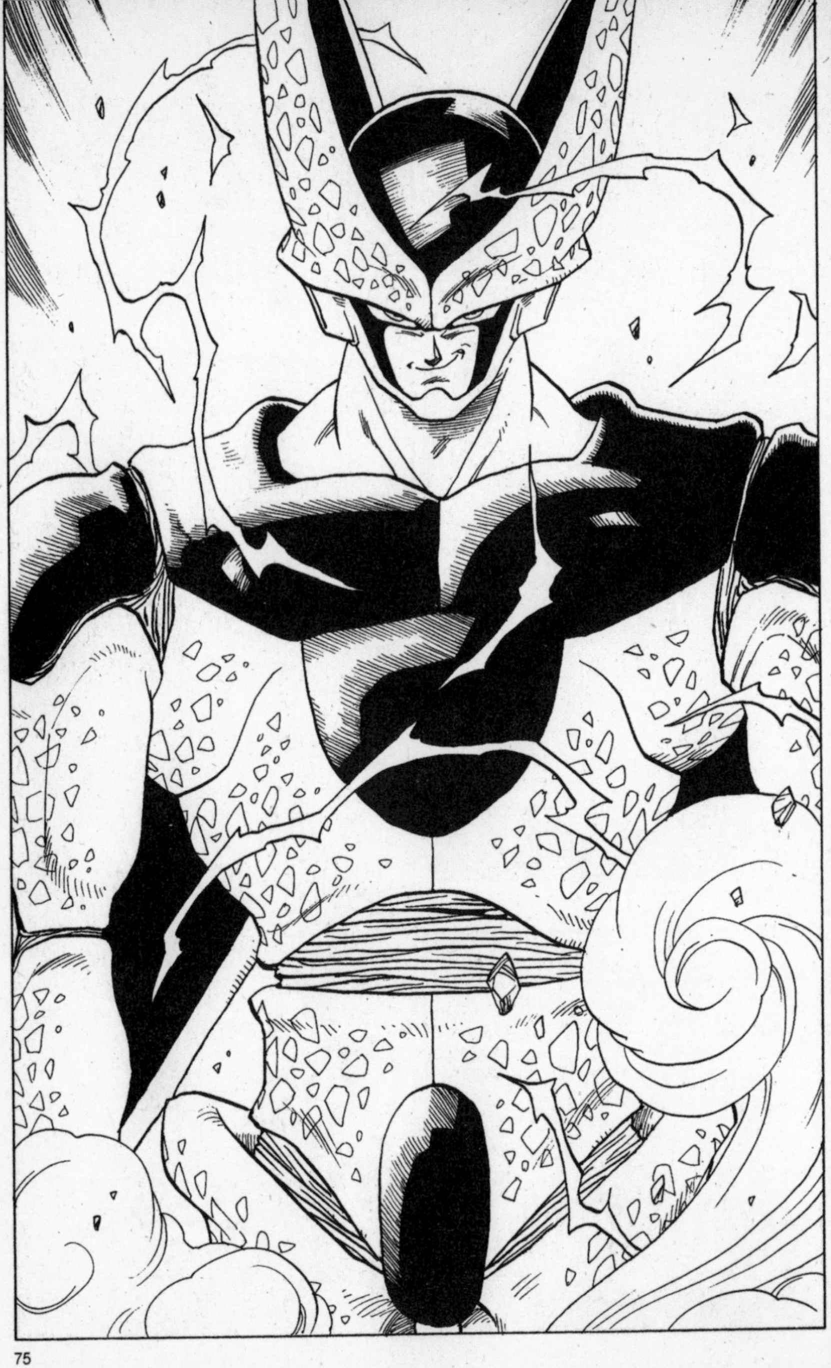

READ THIS WAY

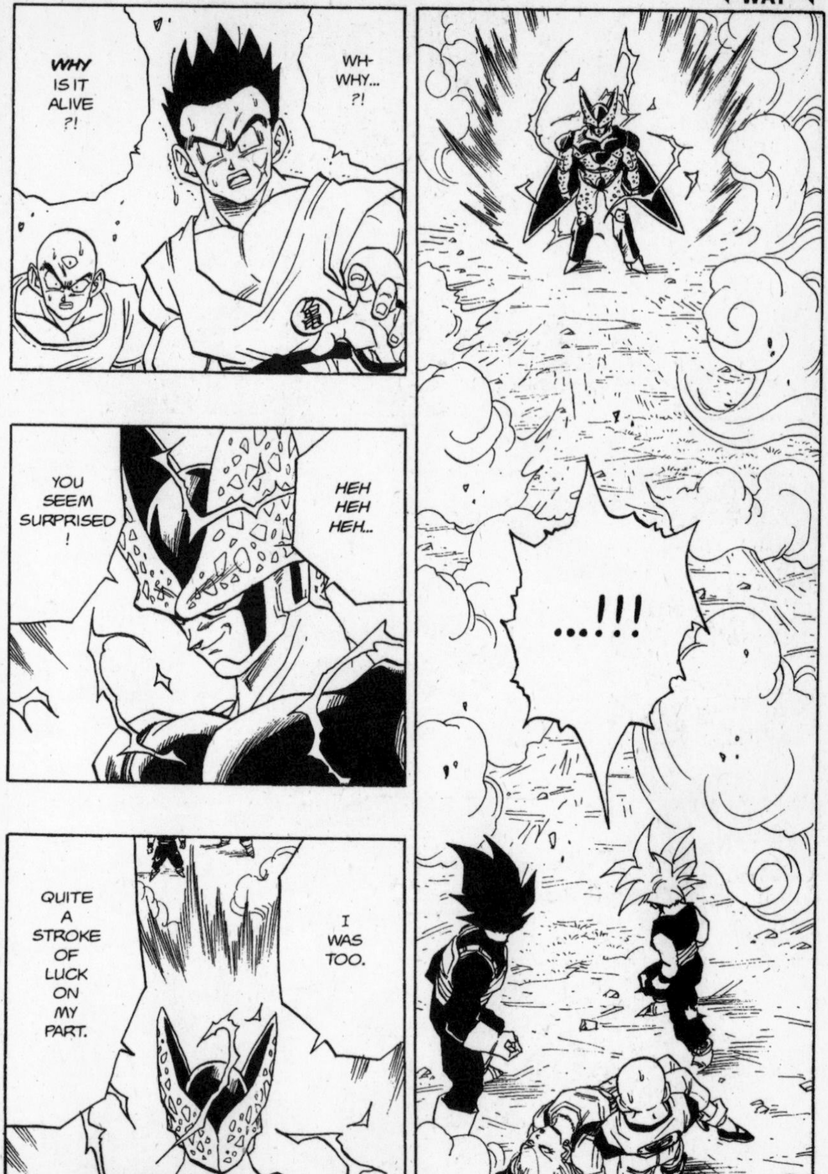
...!!!
WH-WHY...?!
WHY IS IT ALIVE?!
HEH HEH HEH...
YOU SEEM SURPRISED!
I WAS TOO.
QUITE A STROKE OF LUCK ON MY PART.

READ THIS WAY

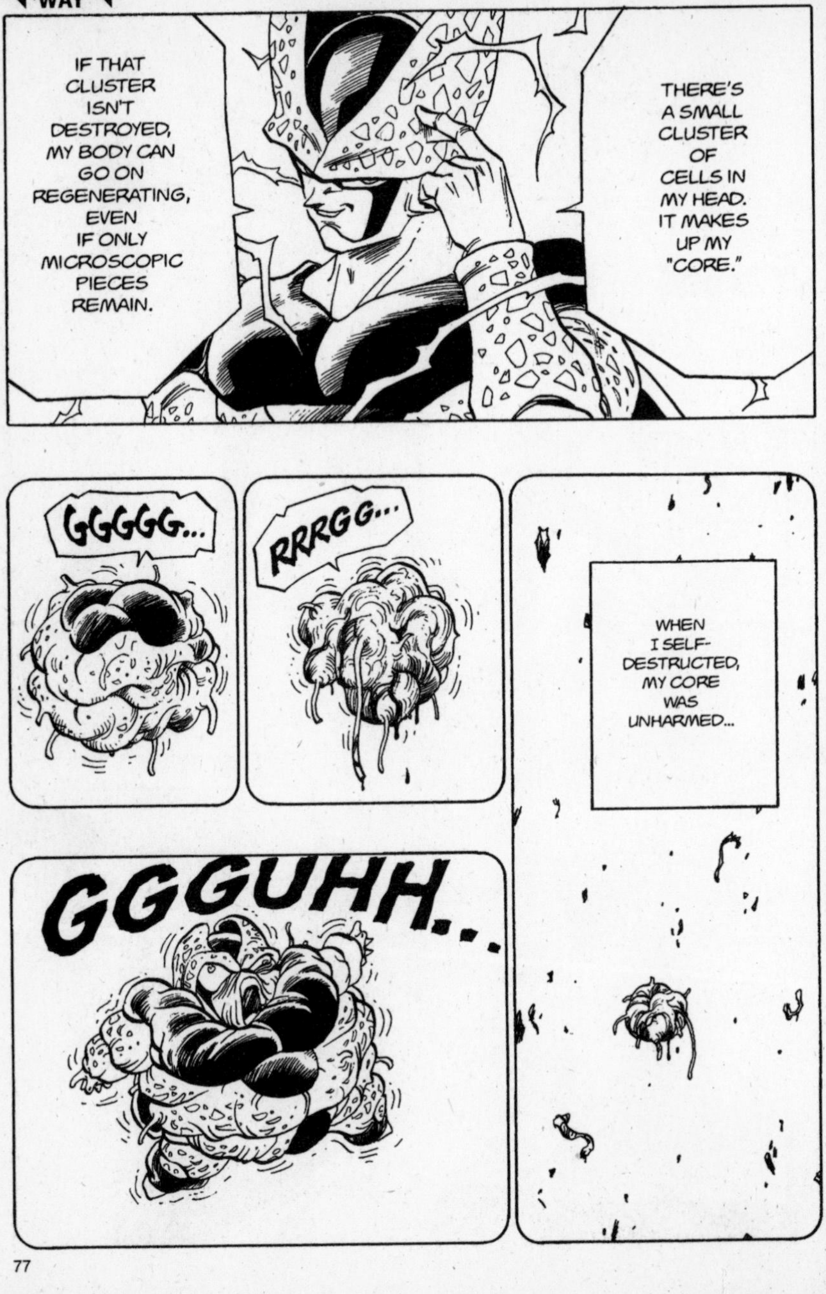
THERE'S A SMALL CLUSTER OF CELLS IN MY HEAD. IT MAKES UP MY "CORE."
IF THAT CLUSTER ISN'T DESTROYED, MY BODY CAN GO ON REGENERATING, EVEN IF ONLY MICROSCOPIC PIECES REMAIN.
WHEN I SELF-DESTRUCTED, MY CORE WAS UNHARMED...
RRRGG...
GGGGG...
GGGUHH...

READ THIS WAY

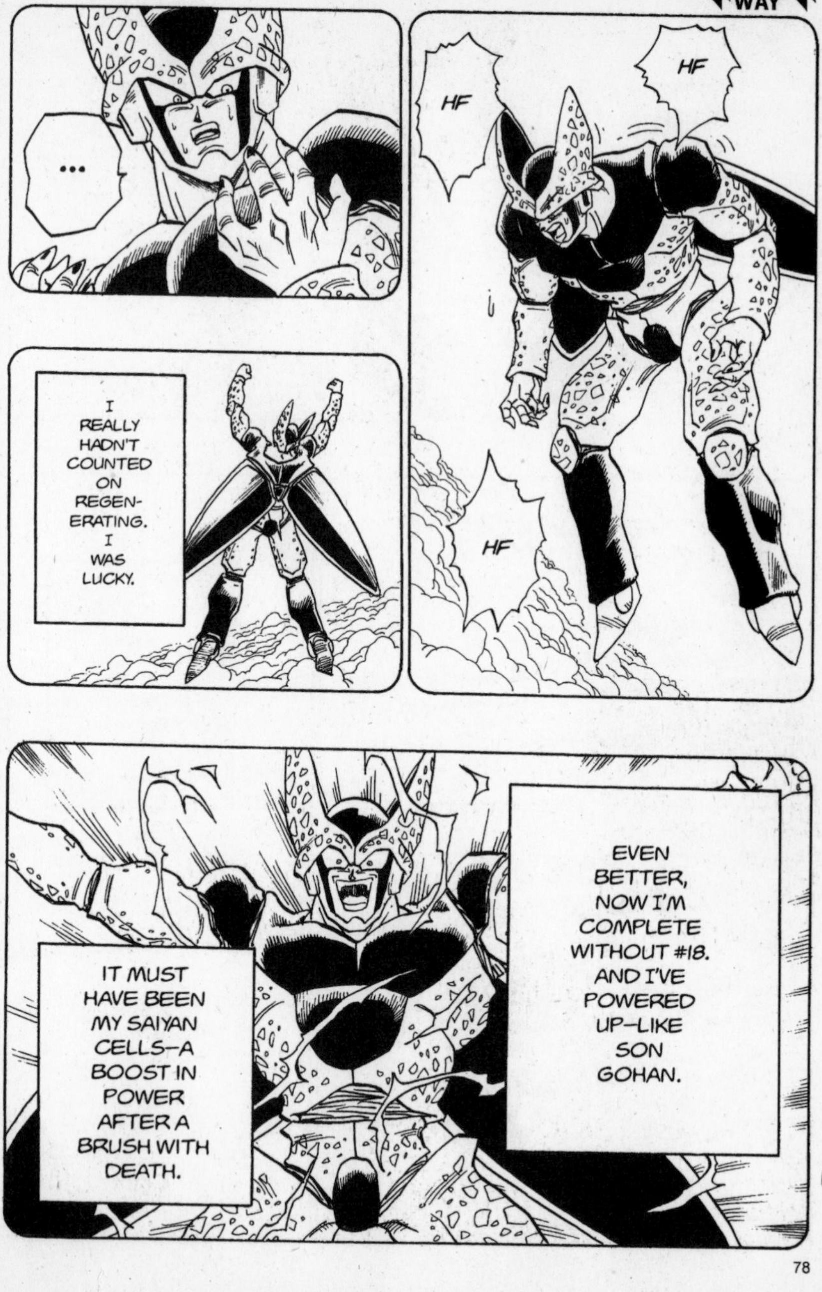
HF
HF
HF
...
I REALLY HADN'T COUNTED ON REGEN-ERATING. I WAS LUCKY.
EVEN BETTER, NOW I'M COMPLETE WITHOUT #18. AND I'VE POWERED UP–LIKE SON GOHAN.
IT MUST HAVE BEEN MY SAIYAN CELLS–A BOOST IN POWER AFTER A BRUSH WITH DEATH.

READ THIS WAY

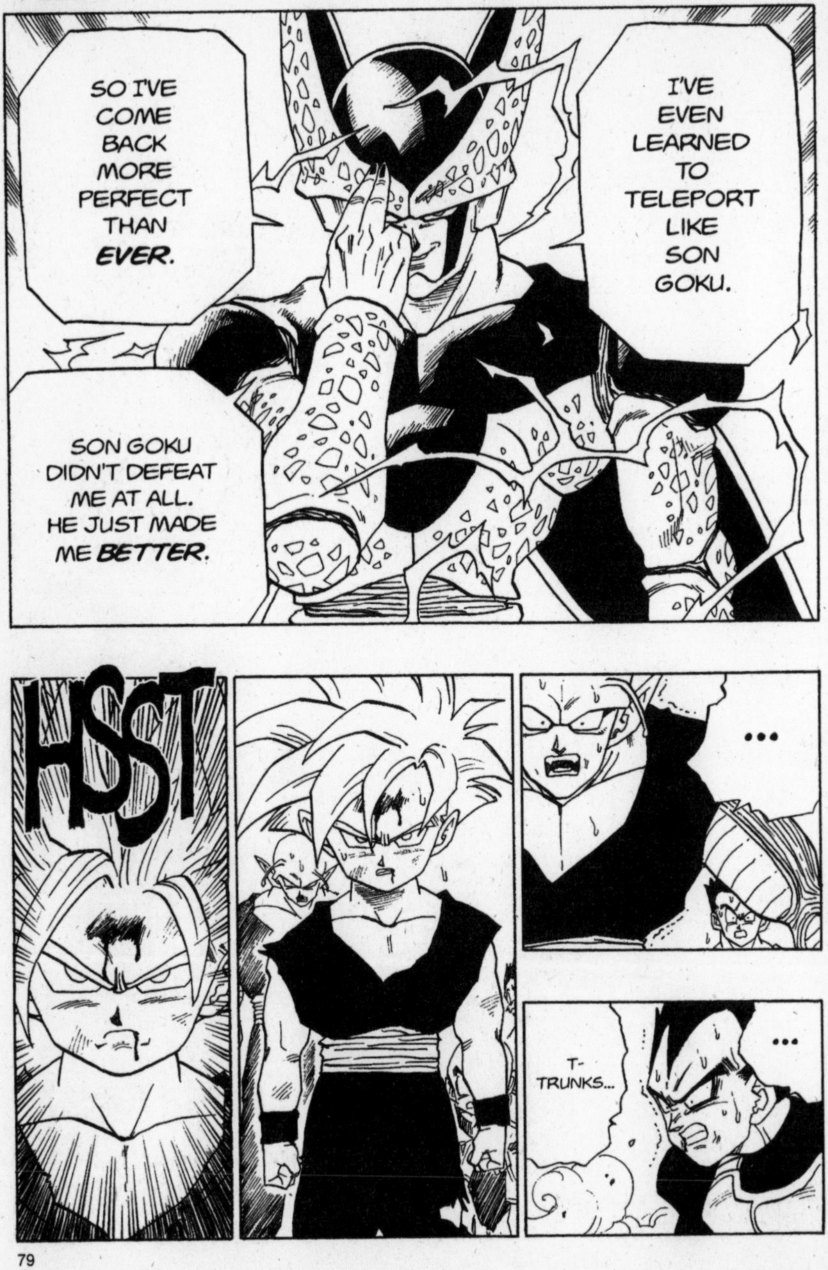
I'VE EVEN LEARNED TO TELEPORT LIKE SON GOKU.
SO I'VE COME BACK MORE PERFECT THAN *EVER*.
SON GOKU DIDN'T DEFEAT ME AT ALL. HE JUST MADE ME *BETTER*.
...
...
T- TRUNKS...
HSST

DBZ:220
The Tables Turn

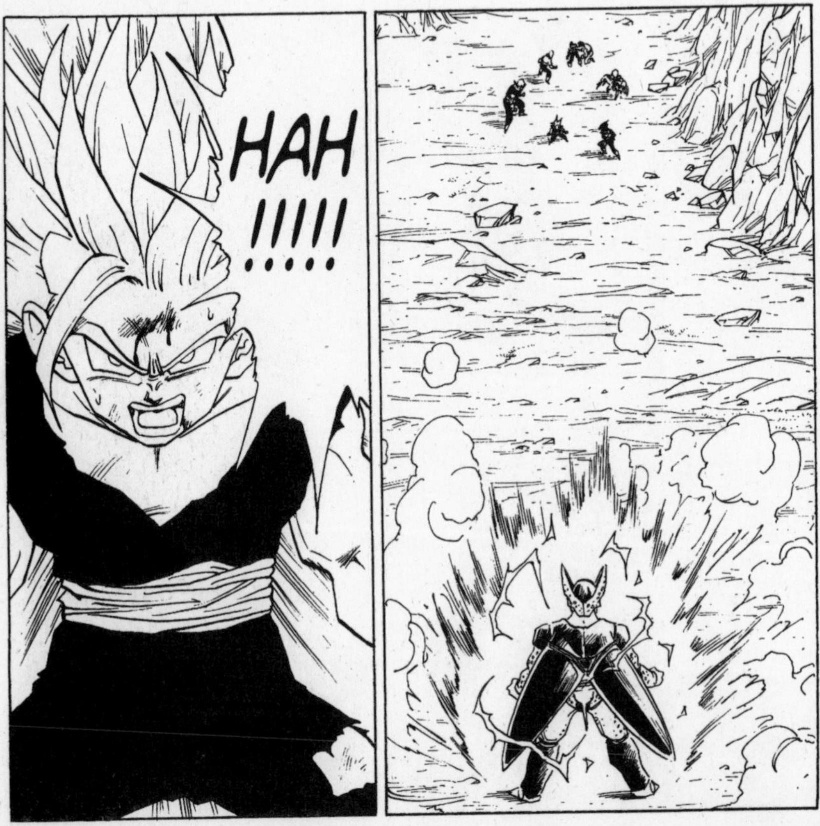
HAH !!!!!

READ THIS WAY

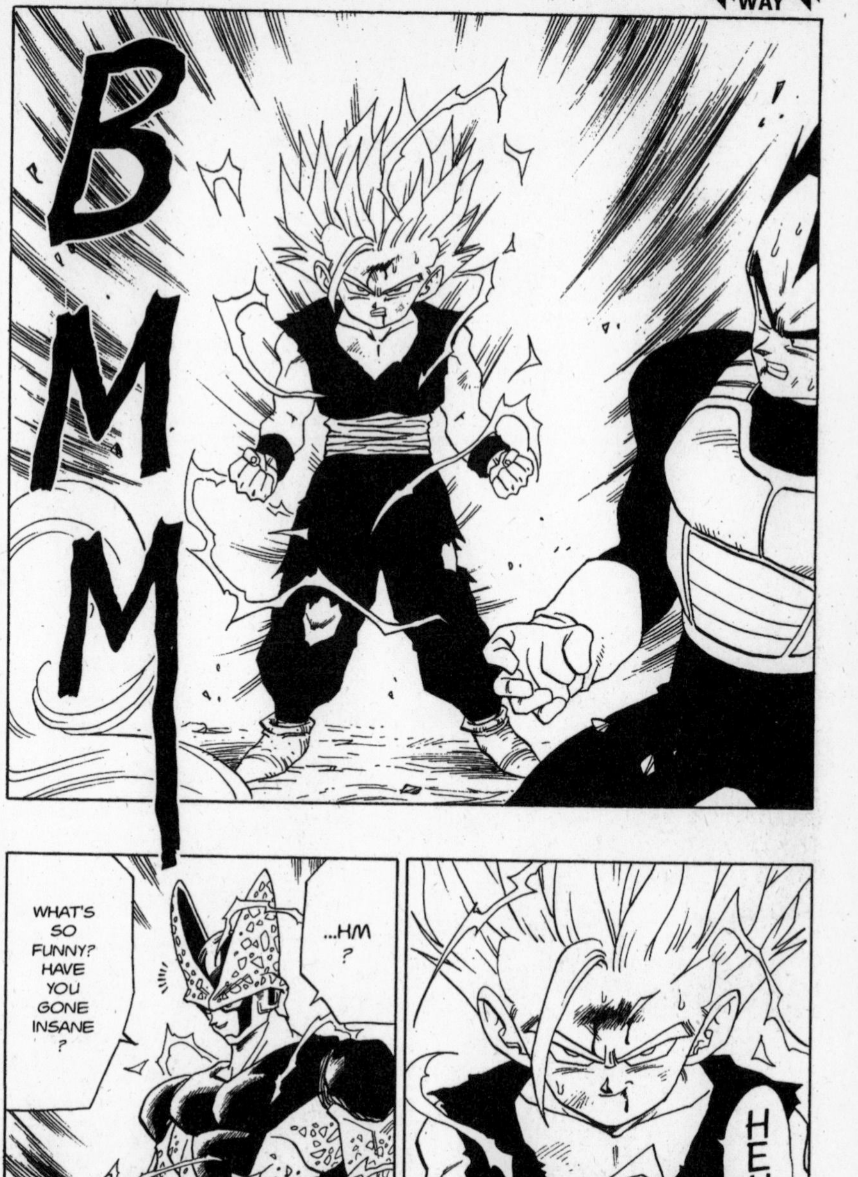
BMMM
HEH
...HM ?
WHAT'S SO FUNNY? HAVE YOU GONE INSANE ?

READ THIS WAY

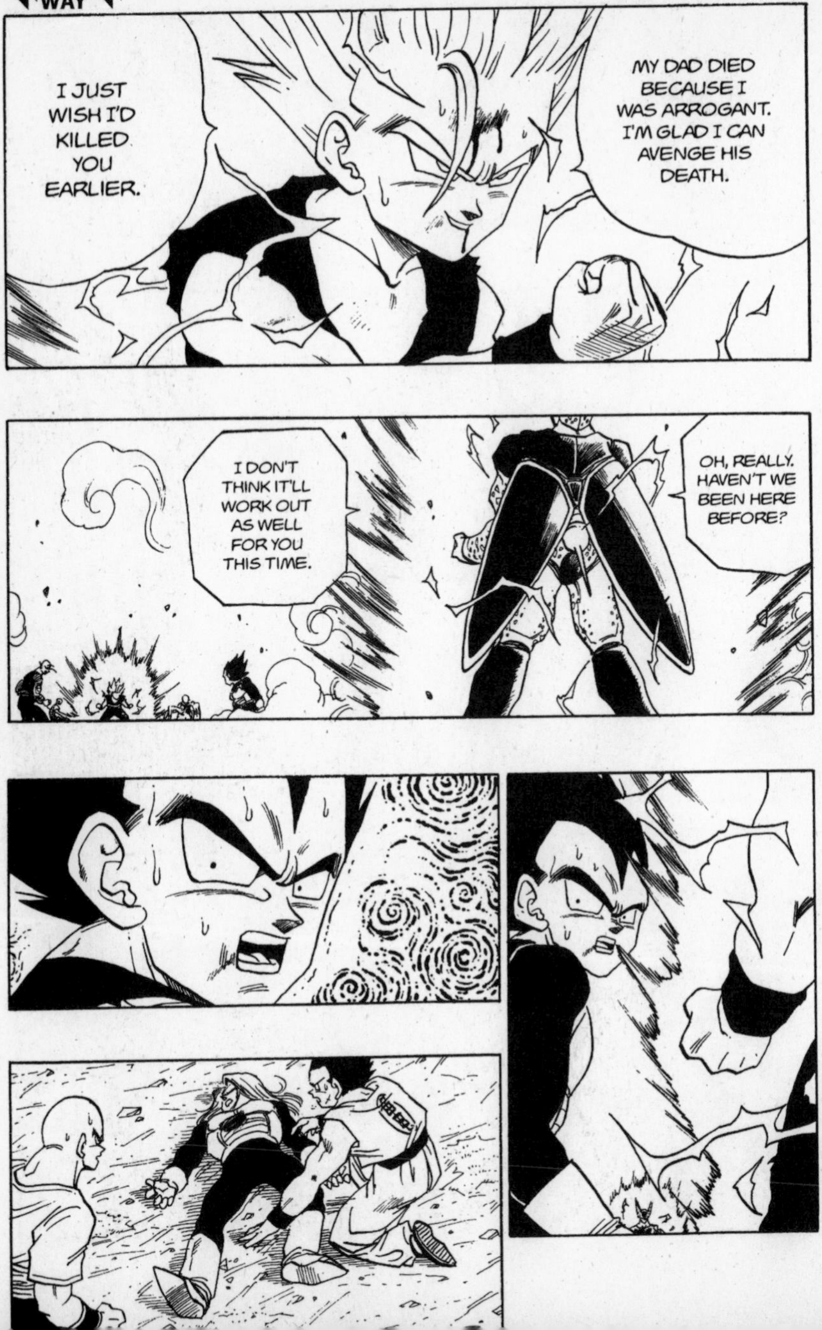
MY DAD DIED BECAUSE I WAS ARROGANT. I'M GLAD I CAN AVENGE HIS DEATH.
I JUST WISH I'D KILLED YOU EARLIER.
OH, REALLY. HAVEN'T WE BEEN HERE BEFORE?
I DON'T THINK IT'LL WORK OUT AS WELL FOR YOU THIS TIME.

READ THIS WAY

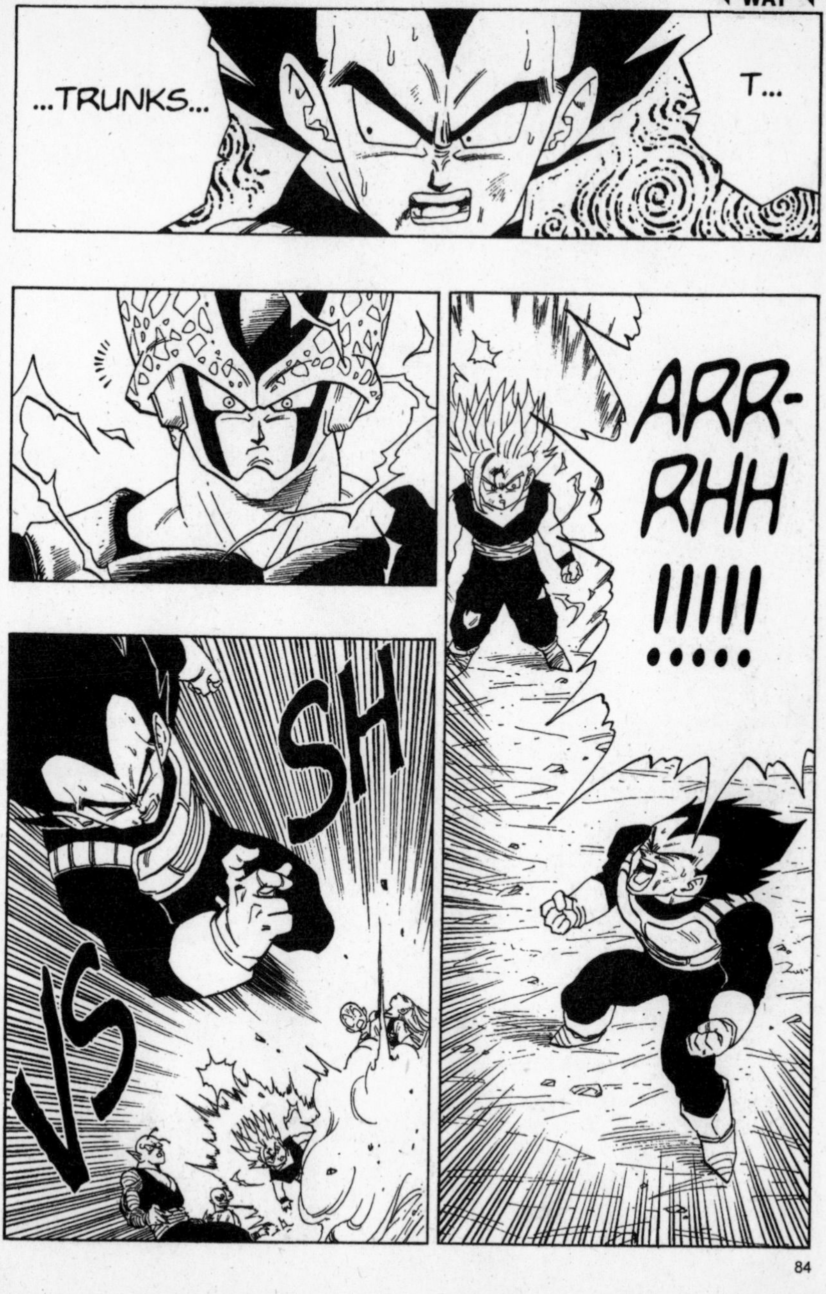
T...
...TRUNKS...
ARR-RHH!!!!!.....
VSSH

READ THIS WAY

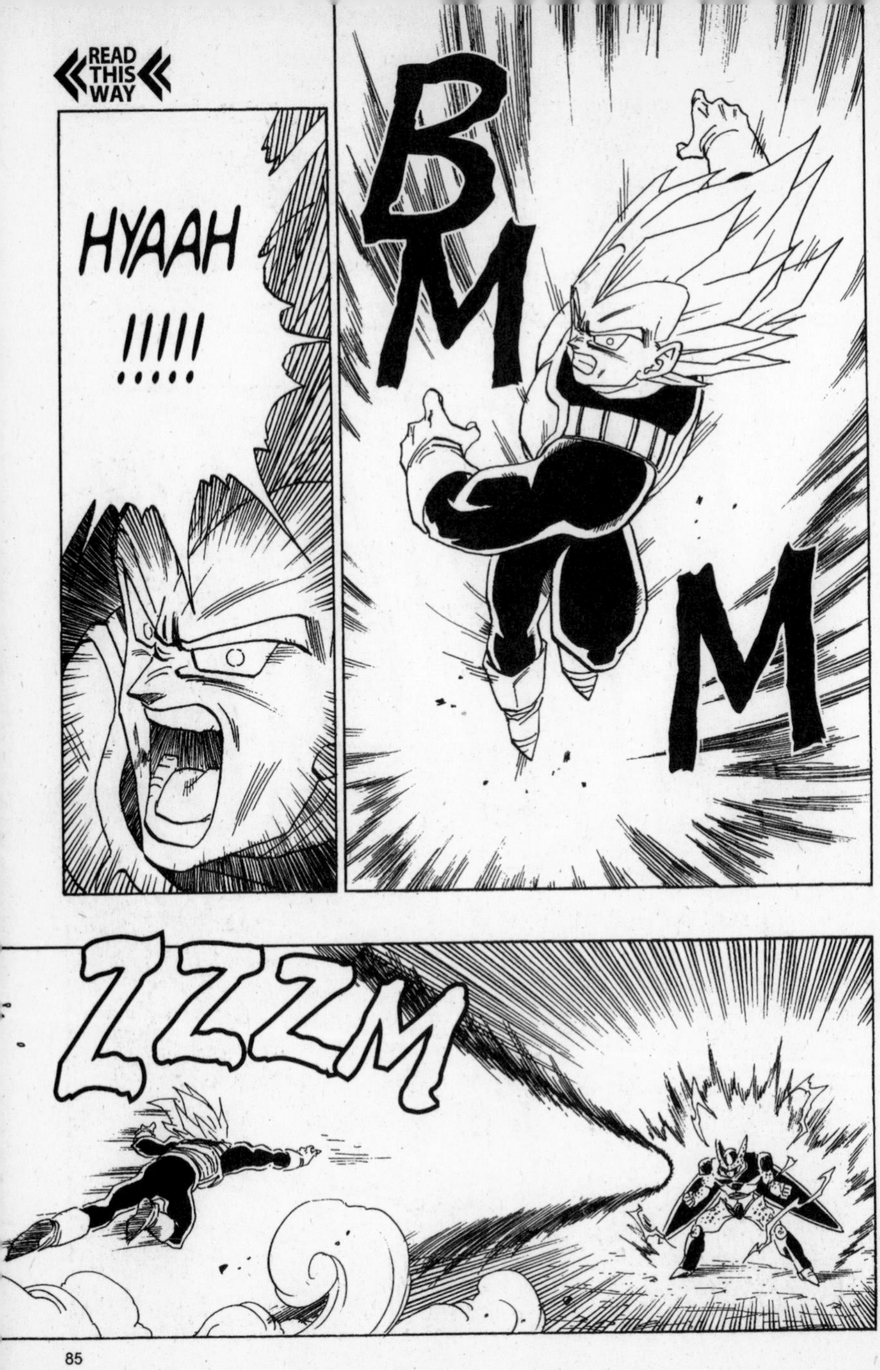

BMM
HYAAH !!!!!
ZZZM

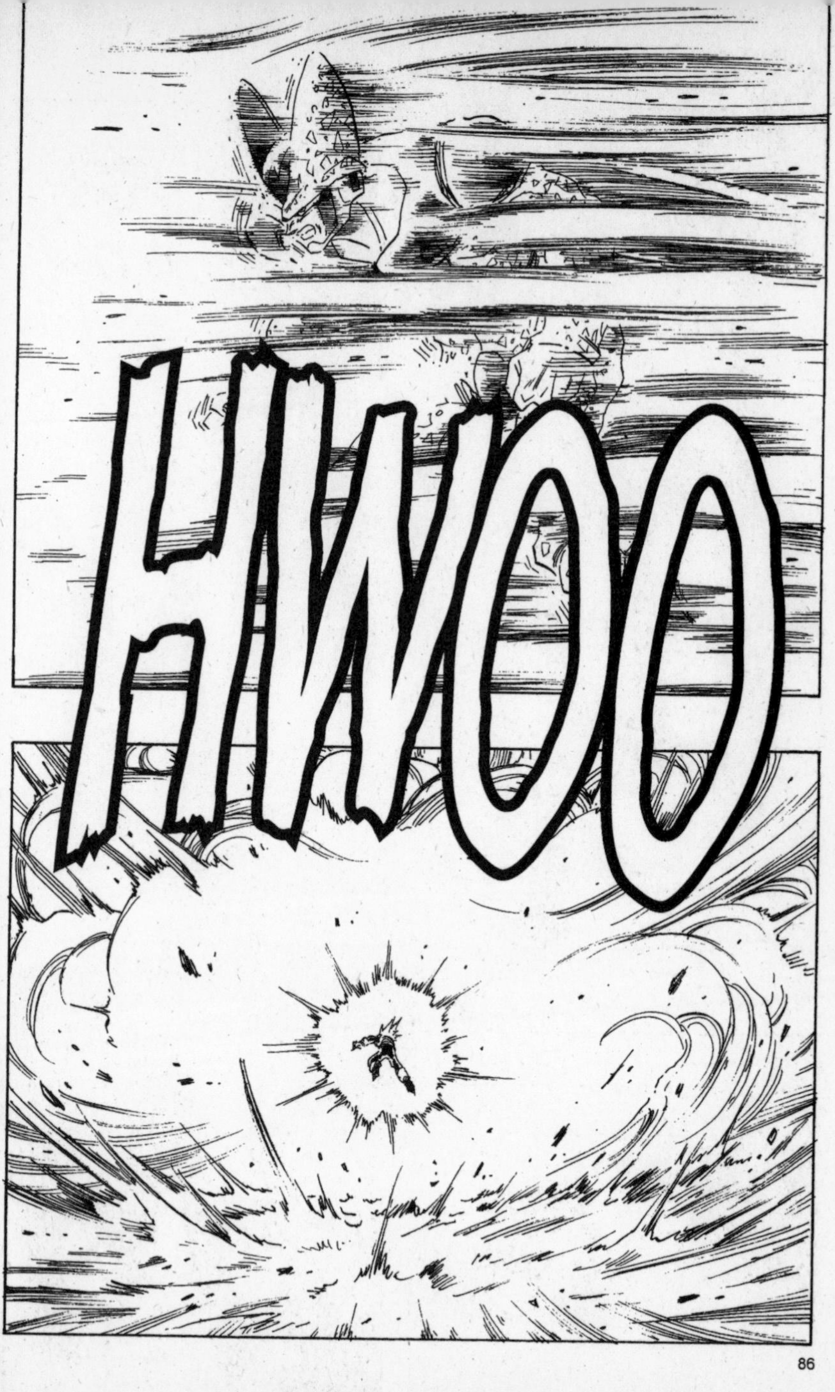
HWOO

READ THIS WAY

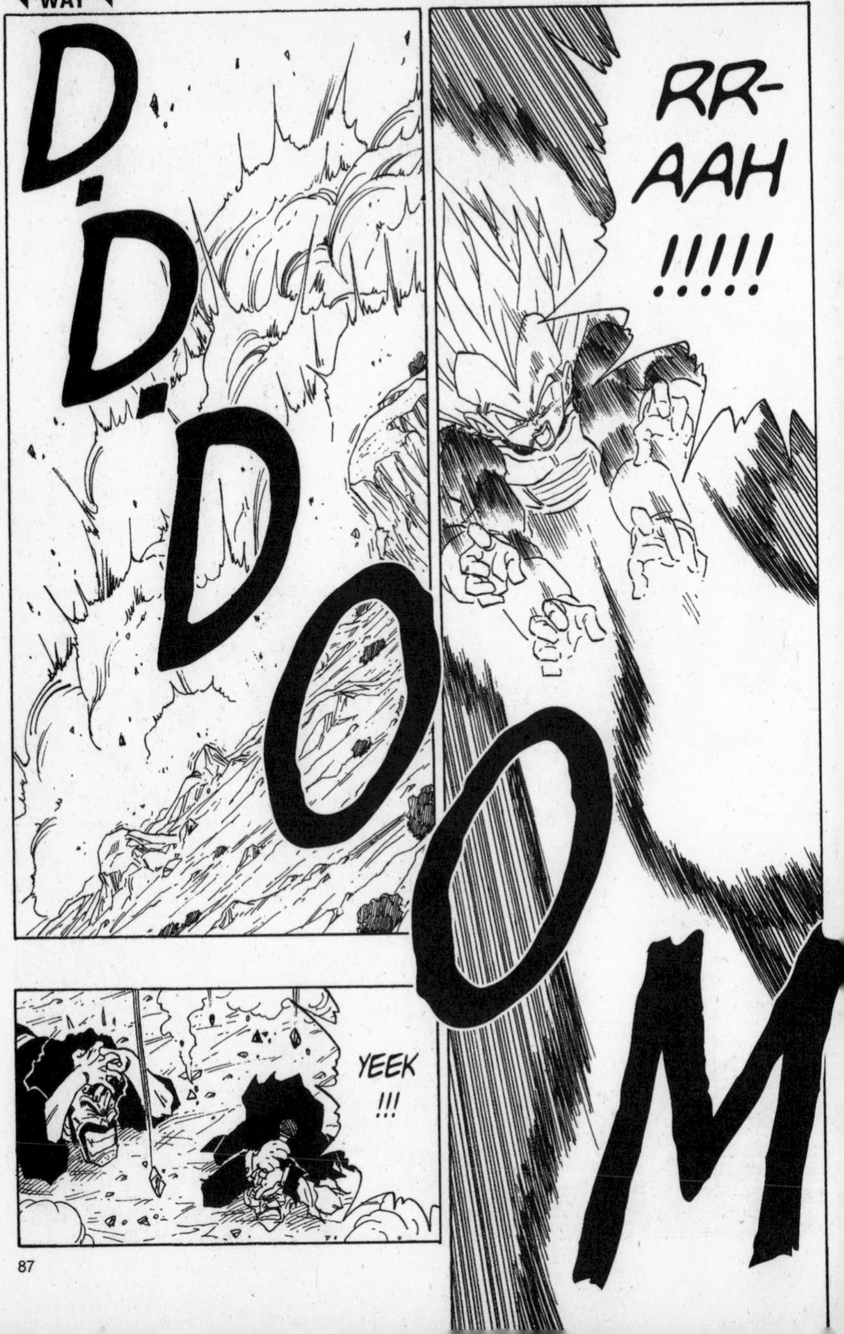
RR-AAH!!!!!
D.D.DOOOM
YEEK!!!

READ THIS WAY

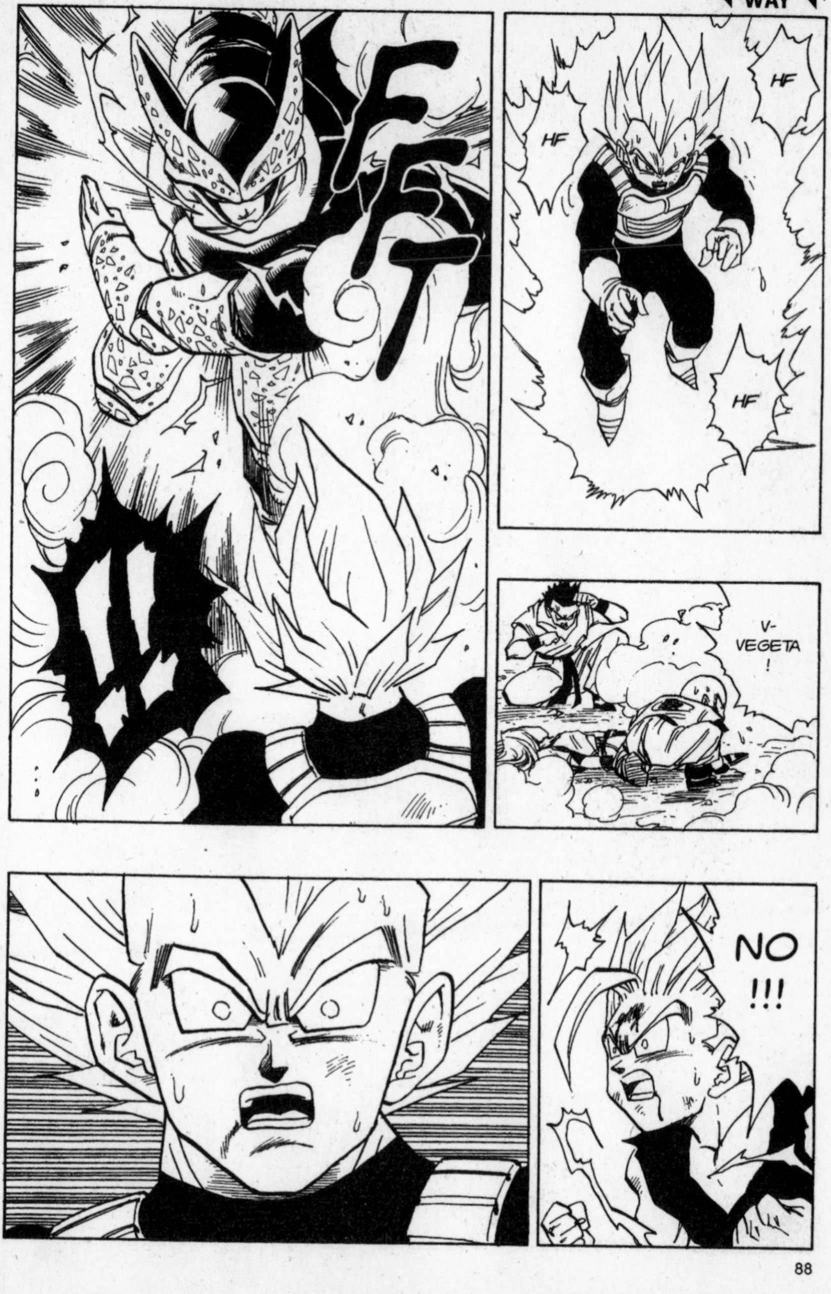
HF
HF
HF
V-
VEGETA
!
FFT
NO
!!!

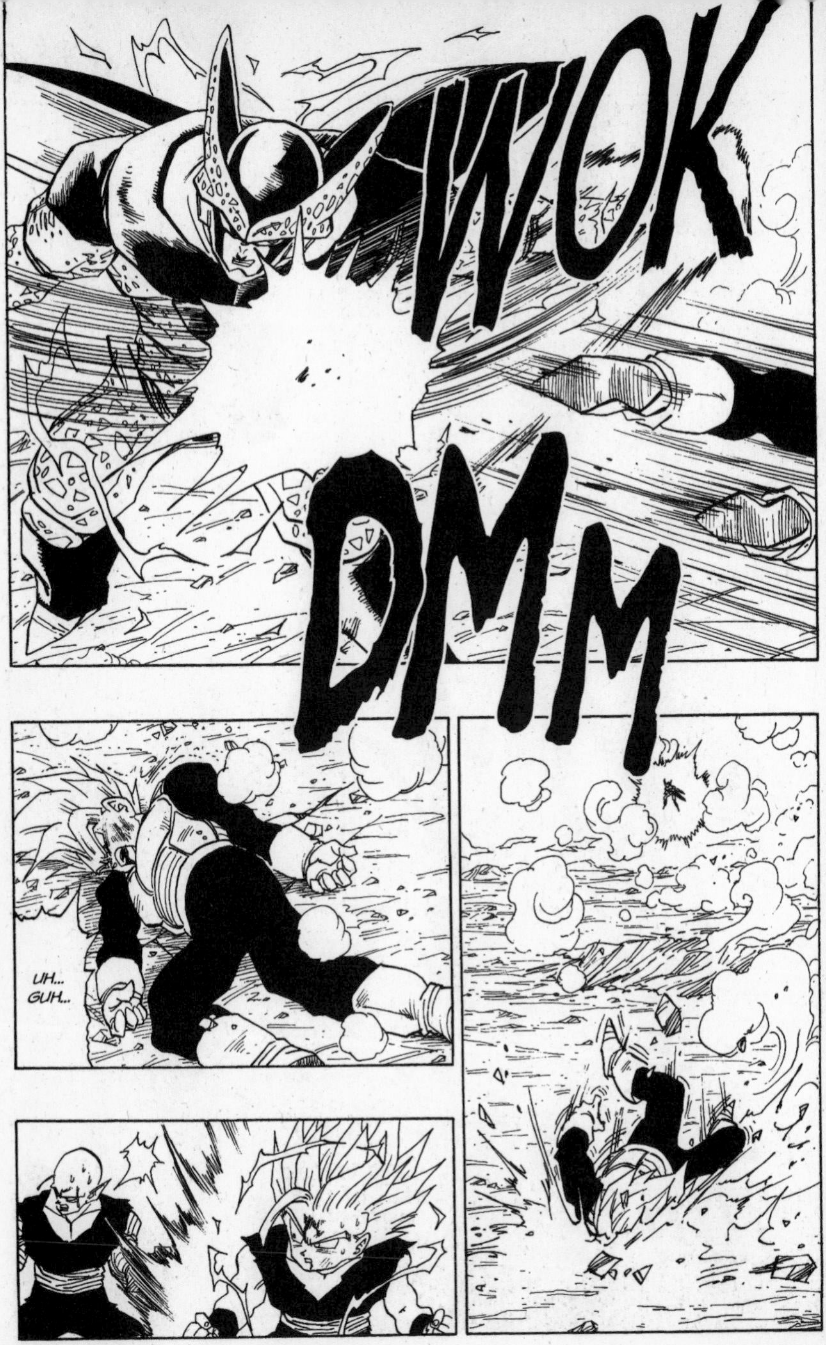
WOK
DMM
UH... GUH...

READ THIS WAY

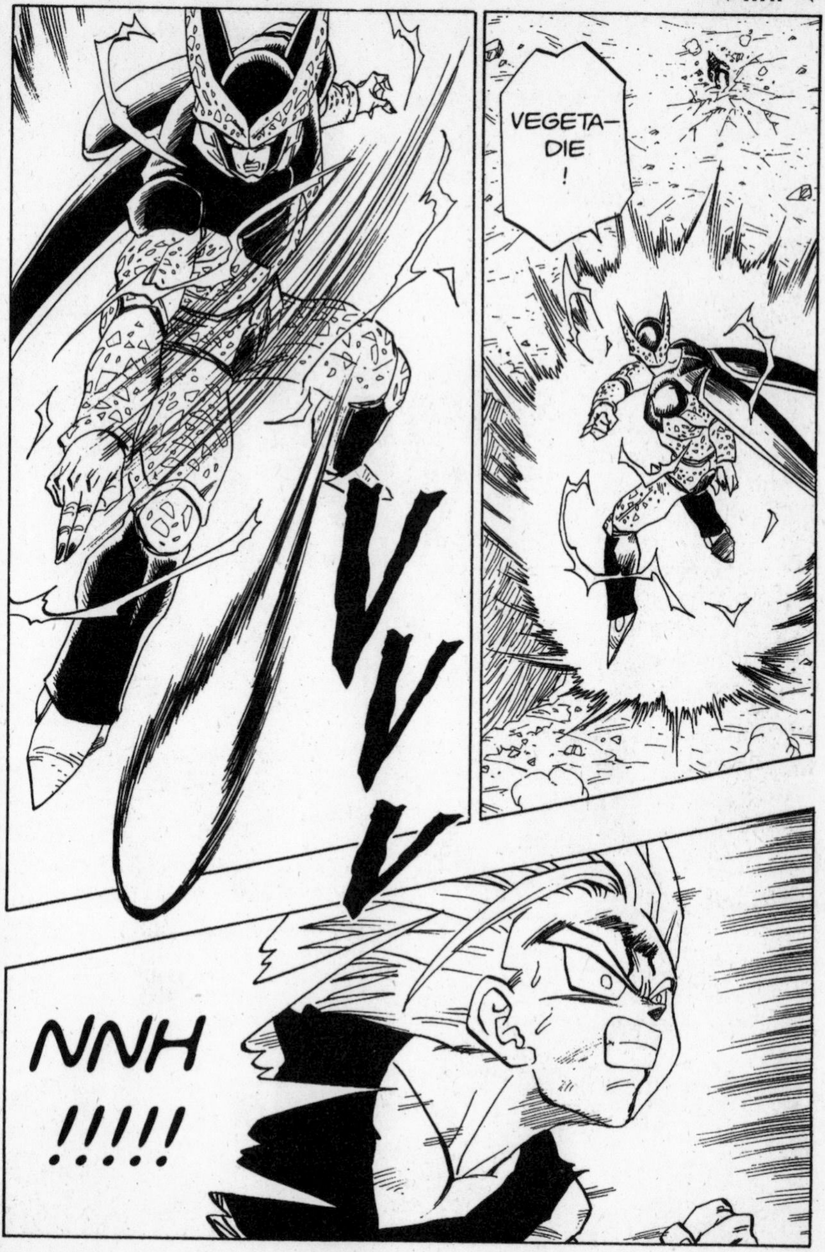
VEGETA-DIE!
NNH!!!!!

READ THIS WAY

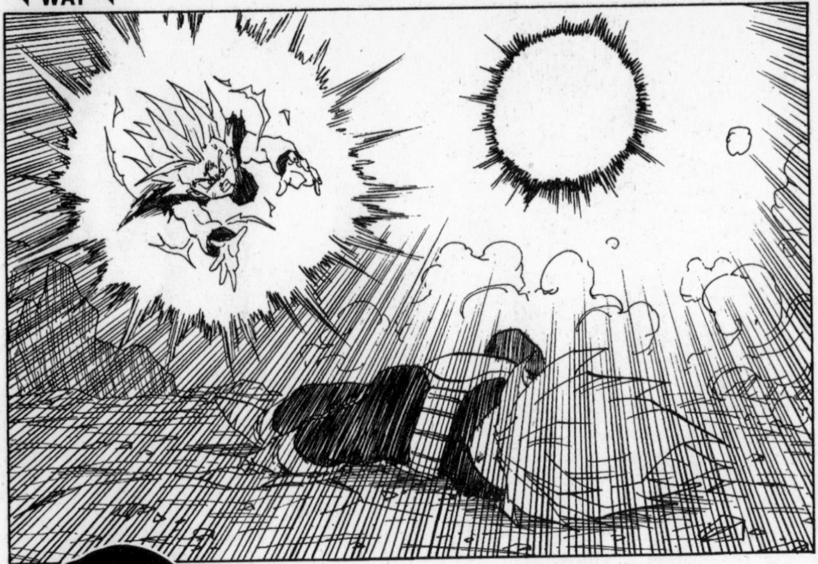

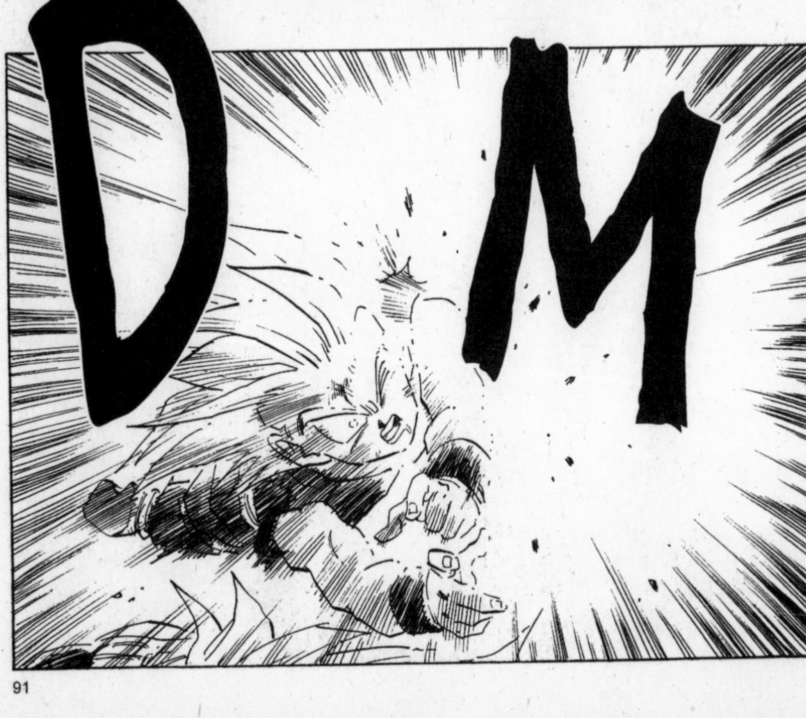
D M

READ THIS WAY

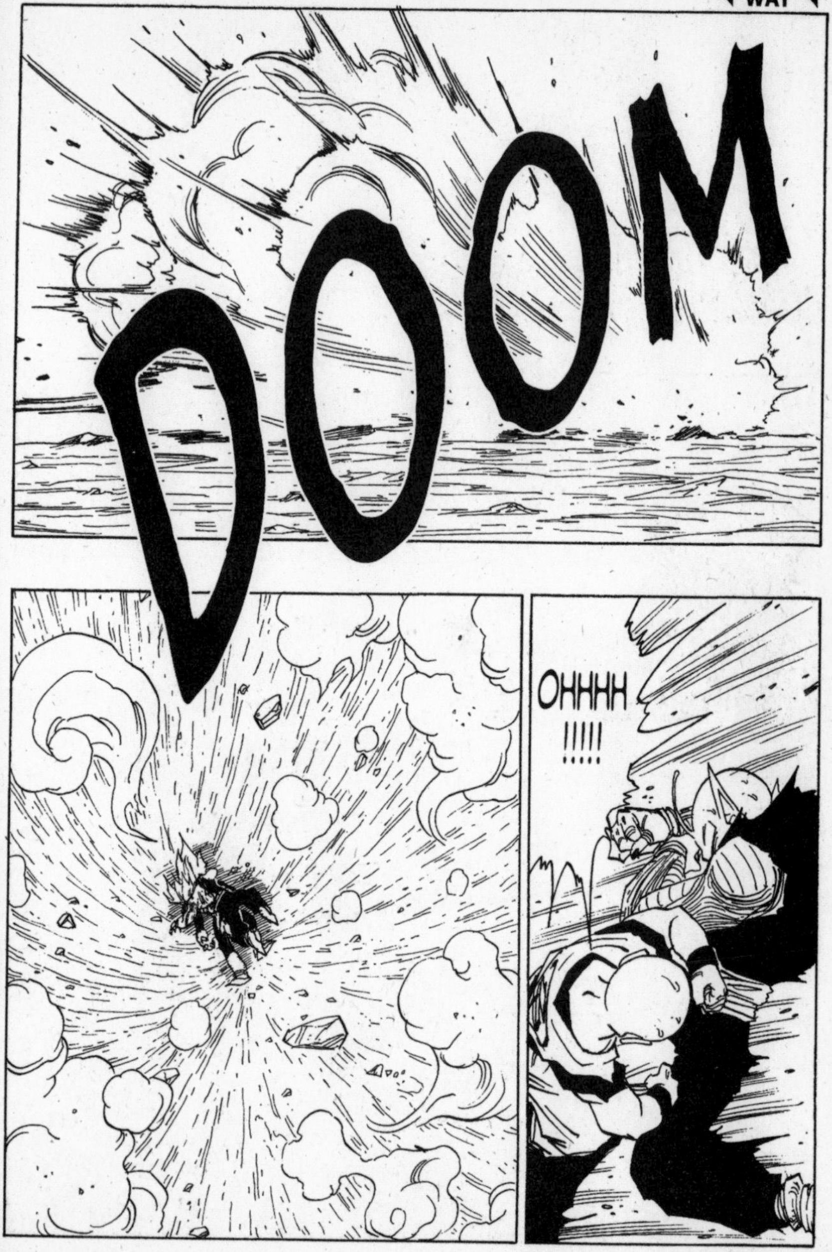
DOOM
OHHHH
!!!!!

READ THIS WAY

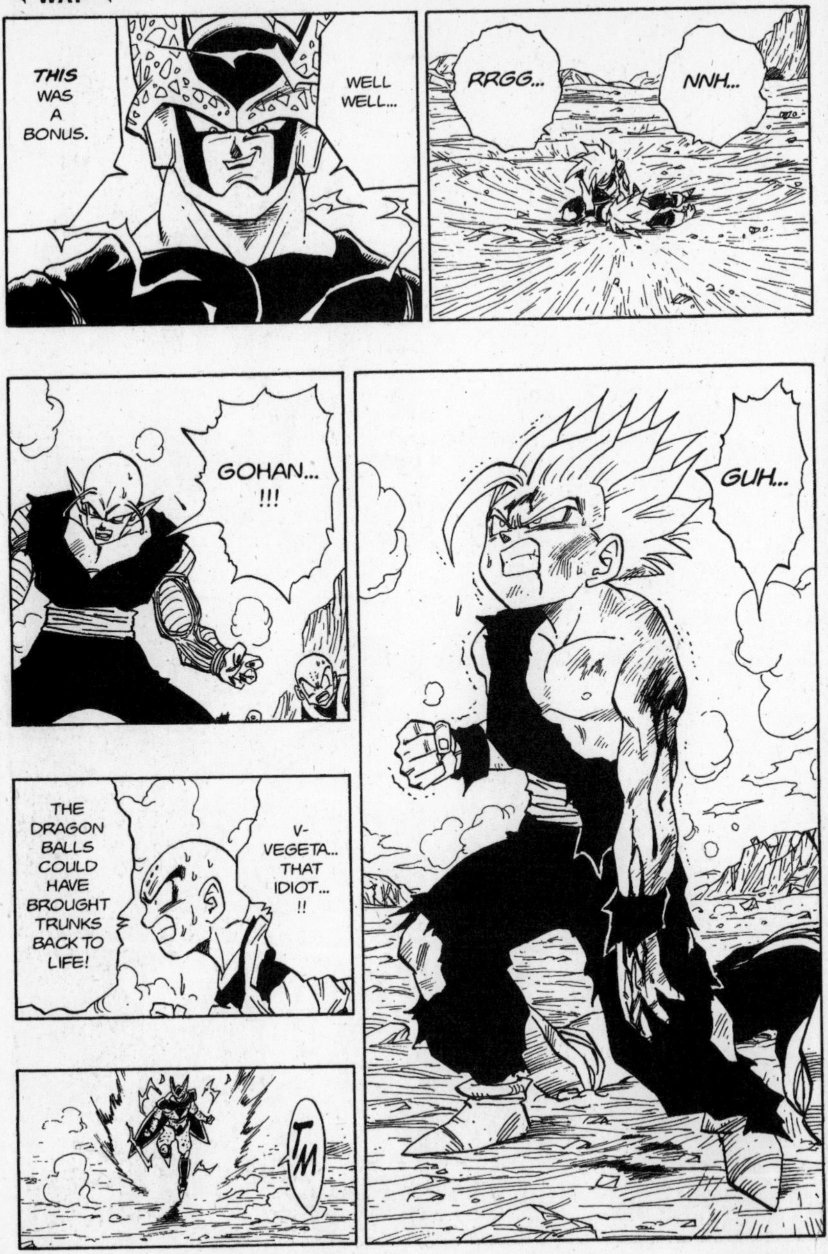

NNH...
RRGG...
WELL WELL...
THIS WAS A BONUS.
GUH...
GOHAN... !!!
V-VEGETA.. THAT IDIOT... !!
THE DRAGON BALLS COULD HAVE BROUGHT TRUNKS BACK TO LIFE!
TM

READ THIS WAY

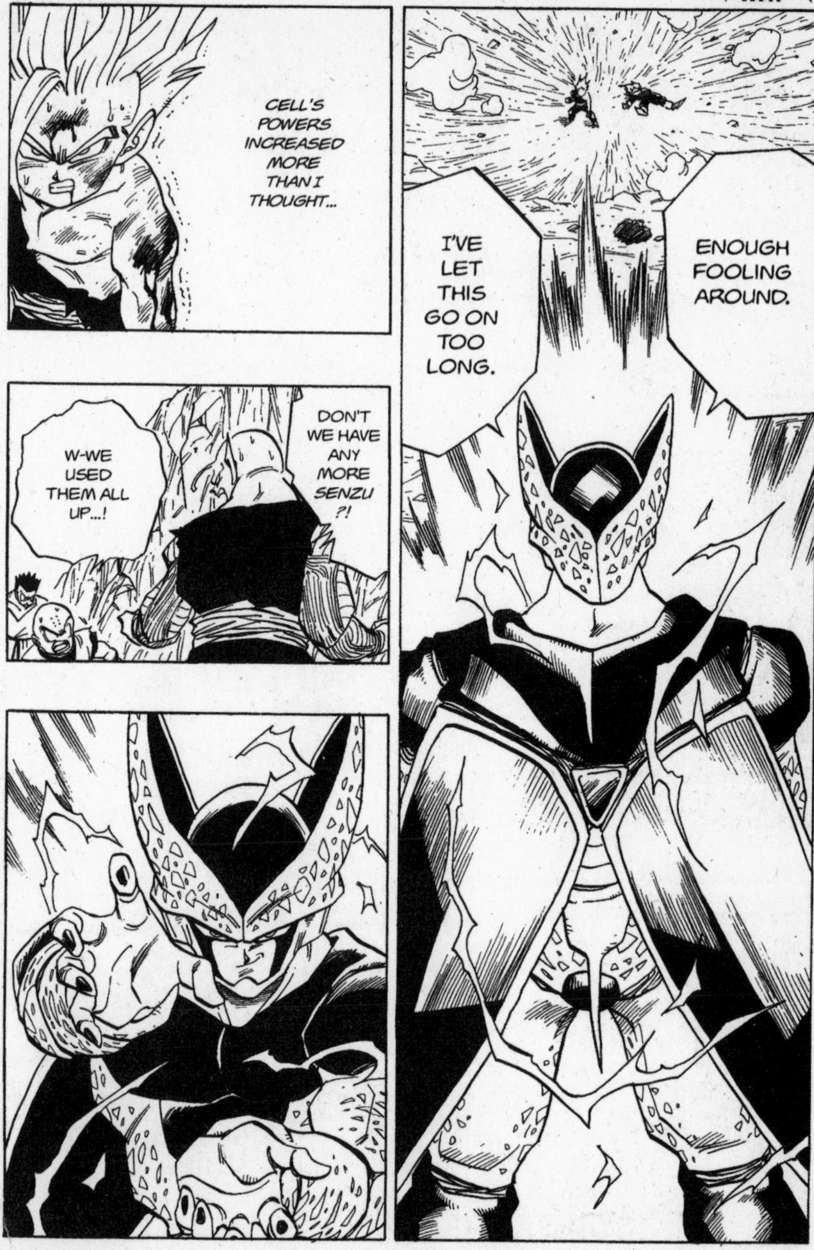

ENOUGH FOOLING AROUND.
I'VE LET THIS GO ON TOO LONG.
CELL'S POWERS INCREASED MORE THAN I THOUGHT...
DON'T WE HAVE ANY MORE SENZU ?!
W-WE USED THEM ALL UP...!

READ THIS WAY

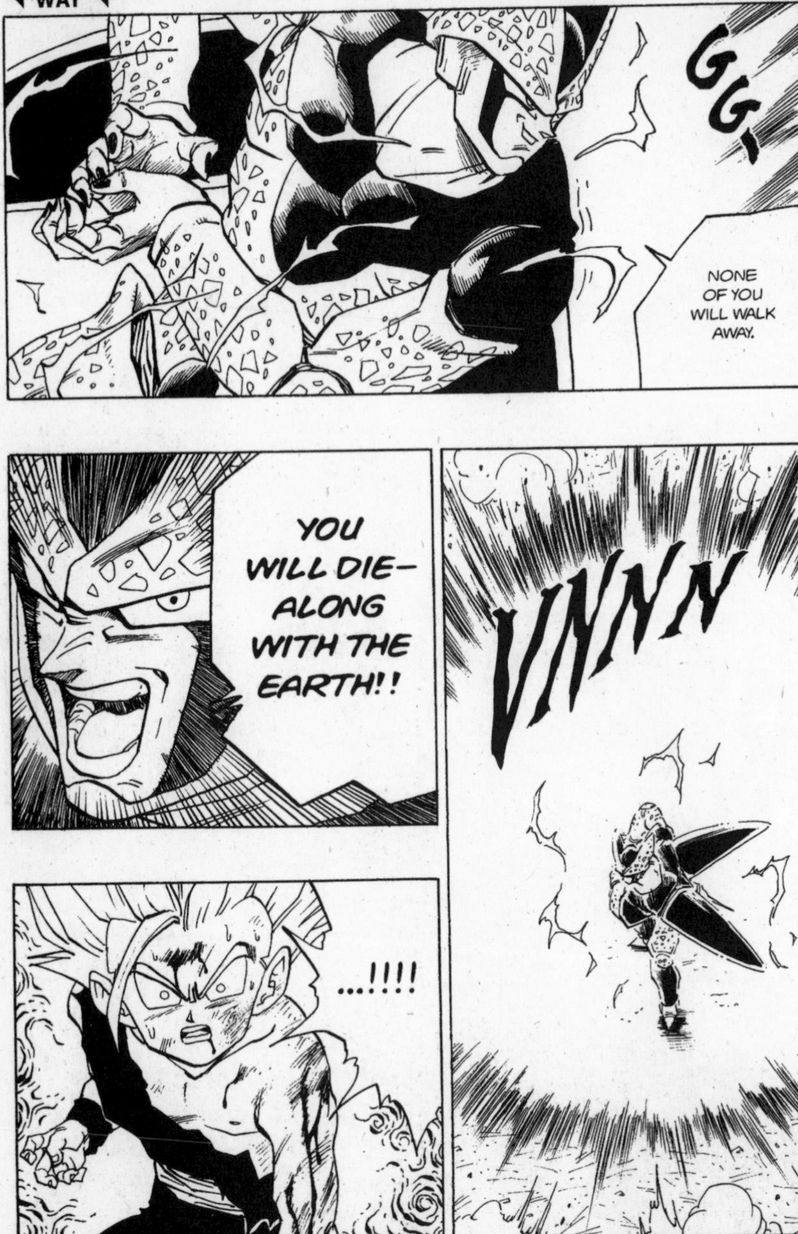
GG-
NONE OF YOU WILL WALK AWAY.
VNNN
YOU WILL DIE— ALONG WITH THE EARTH!!
...!!!!

NEXT: A Message from Goku

DEATH TO THE EARTH !!

RRRRMMM.....

DAD, I'M SORRY... I SHOULD HAVE BEEN ABLE TO SAVE THE EARTH FROM CELL... BUT I FAILED.

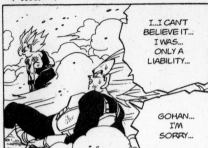

READ THIS WAY
...
I...I CAN'T BELIEVE IT... I WAS... ONLY A LIABILITY...
GOHAN... I'M SORRY...
VEGETA... APOLOGIZED?
HE KNOWS. HE KNOWS THERE'S NO HOPE.
C... CURSE IT...
CURSE IT!!!!!
I CURSE OUR POWERLESS-NESS!!!

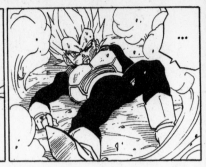

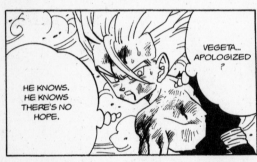

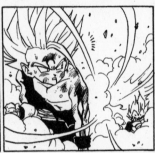

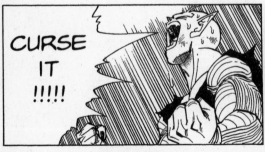

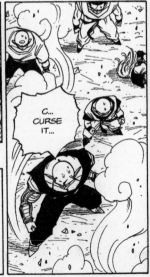

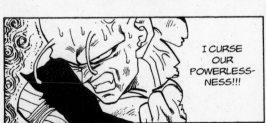

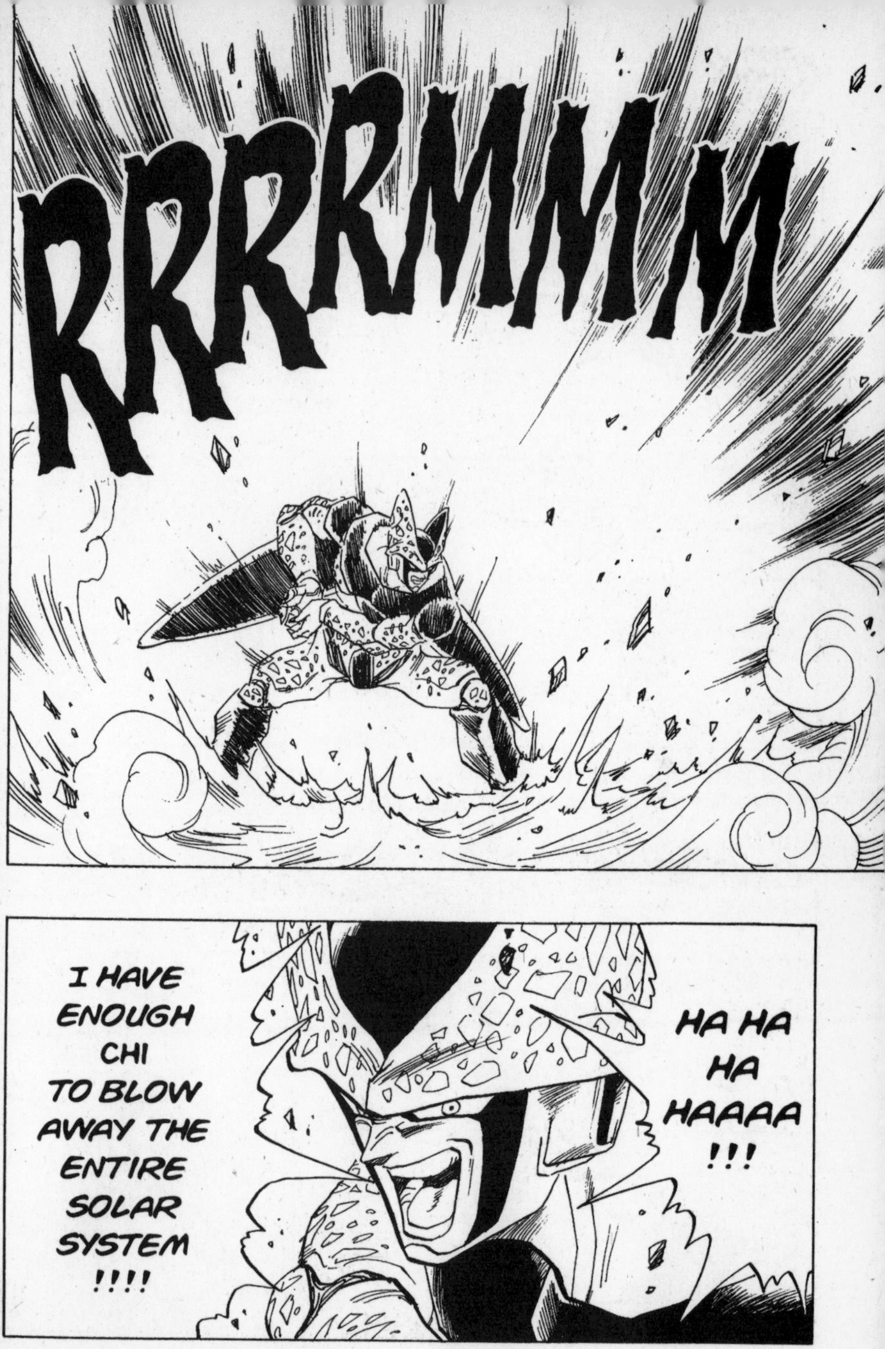
RRRRMMMM
HA HA HA HAAAA!!!
I HAVE ENOUGH CHI TO BLOW AWAY THE ENTIRE SOLAR SYSTEM!!!!

READ THIS WAY

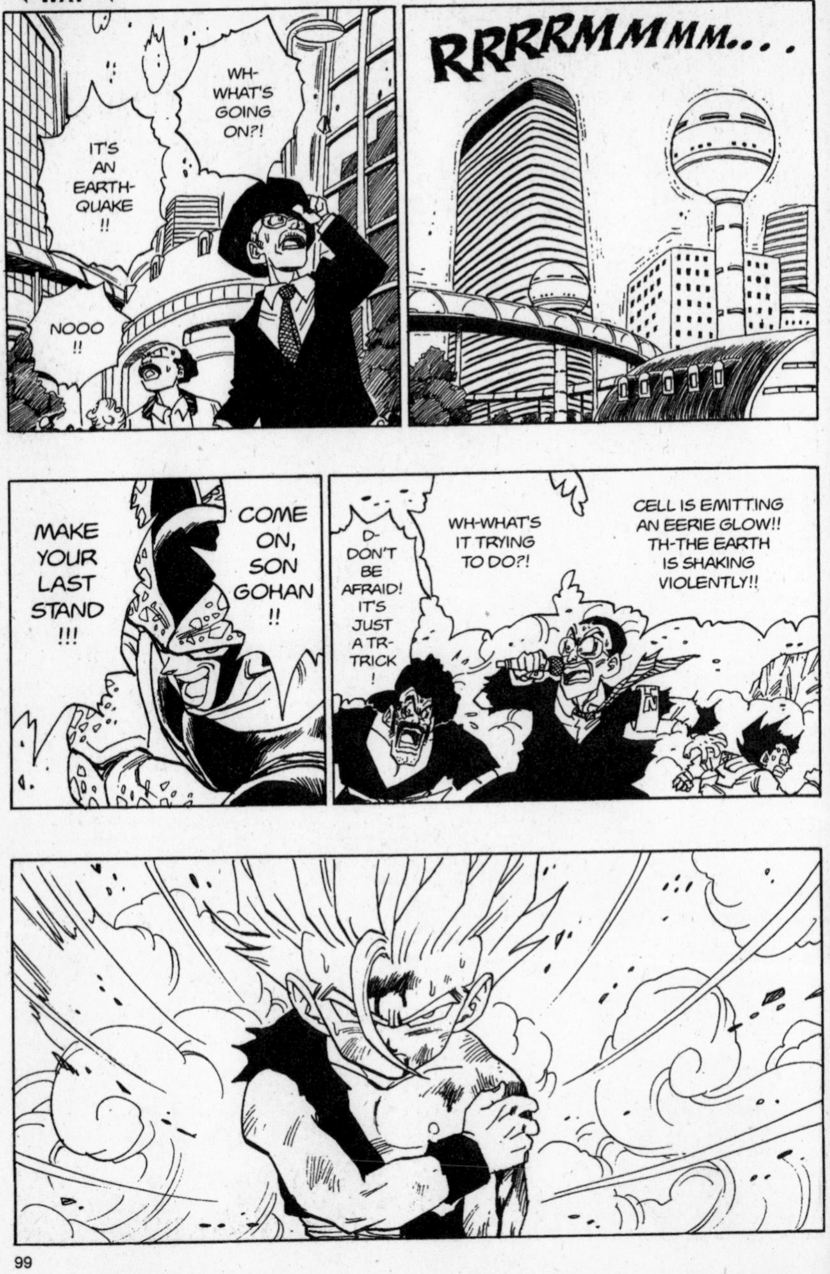

RRRRMMMMM...
WH- WHAT'S GOING ON?!
IT'S AN EARTH-QUAKE !!
NOOO !!
CELL IS EMITTING AN EERIE GLOW!! TH-THE EARTH IS SHAKING VIOLENTLY!!
WH-WHAT'S IT TRYING TO DO?!
D- DON'T BE AFRAID! IT'S JUST A TR- TRICK !
COME ON, SON GOHAN !!
MAKE YOUR LAST STAND !!!

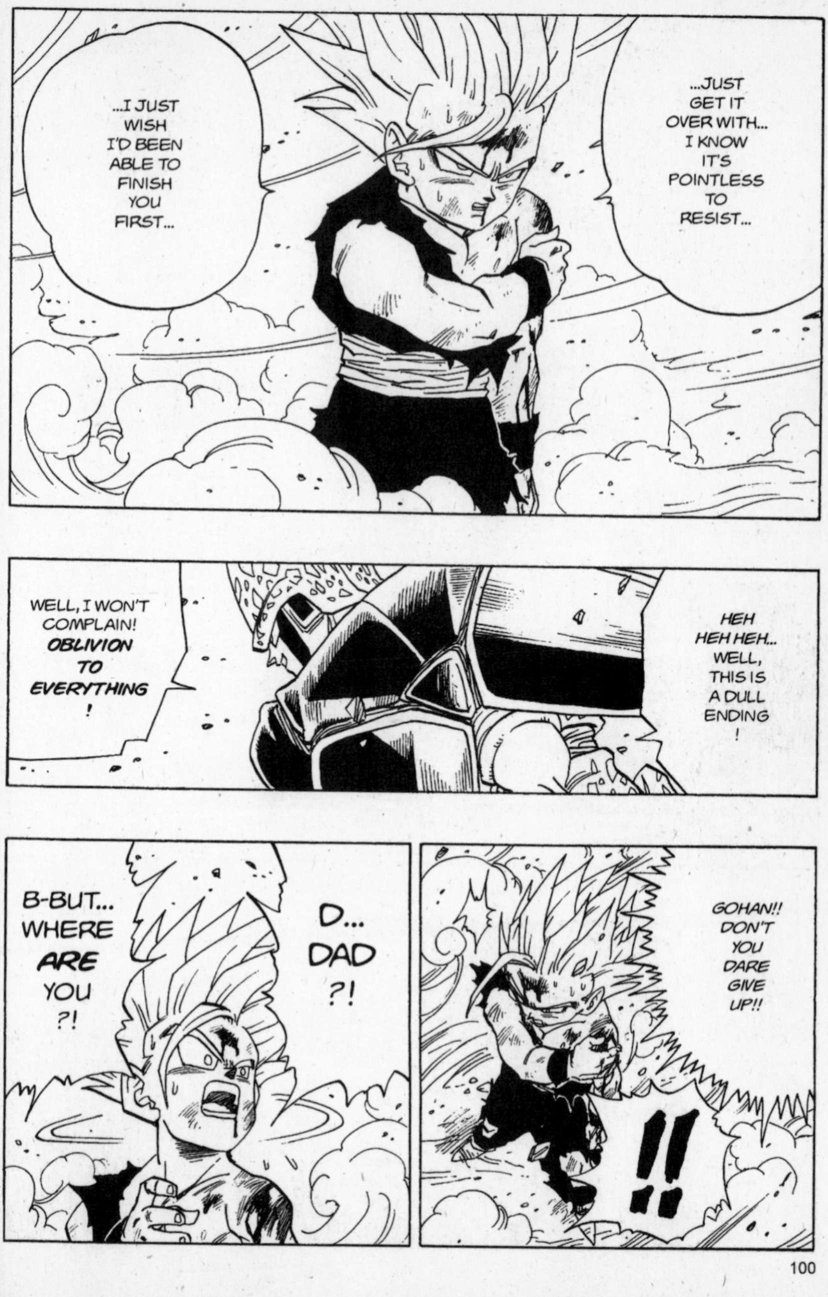
...JUST GET IT OVER WITH... I KNOW IT'S POINTLESS TO RESIST...
...I JUST WISH I'D BEEN ABLE TO FINISH YOU FIRST...
HEH HEH HEH... WELL, THIS IS A DULL ENDING!
WELL, I WON'T COMPLAIN! OBLIVION TO EVERYTHING!
GOHAN!! DON'T YOU DARE GIVE UP!!
!!
D... DAD?!
B-BUT... WHERE ARE YOU?!

READ THIS WAY

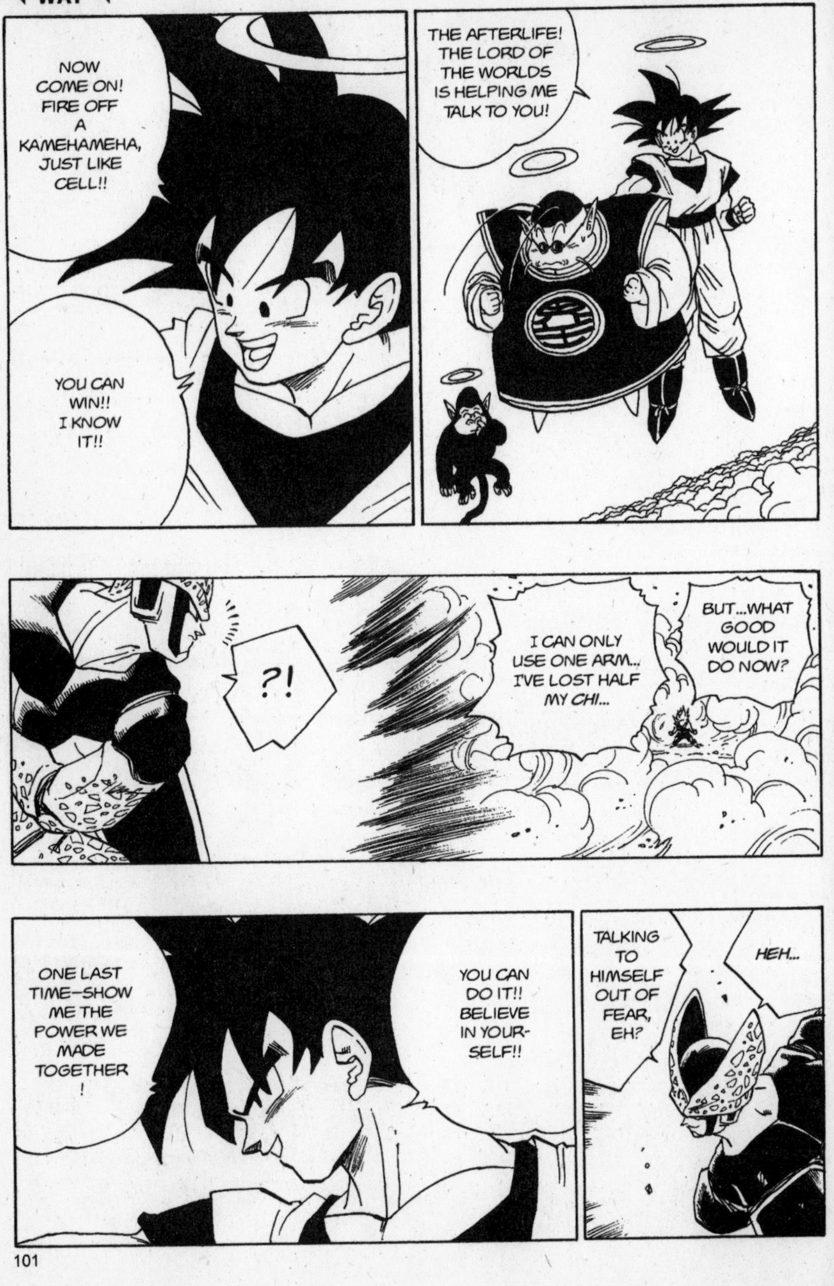
THE AFTERLIFE! THE LORD OF THE WORLDS IS HELPING ME TALK TO YOU!
NOW COME ON! FIRE OFF A KAMEHAMEHA, JUST LIKE CELL!!
YOU CAN WIN!! I KNOW IT!!
BUT...WHAT GOOD WOULD IT DO NOW?
I CAN ONLY USE ONE ARM... I'VE LOST HALF MY *CHI*...
?!
HEH...
TALKING TO HIMSELF OUT OF FEAR, EH?
YOU CAN DO IT!! BELIEVE IN YOURSELF!!
ONE LAST TIME—SHOW ME THE POWER WE MADE TOGETHER!

READ THIS WAY

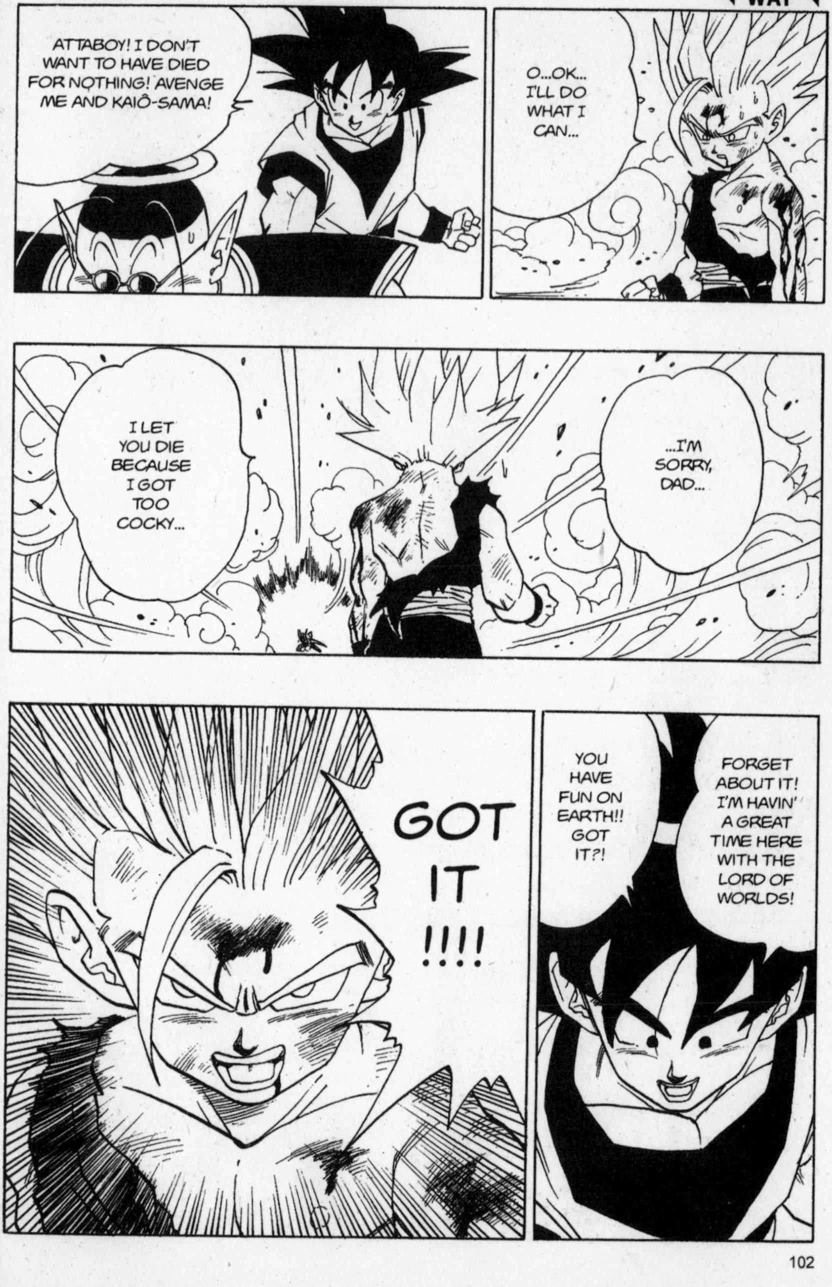
O...OK... I'LL DO WHAT I CAN...
ATTABOY! I DON'T WANT TO HAVE DIED FOR NOTHING! AVENGE ME AND KAIÔ-SAMA!
...I'M SORRY, DAD...
I LET YOU DIE BECAUSE I GOT TOO COCKY...
FORGET ABOUT IT! I'M HAVIN' A GREAT TIME HERE WITH THE LORD OF WORLDS!
YOU HAVE FUN ON EARTH!! GOT IT?!
GOT IT !!!!

READ THIS WAY

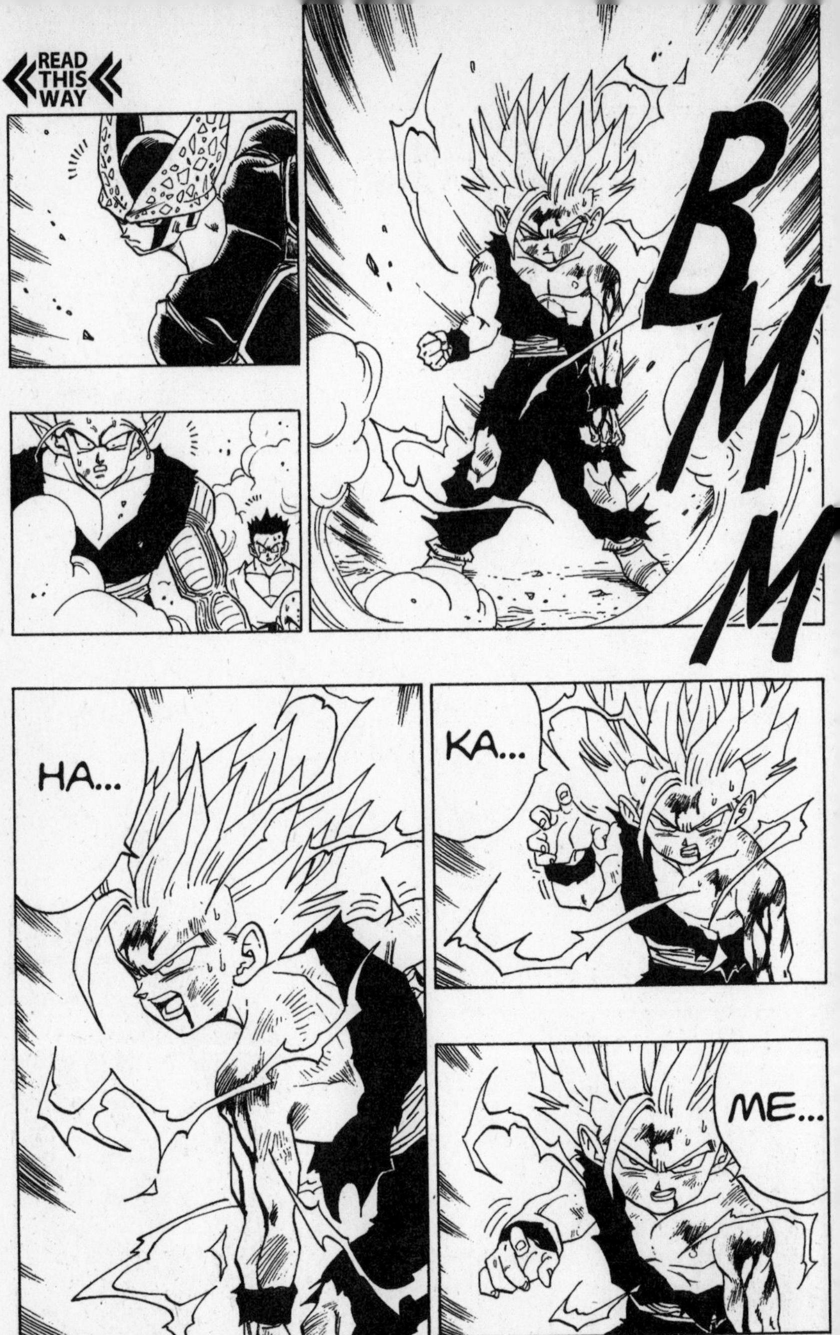
BMM
KA...
ME...
HA...

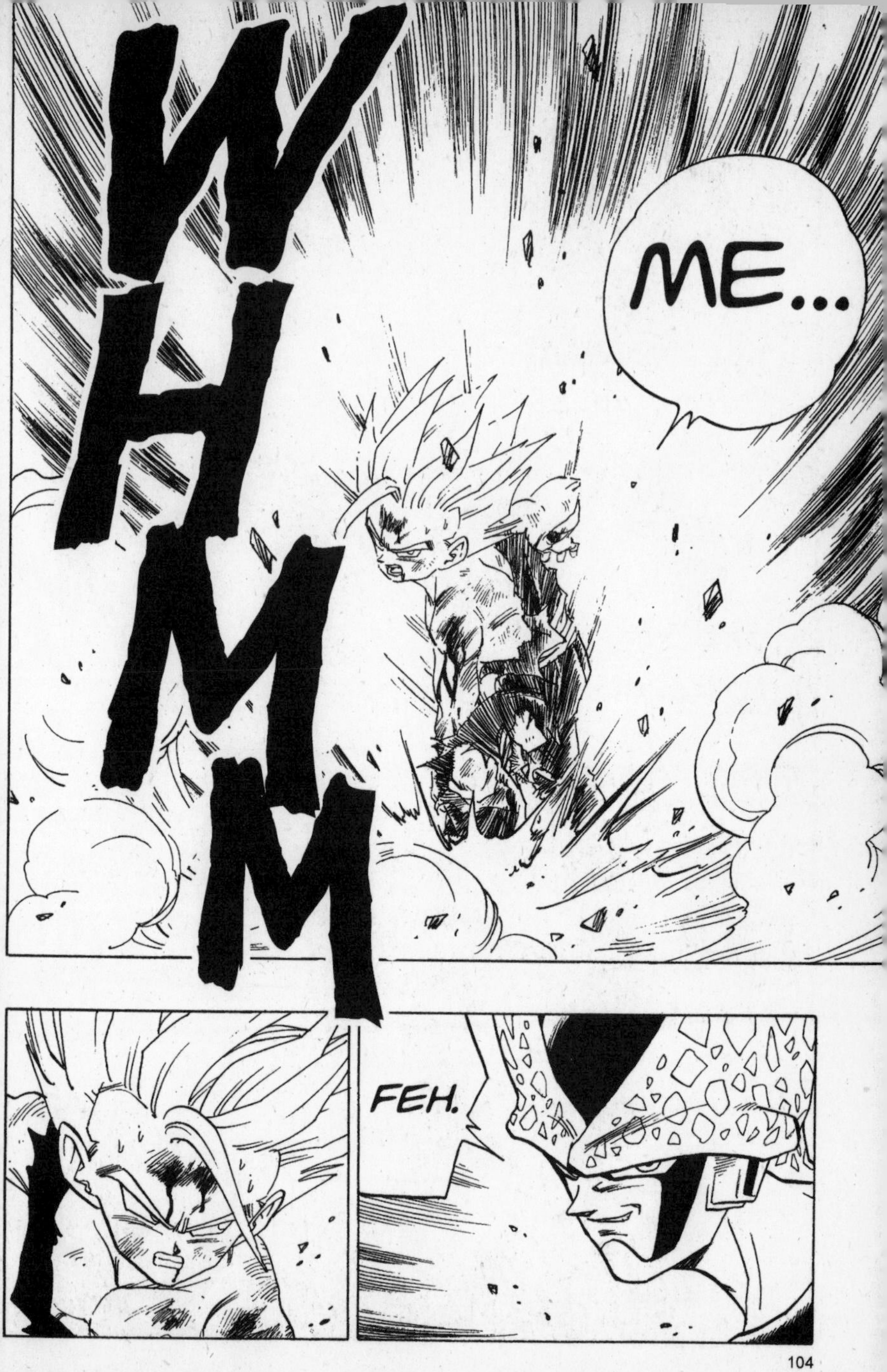
ME...
WHMMM
FEH.

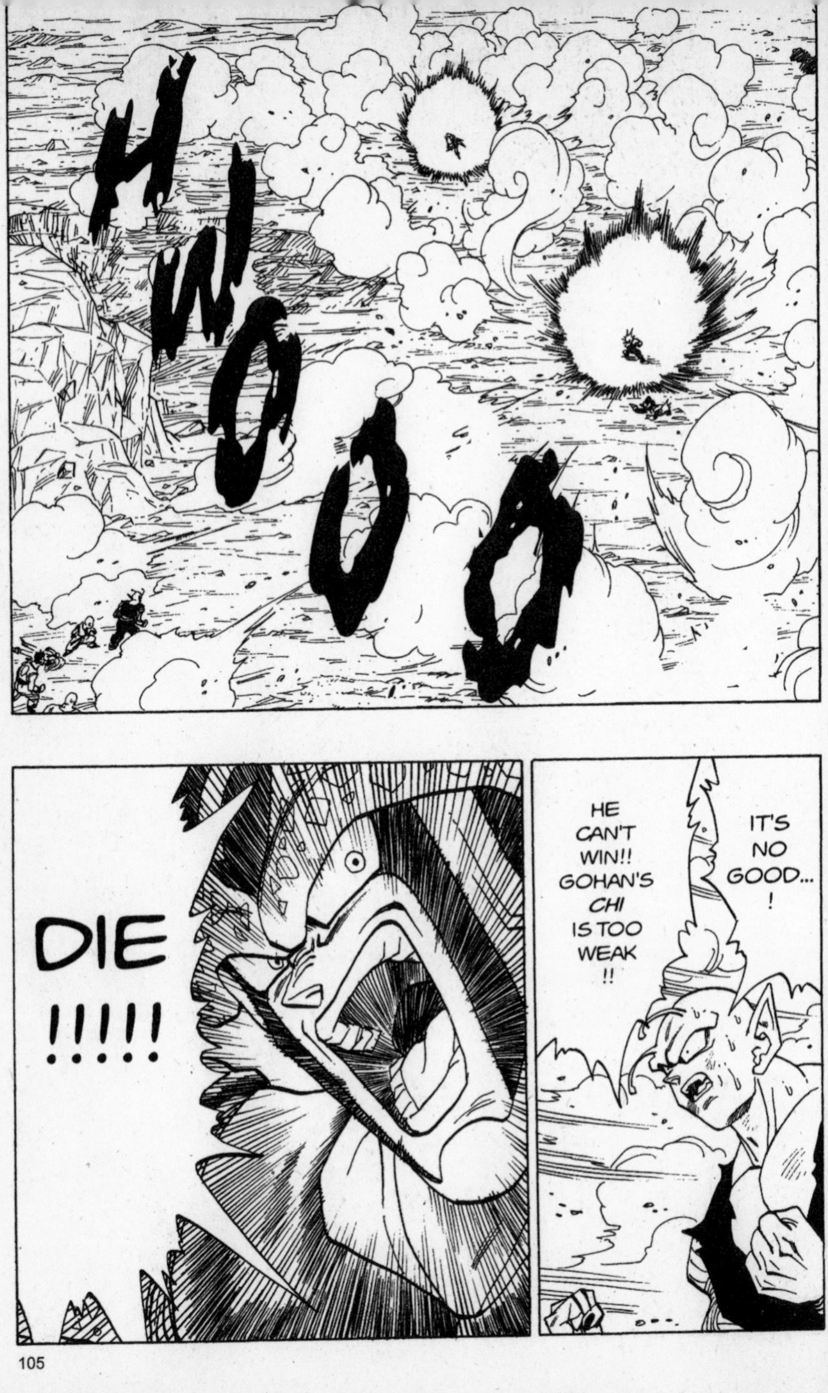
HWOOO
IT'S NO GOOD...!
HE CAN'T WIN!! GOHAN'S *CHI* IS TOO WEAK!!
DIE!!!!!

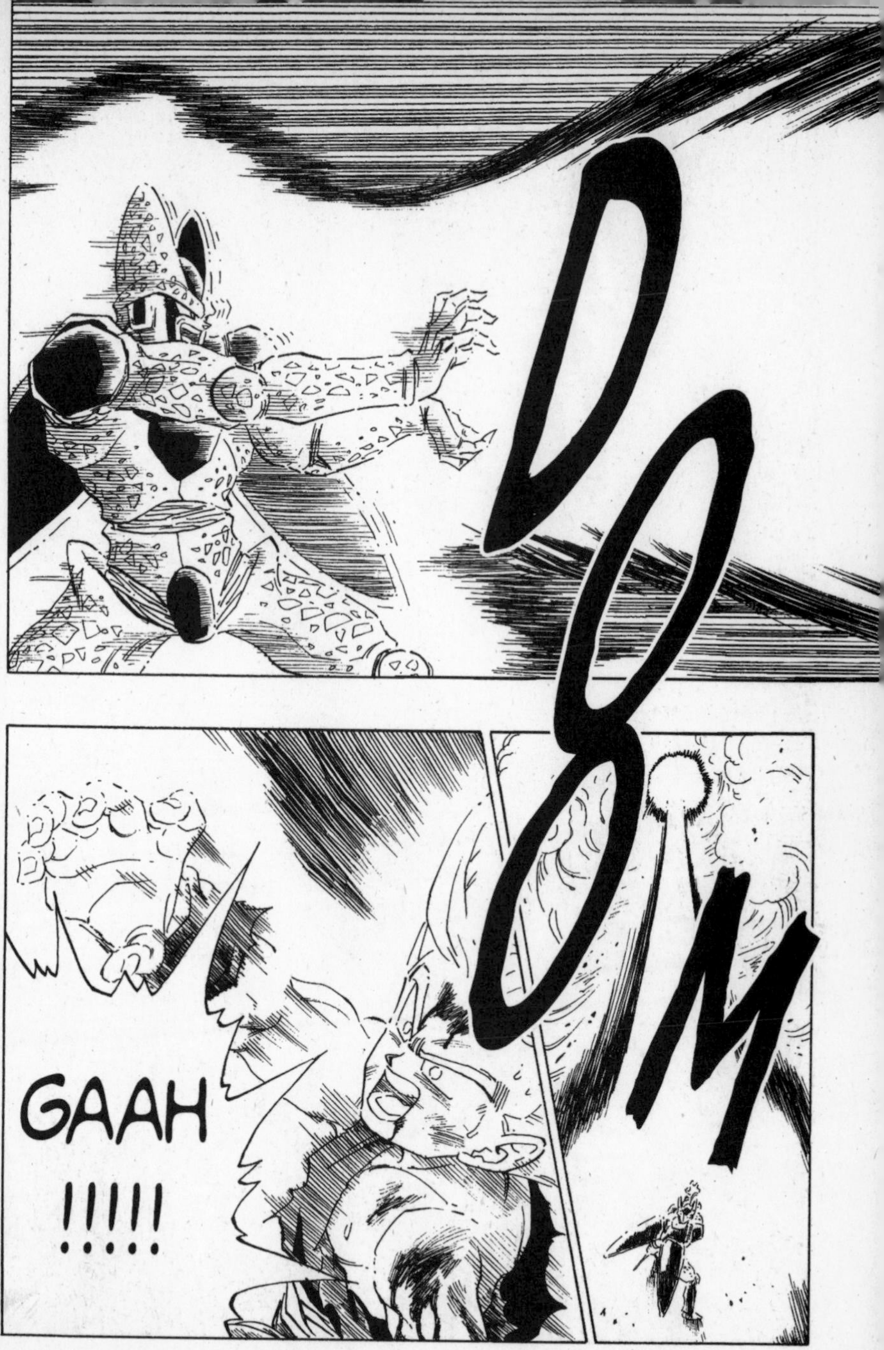
DOOM
GAAH !!!!!

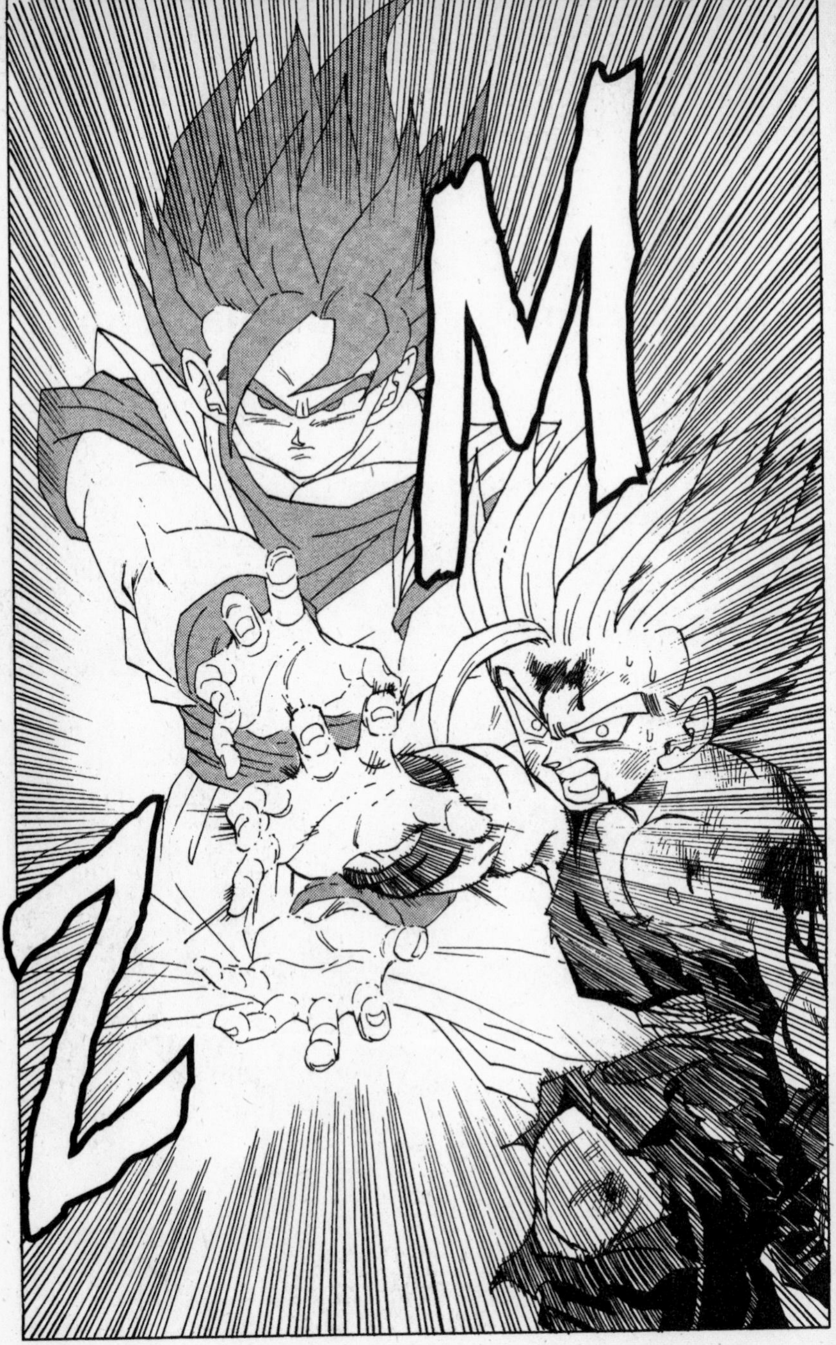
ZM

DBZ:222
Kamehameha vs. Kamehameha

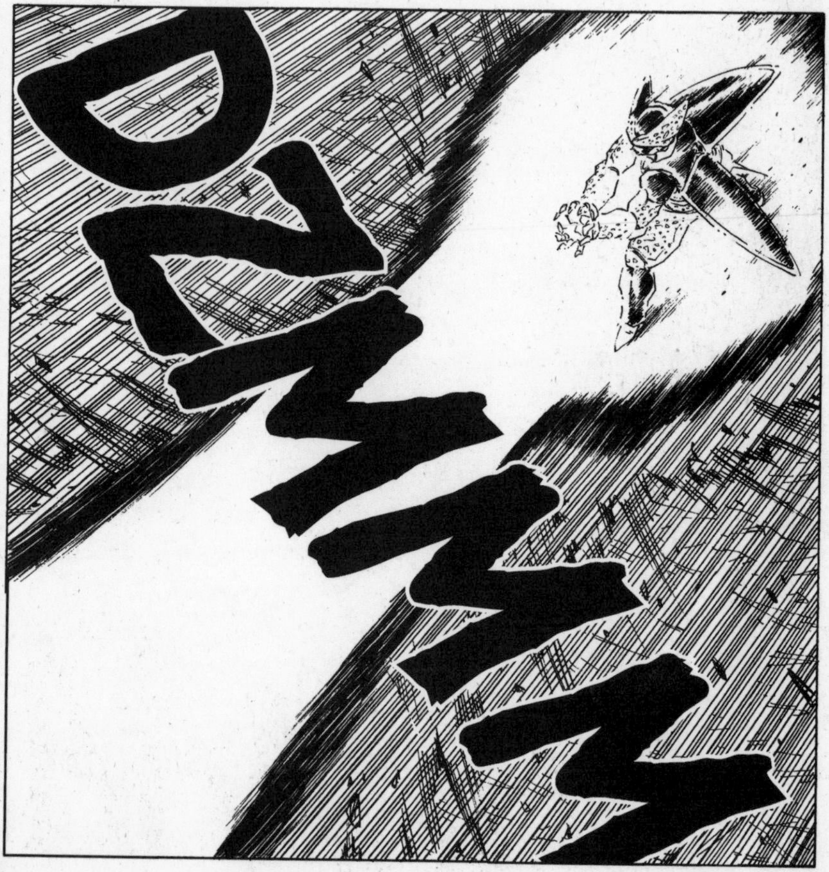
DZNNN

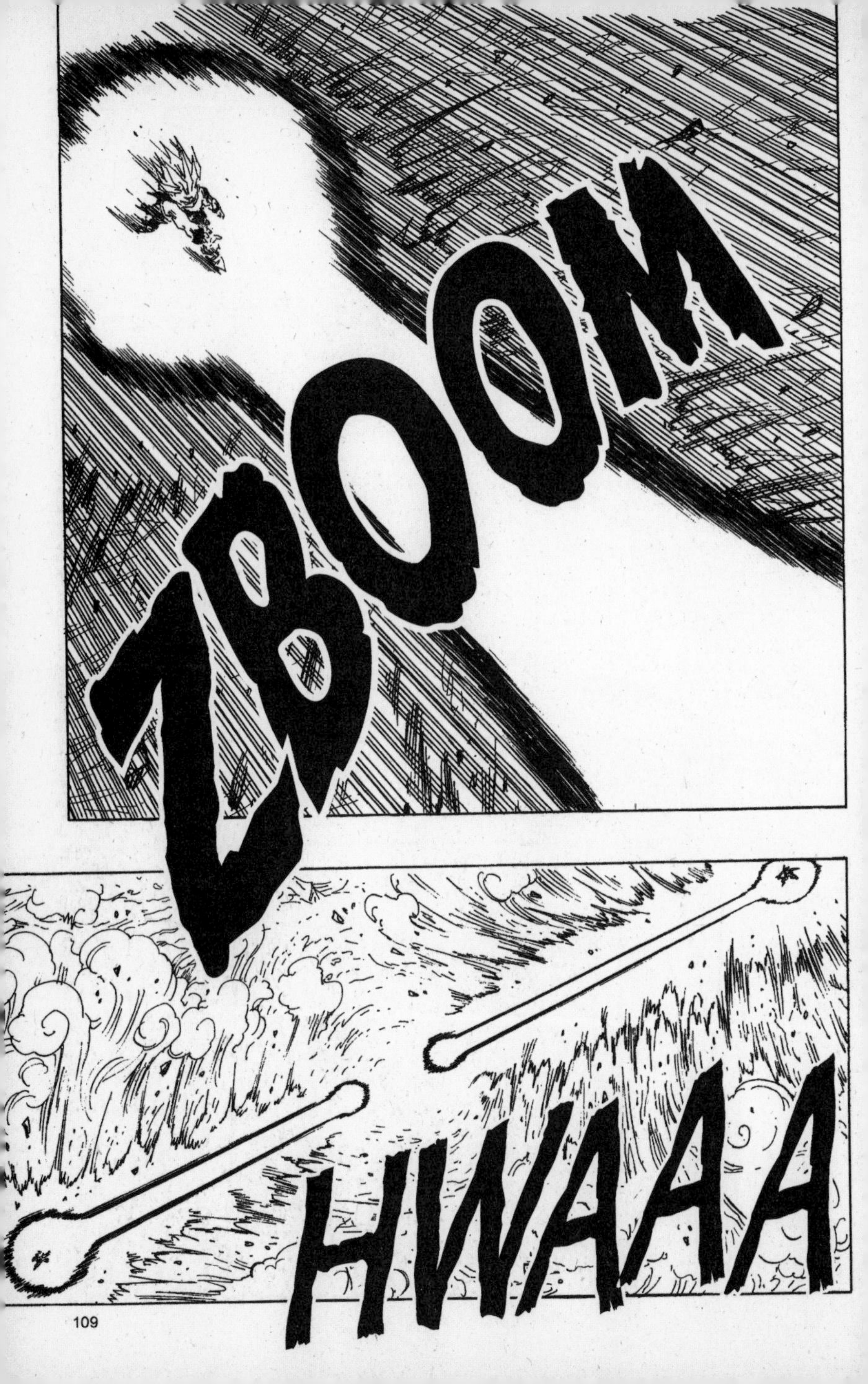
ZBOOM
HWAAA

READ THIS WAY

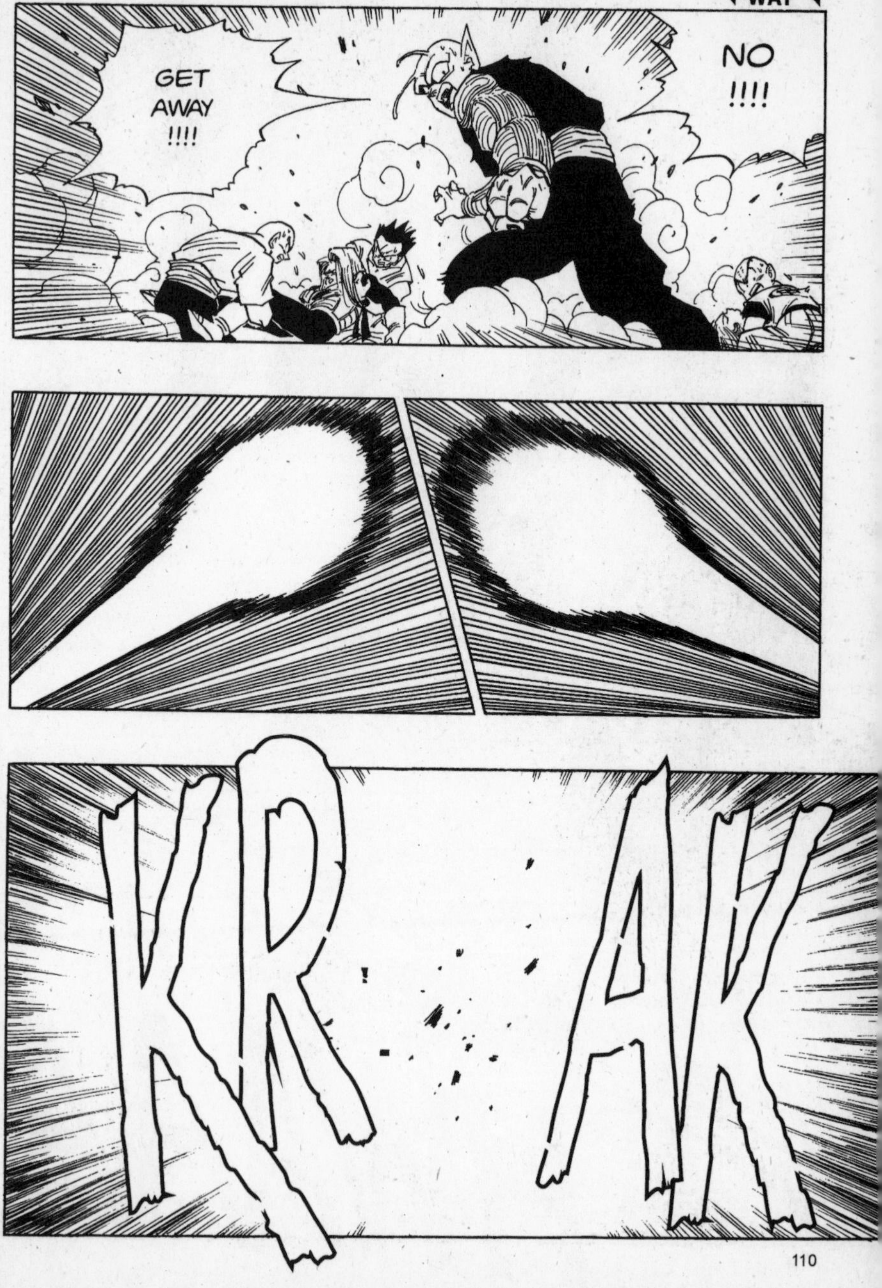
NO !!!!
GET AWAY !!!!
KRAK

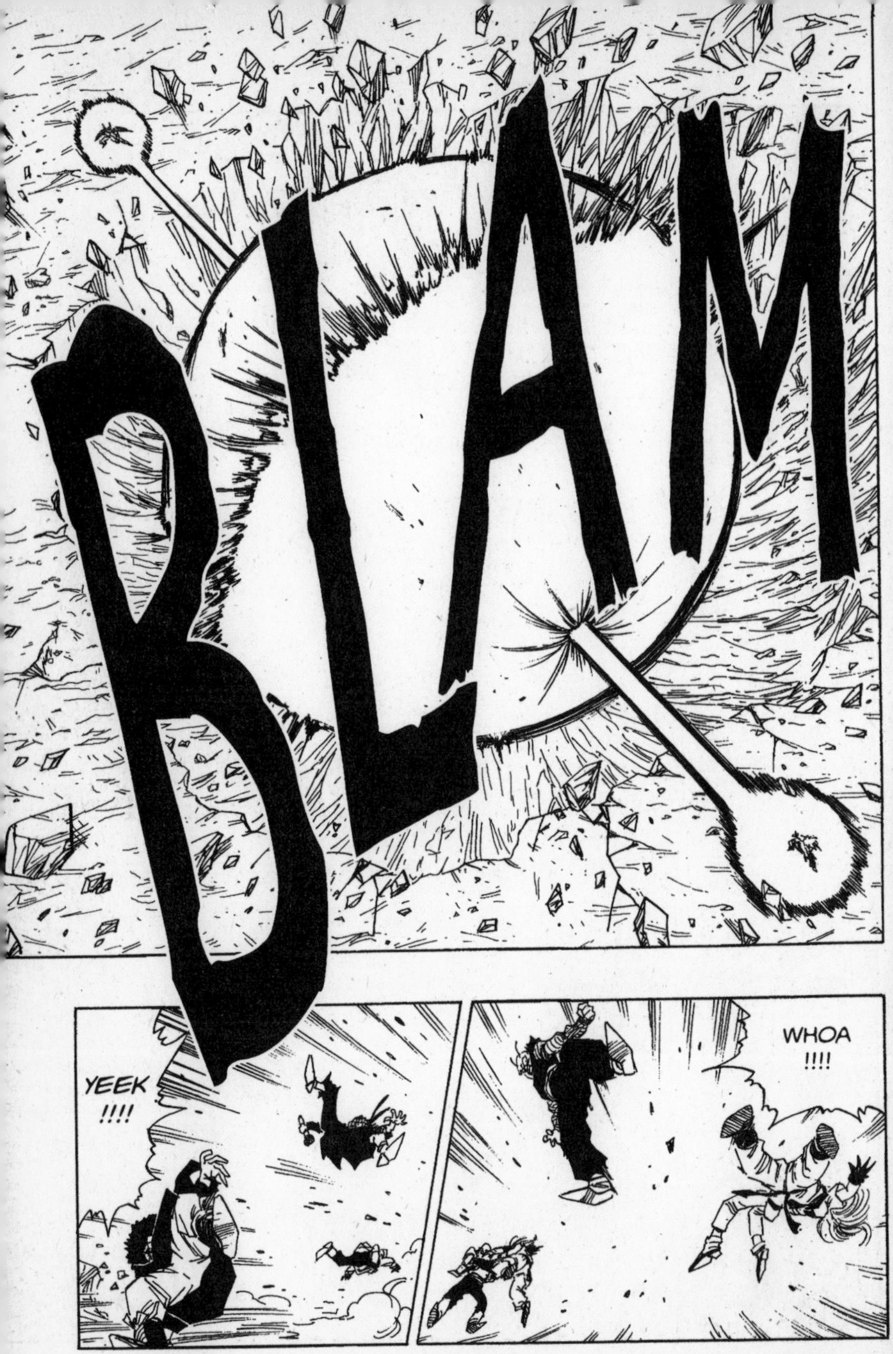
BLAM
WHOA !!!!
YEEK !!!!

READ THIS WAY

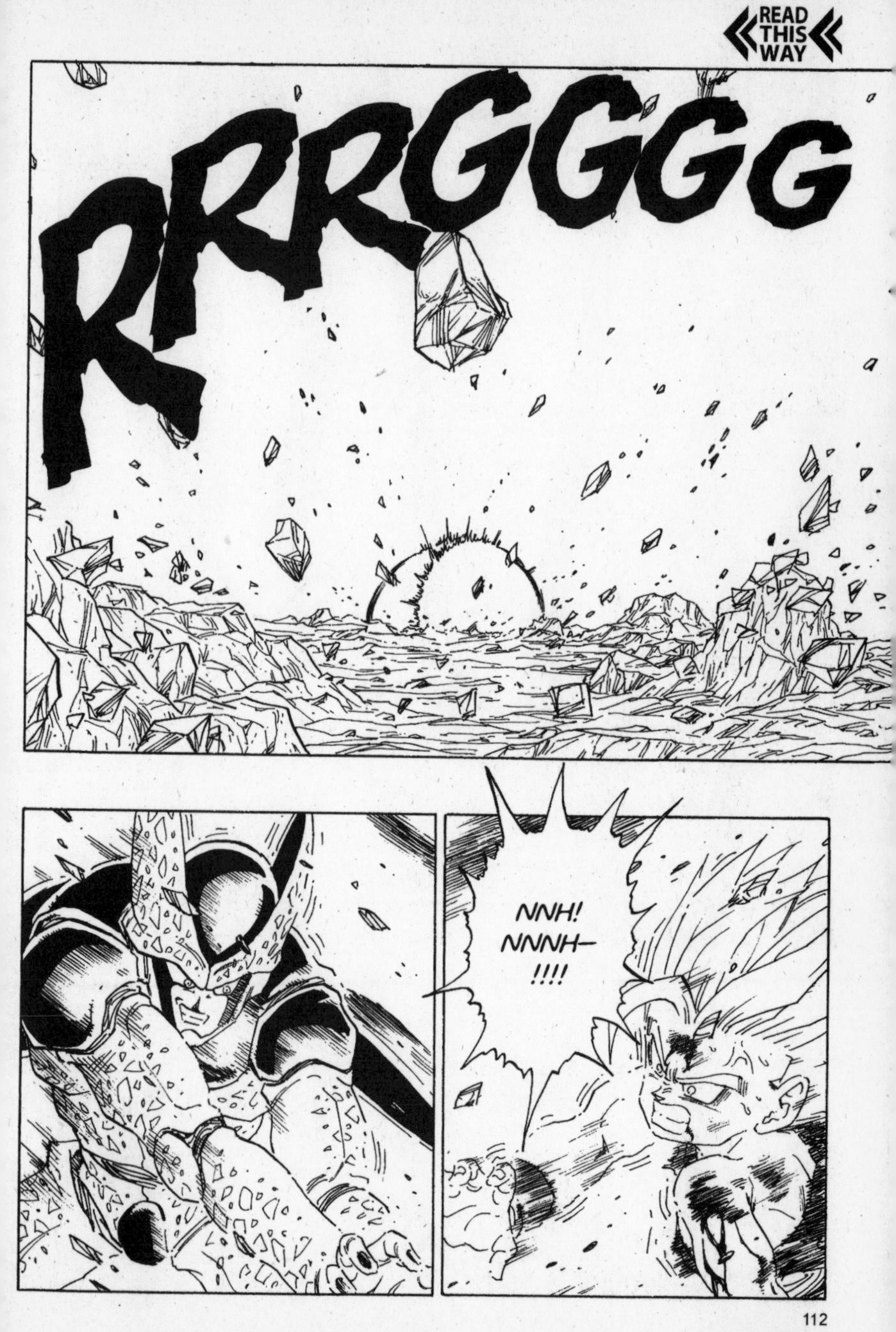
RRRGGGG
NNH! NNNH—!!!!

READ THIS WAY

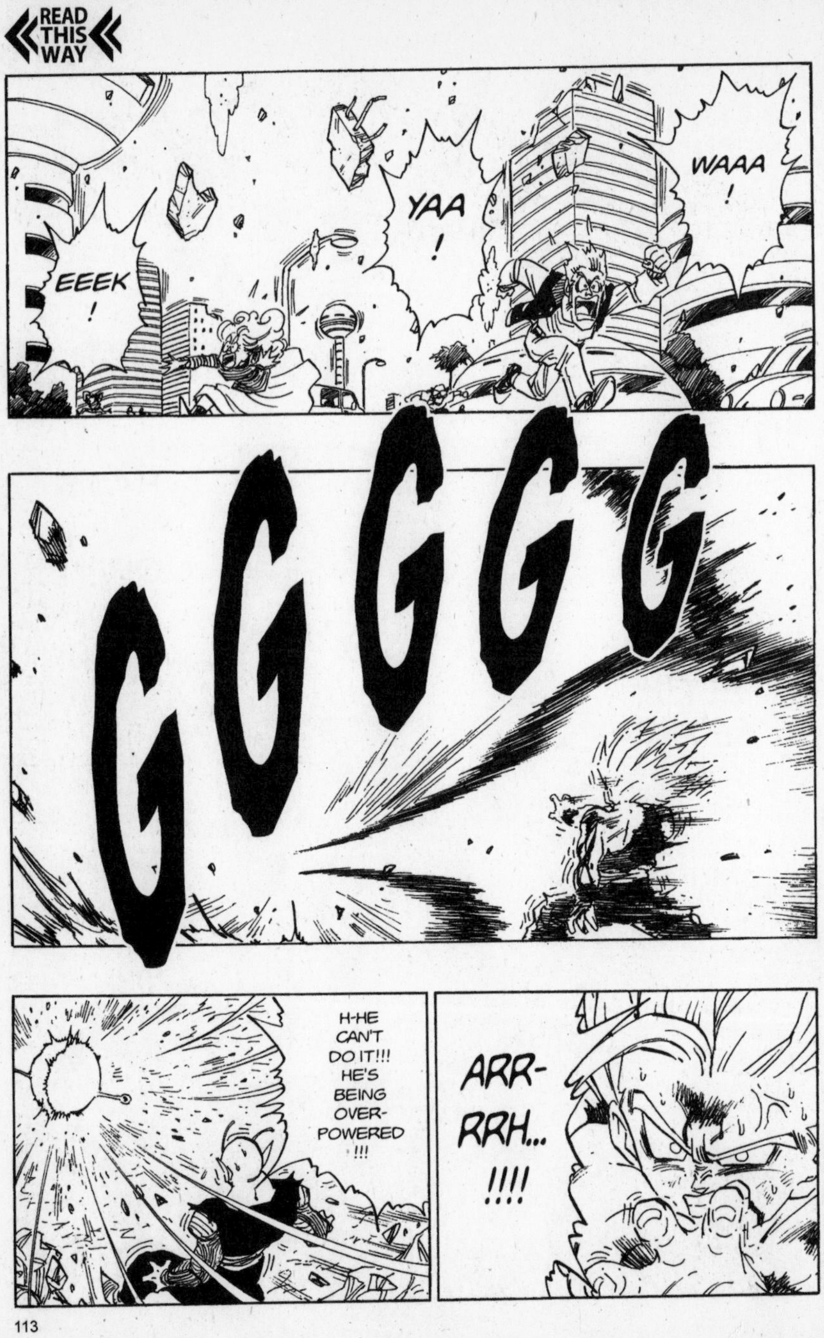
WAAA!
YAA!
EEEK!
GGGG
ARR-RRH...!!!!
H-HE CAN'T DO IT!!! HE'S BEING OVER-POWERED!!!

READ THIS WAY

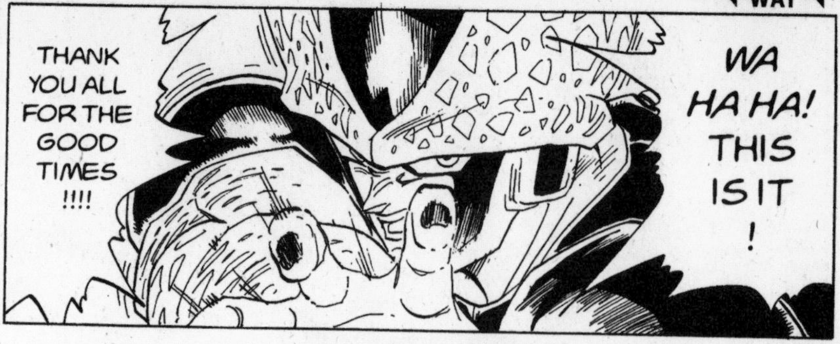
WA HA HA! THIS IS IT!
THANK YOU ALL FOR THE GOOD TIMES!!!!

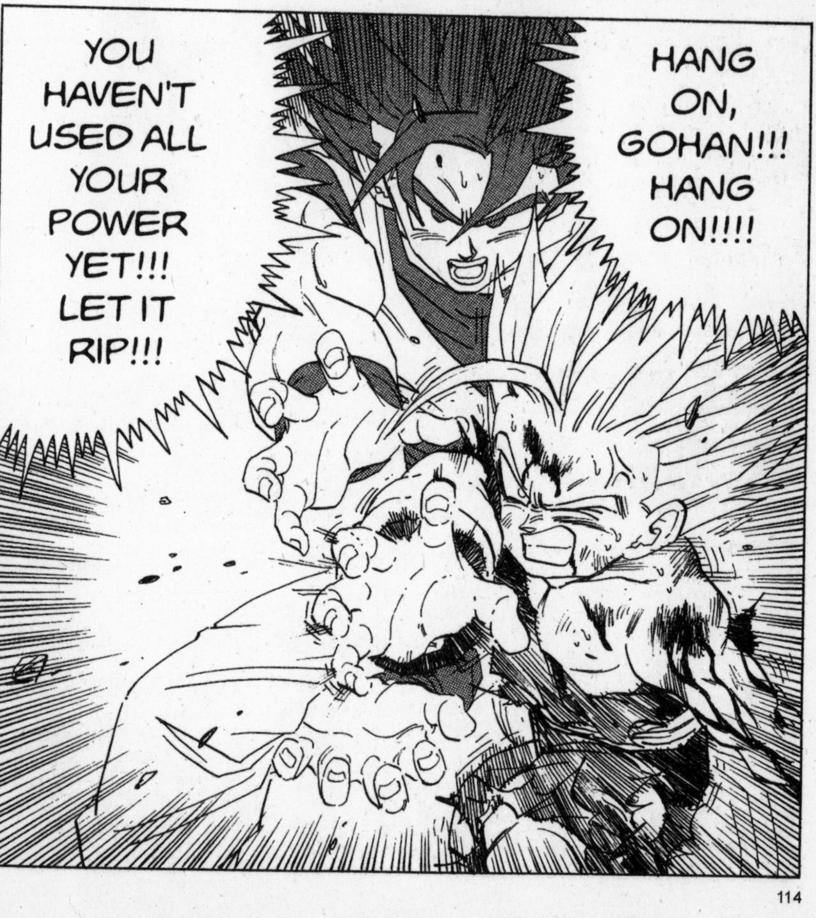
HANG ON, GOHAN!!! HANG ON!!!!
YOU HAVEN'T USED ALL YOUR POWER YET!!! LET IT RIP!!!

READ THIS WAY

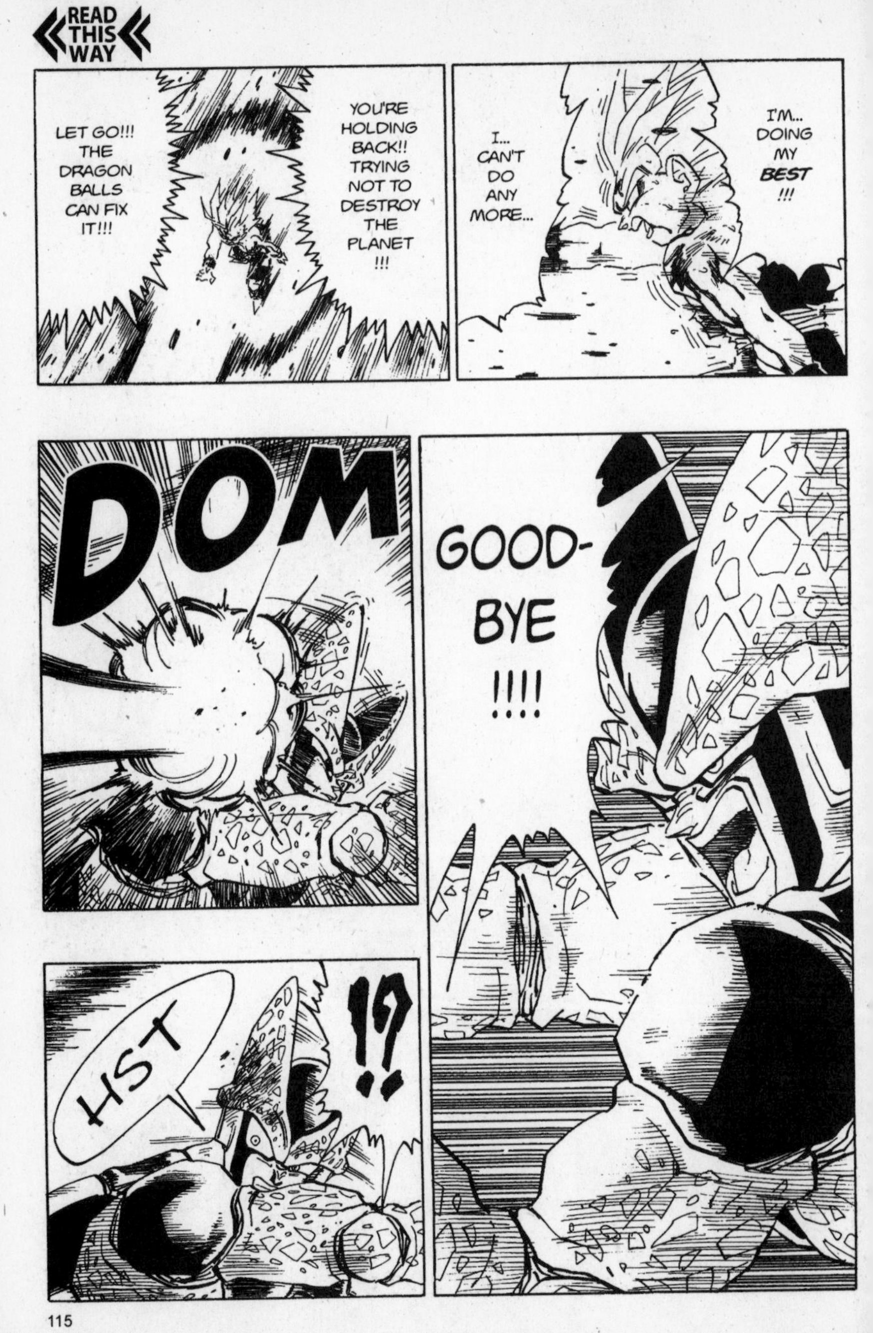
I'M... DOING MY BEST!!!
I... CAN'T DO ANY MORE...
YOU'RE HOLDING BACK!! TRYING NOT TO DESTROY THE PLANET!!!
LET GO!!! THE DRAGON BALLS CAN FIX IT!!!
GOOD-BYE!!!!
DOM
HST
!?

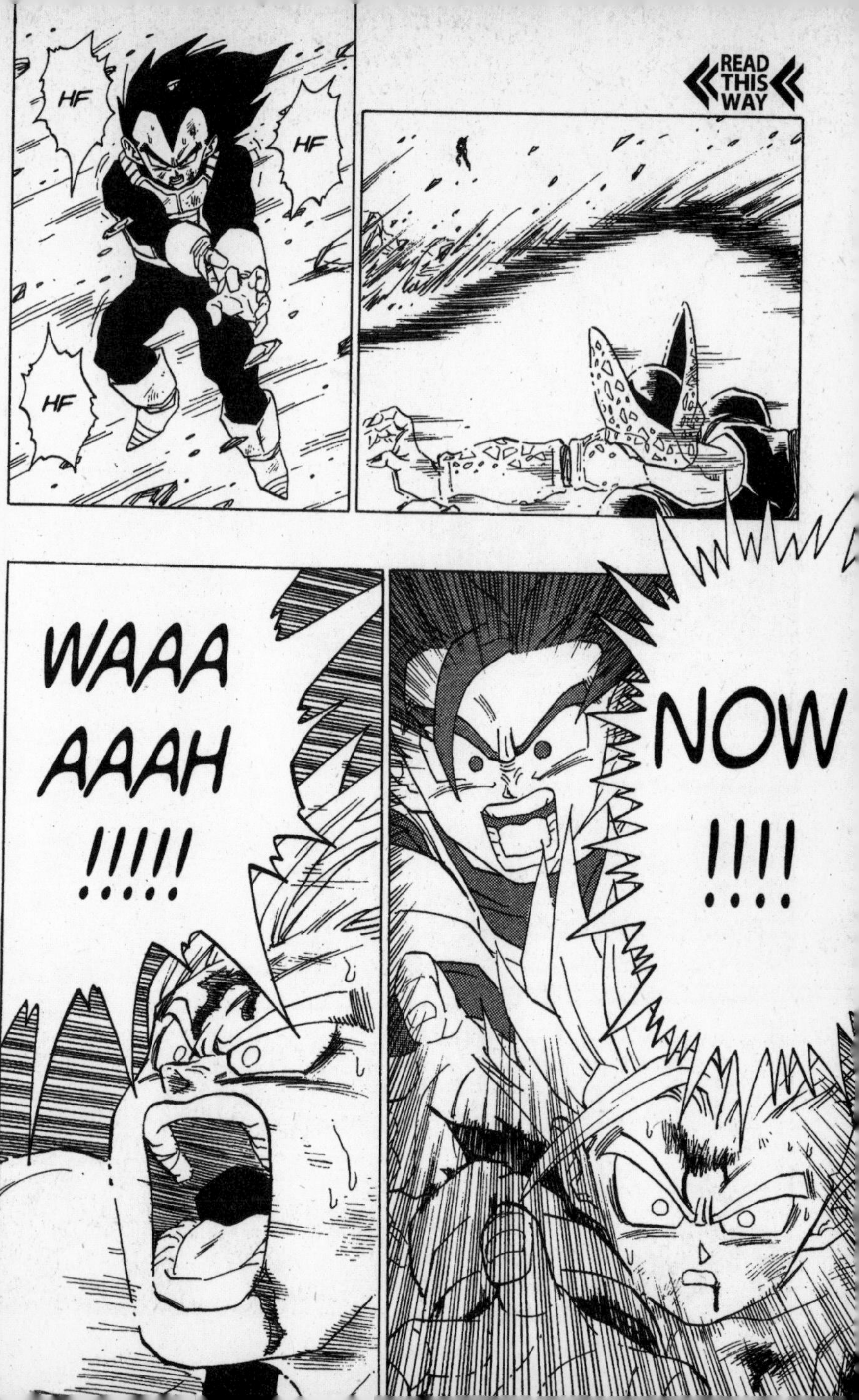
READ THIS WAY
HF
HF
HF
NOW!!!!
WAAAAAAH!!!!!

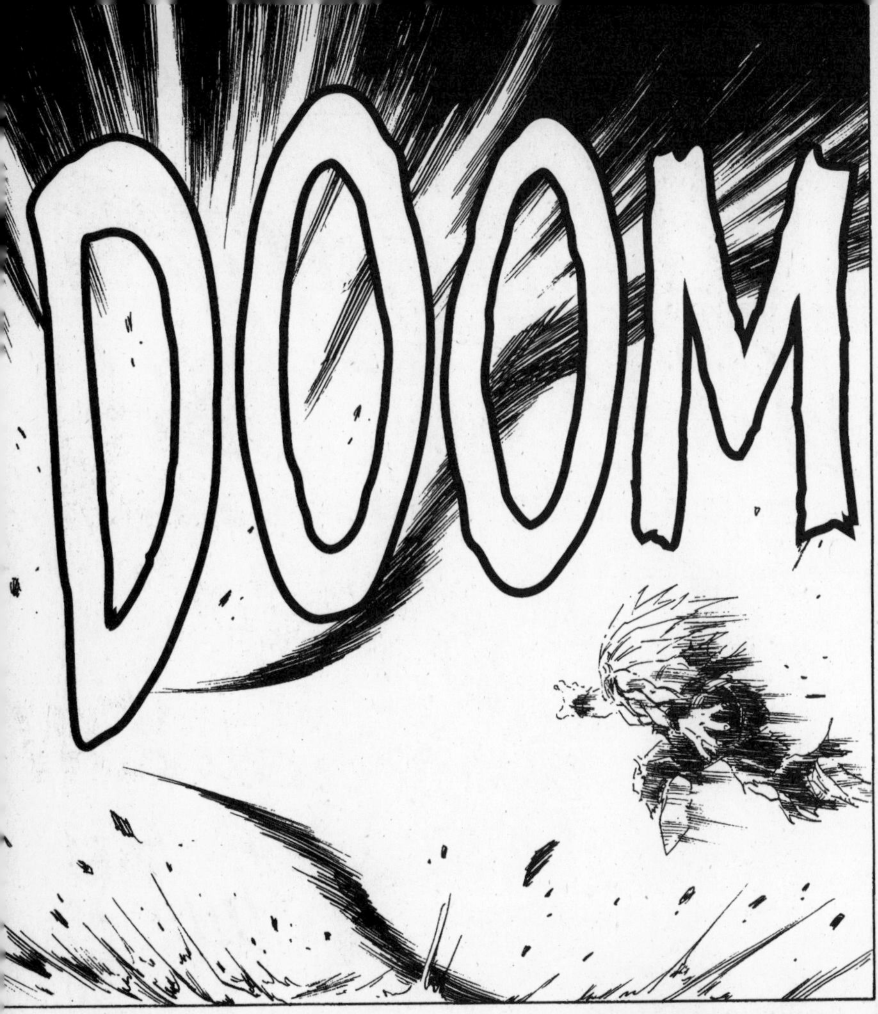
DOOM
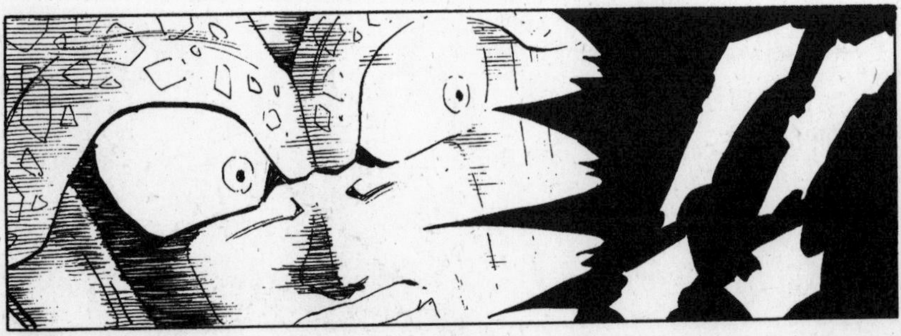

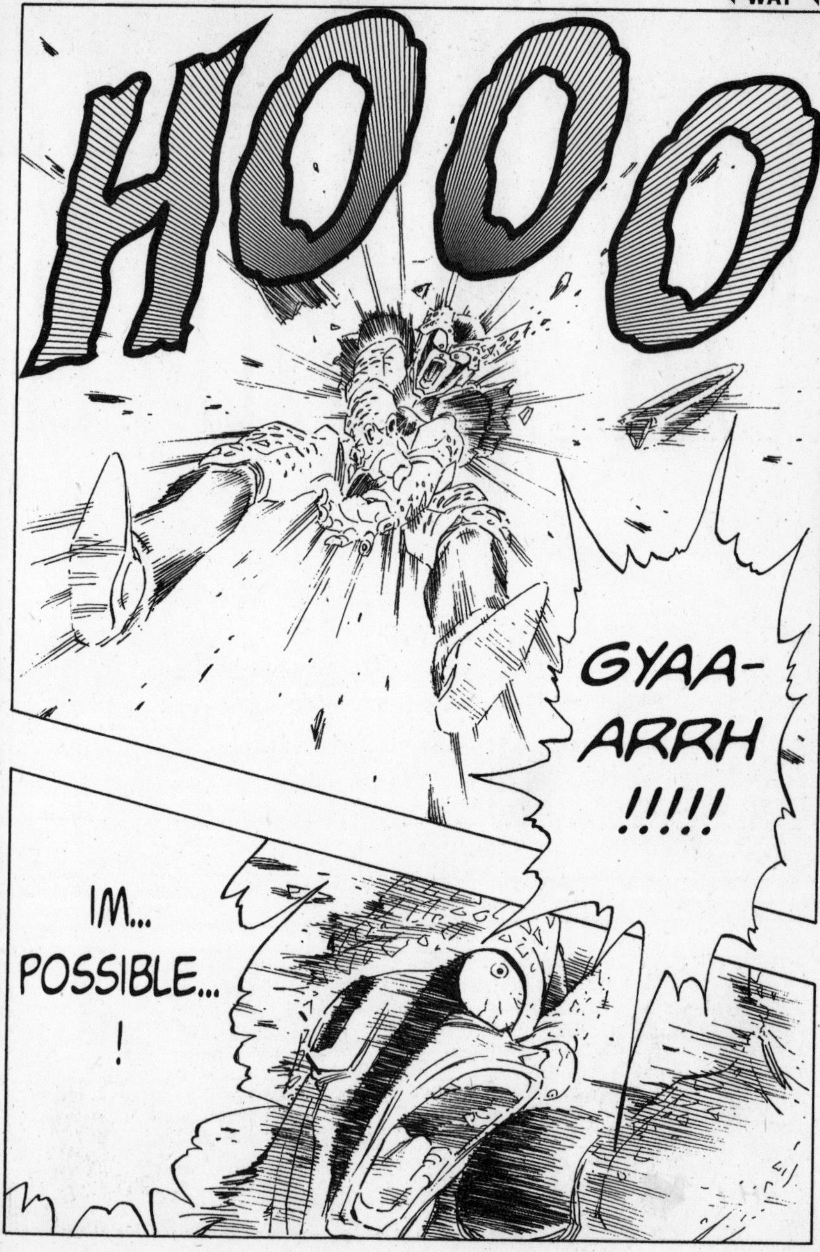
HOOO
GYAA-ARRH!!!!!
IM... POSSIBLE...!

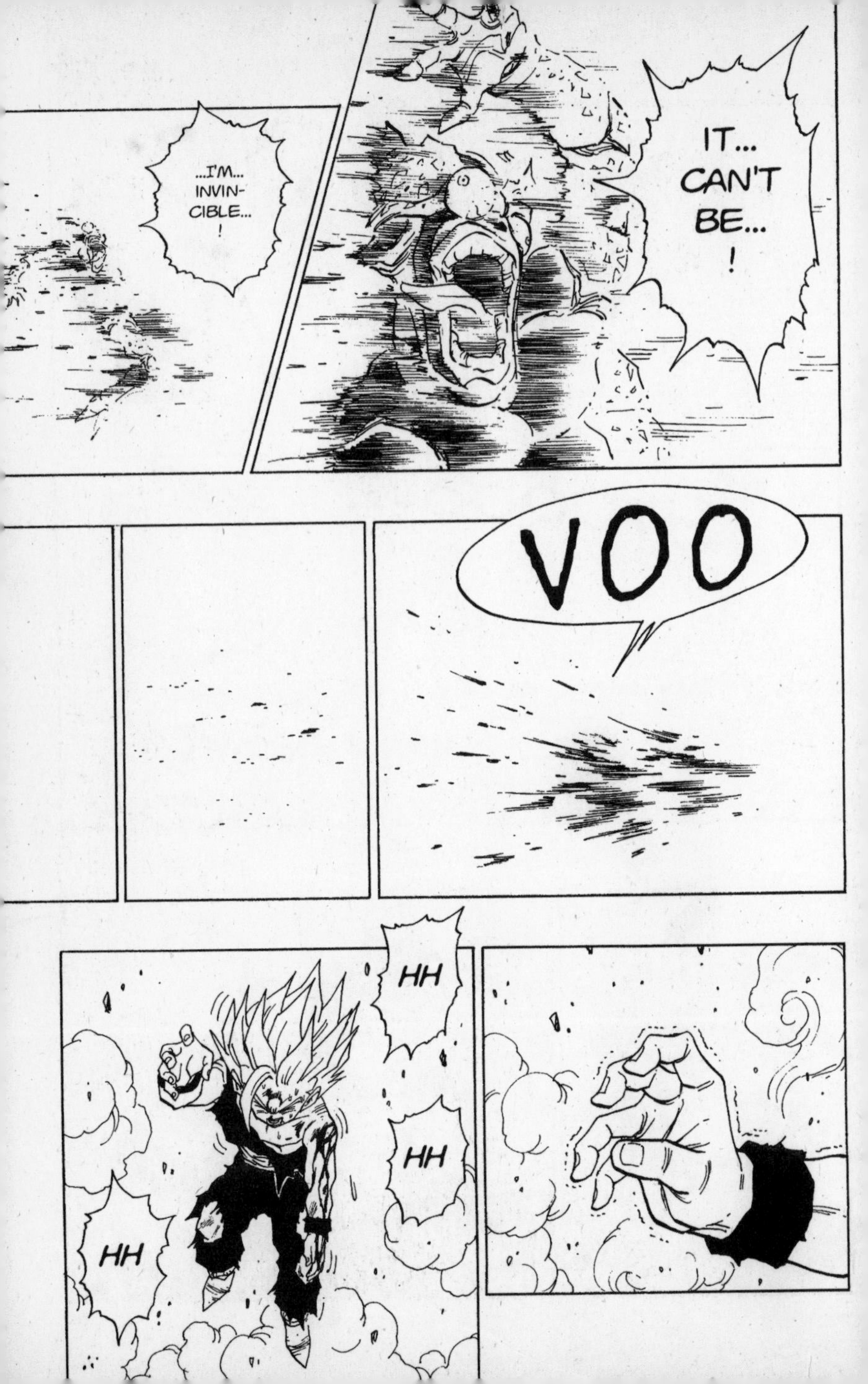
IT... CAN'T BE... !
...I'M... INVIN-CIBLE... !
VOO
HH
HH
HH

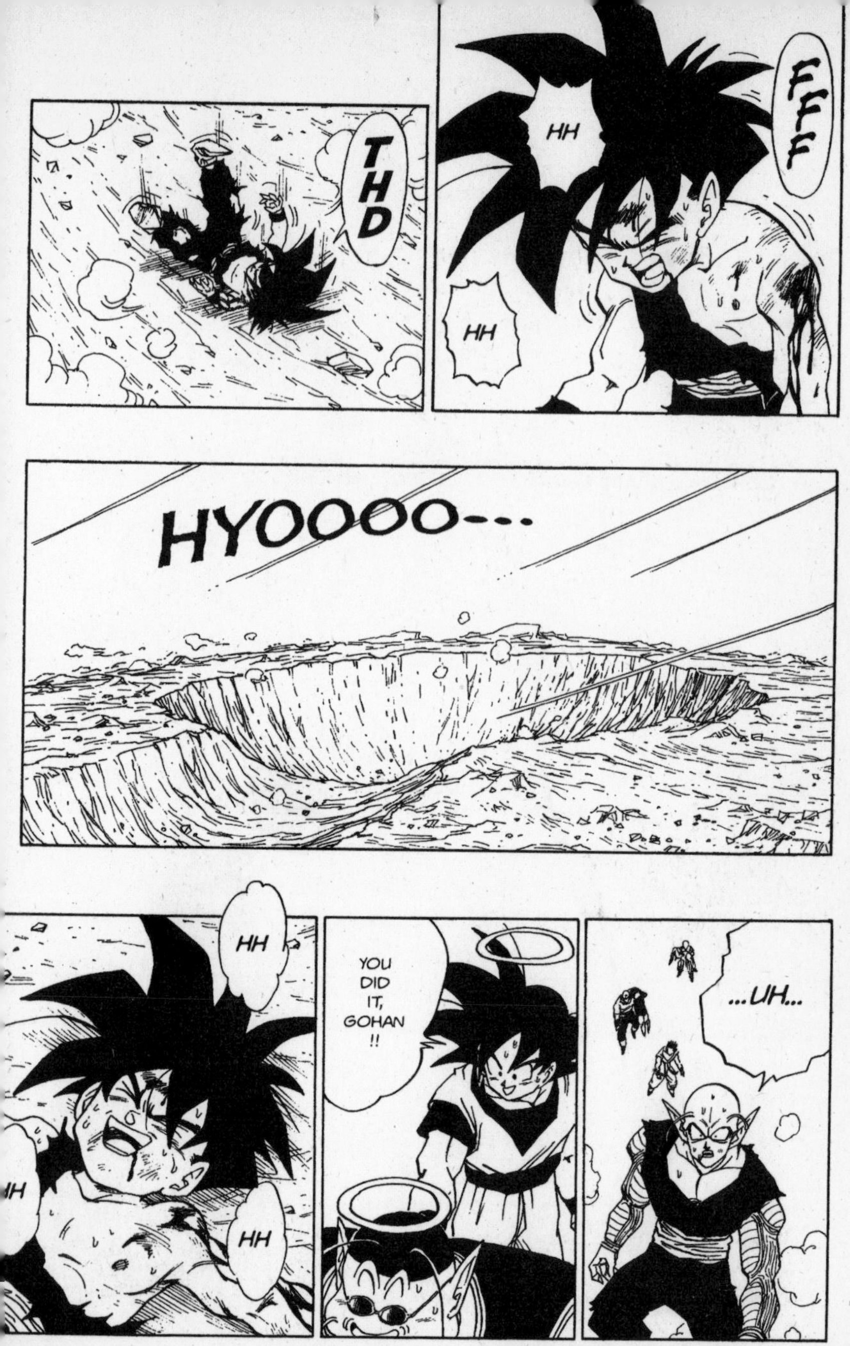
FFF
HH
HH
THD
HYOOOO---.
...UH...
YOU DID IT, GOHAN !!
HH
HH

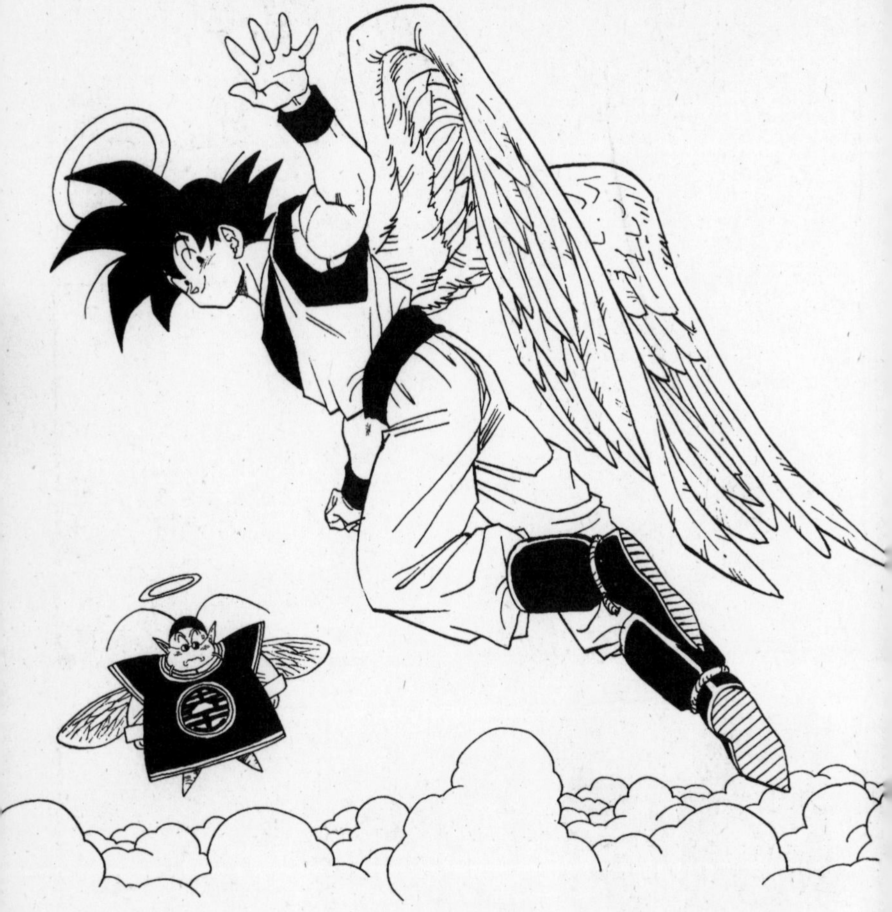

DBZ:223 • Finale

READ THIS WAY

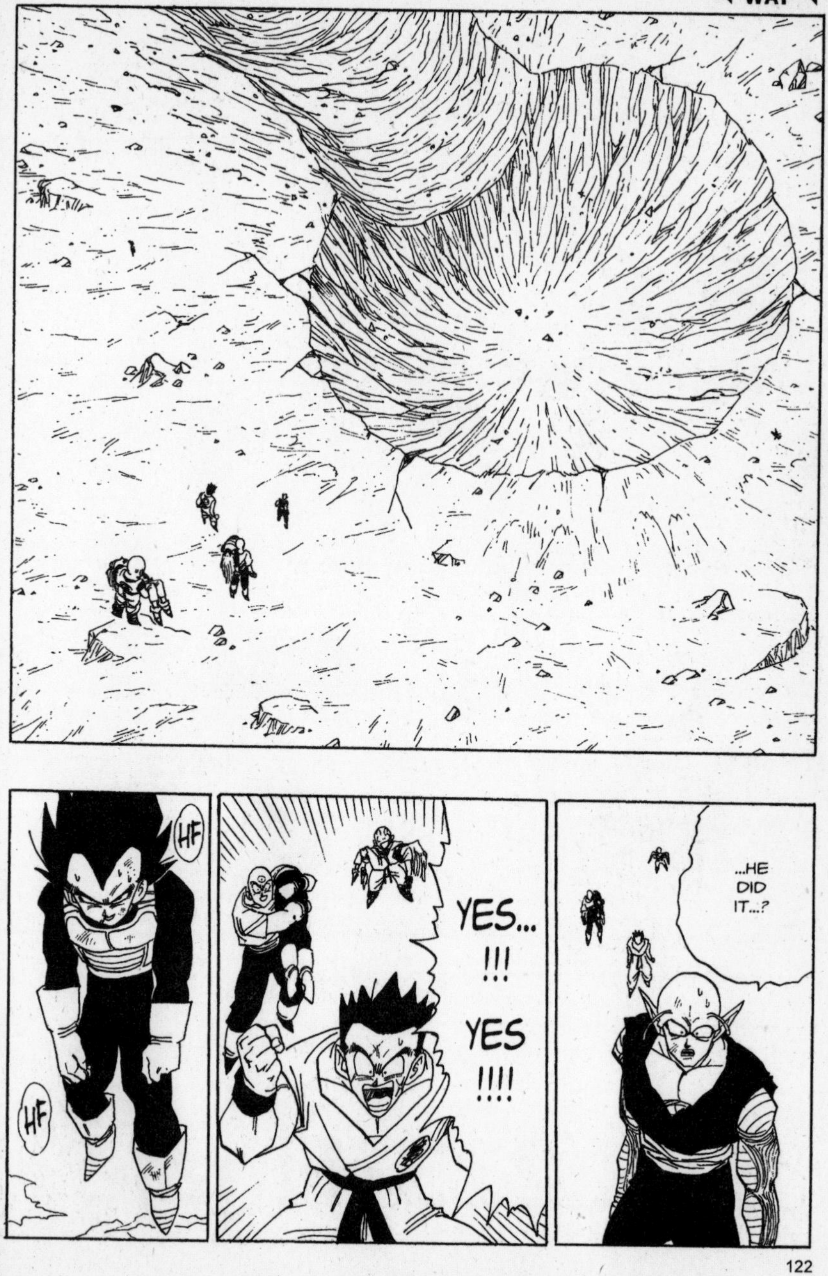
...HE DID IT...?
YES... !!!
YES !!!!
HF
HF

READ THIS WAY

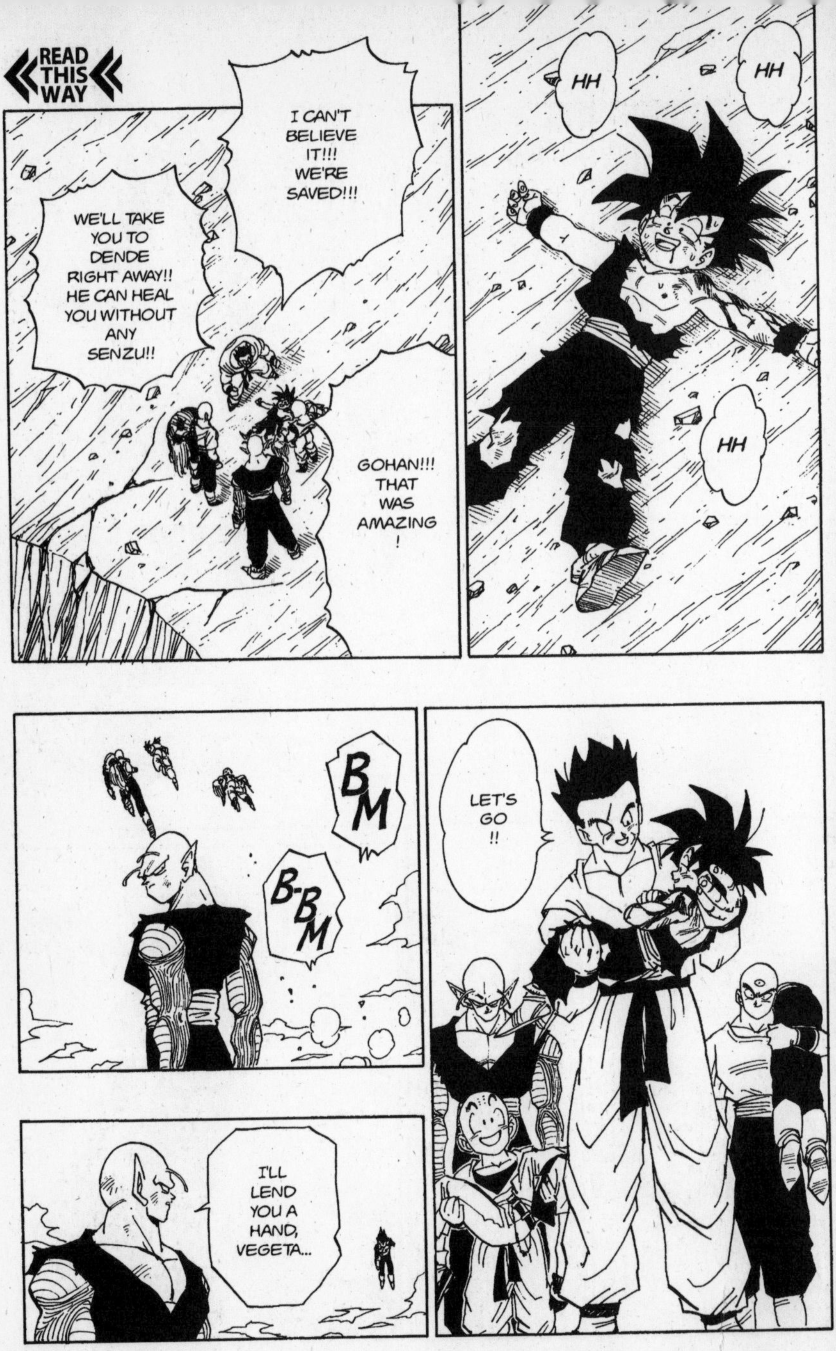
HH
HH
HH
I CAN'T BELIEVE IT!!! WE'RE SAVED!!!
WE'LL TAKE YOU TO DENDE RIGHT AWAY!! HE CAN HEAL YOU WITHOUT ANY SENZU!!
GOHAN!!! THAT WAS AMAZING!
LET'S GO!!
BM
B-BM
I'LL LEND YOU A HAND, VEGETA...

READ THIS WAY

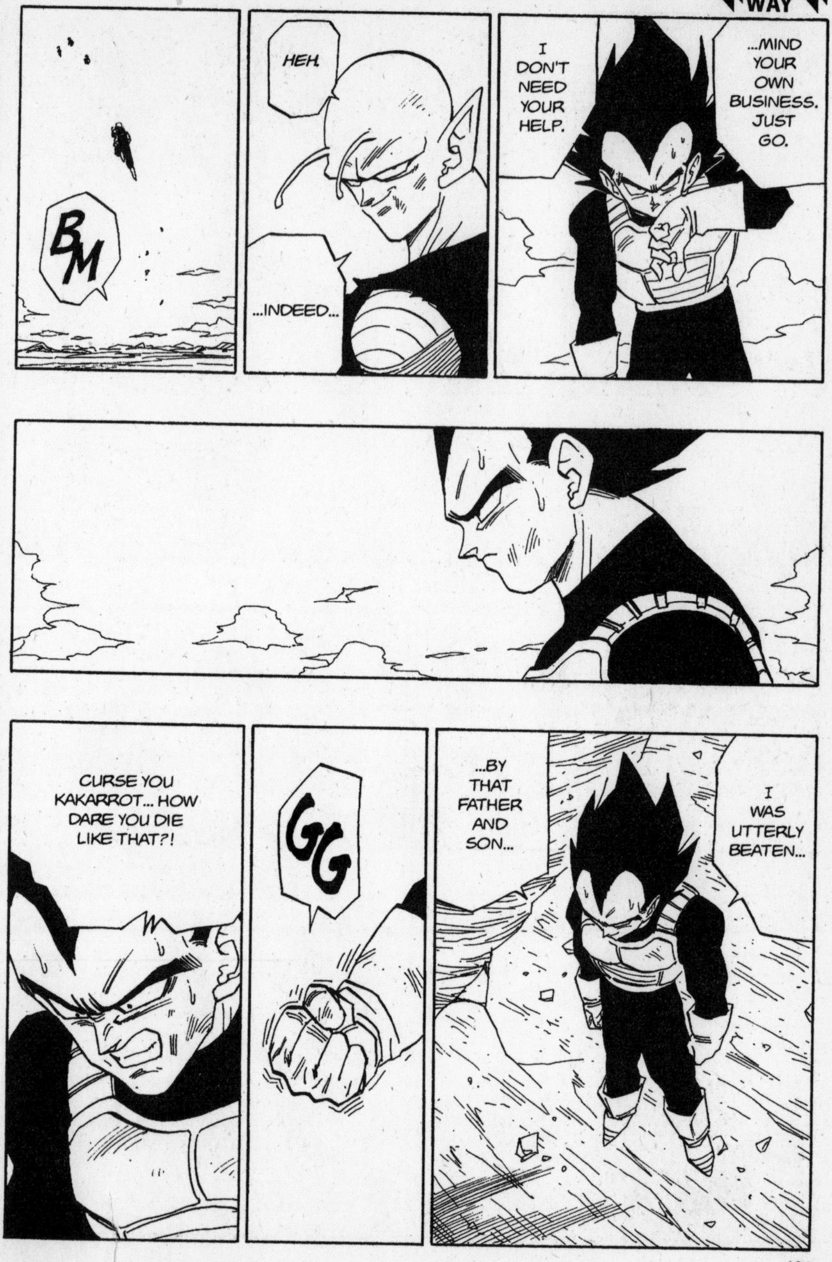
...MIND YOUR OWN BUSINESS. JUST GO.
I DON'T NEED YOUR HELP.
HEH.
...INDEED...
BM
I WAS UTTERLY BEATEN...
...BY THAT FATHER AND SON...
GG
CURSE YOU KAKARROT... HOW DARE YOU DIE LIKE THAT?!

READ THIS WAY

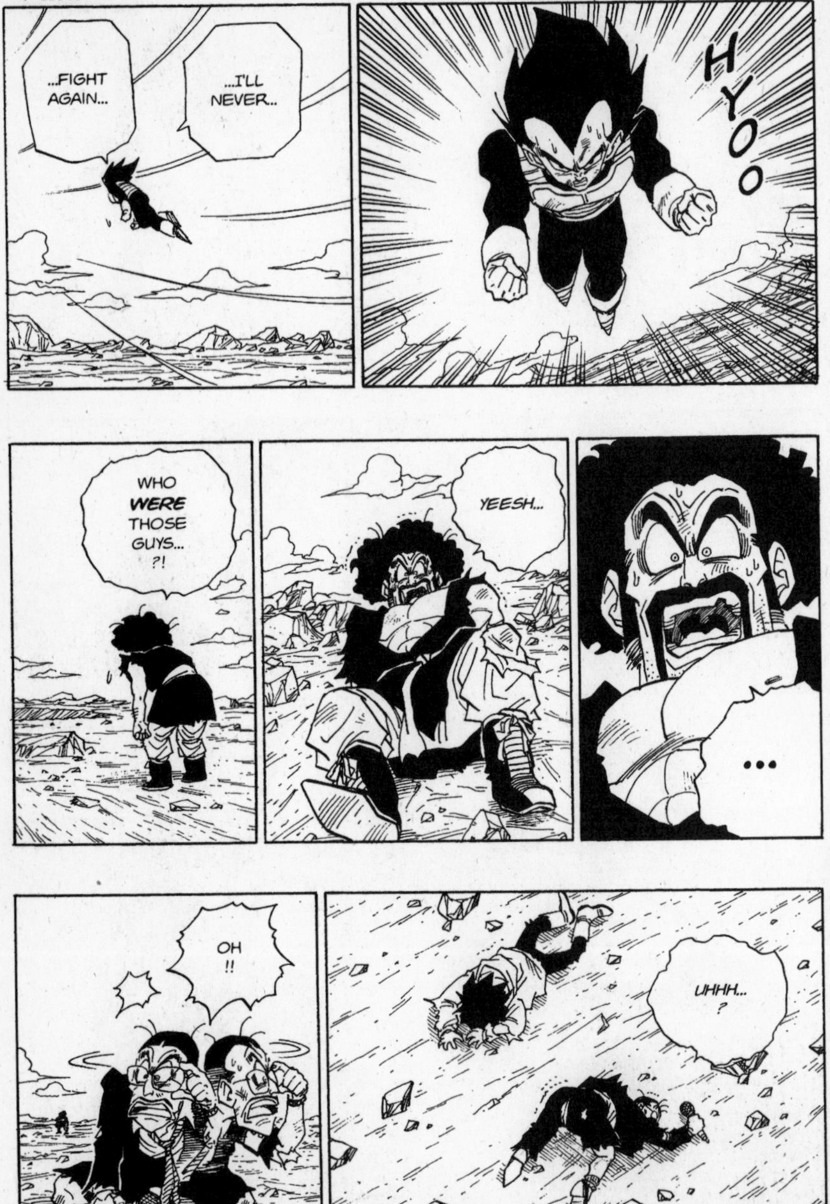
HYOOO
...I'LL NEVER...
...FIGHT AGAIN...
...
YEESH...
WHO WERE THOSE GUYS...?!
UHHH...?
OH!!

READ THIS WAY

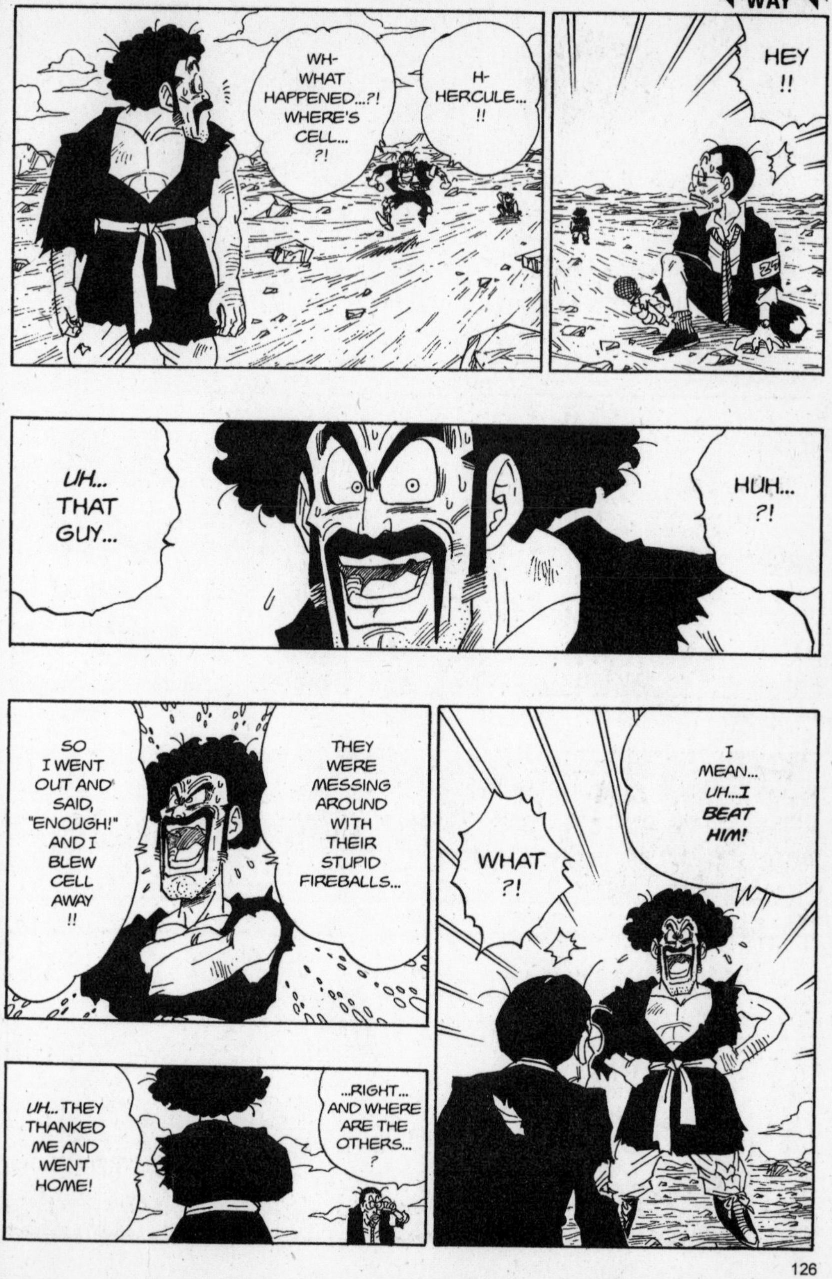
HEY !!
H- HERCULE... !!
WH- WHAT HAPPENED...?! WHERE'S CELL... ?!
HUH... ?!
UH... THAT GUY...
I MEAN... UH...I BEAT HIM!
WHAT ?!
THEY WERE MESSING AROUND WITH THEIR STUPID FIREBALLS...
SO I WENT OUT AND SAID, "ENOUGH!" AND I BLEW CELL AWAY !!
...RIGHT... AND WHERE ARE THE OTHERS... ?
UH... THEY THANKED ME AND WENT HOME!

READ THIS WAY

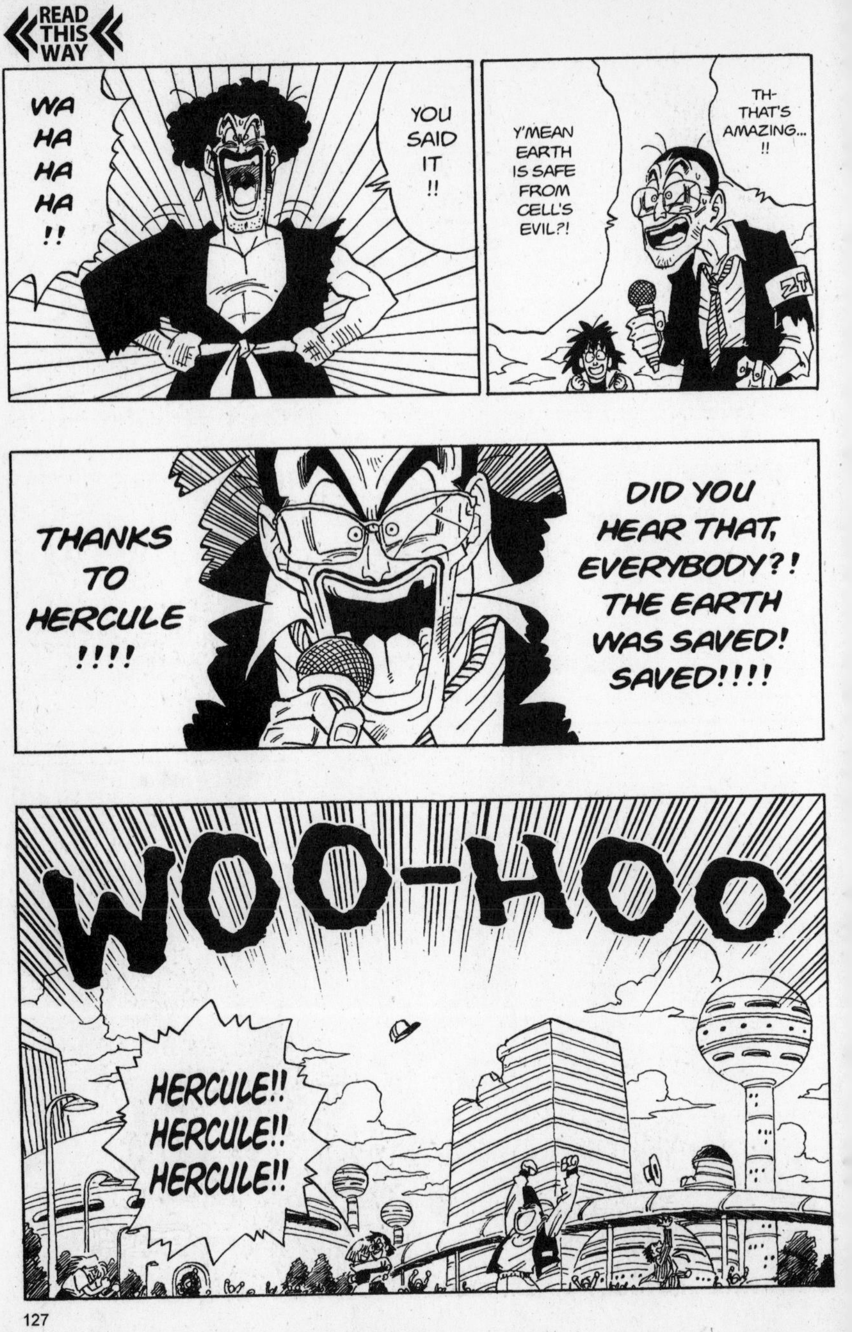
TH- THAT'S AMAZING...!!
Y'MEAN EARTH IS SAFE FROM CELL'S EVIL?!
YOU SAID IT!!
WA HA HA HA!!
DID YOU HEAR THAT, EVERYBODY?! THE EARTH WAS SAVED! SAVED!!!!
THANKS TO HERCULE!!!!
WOO-HOO
HERCULE!! HERCULE!! HERCULE!!

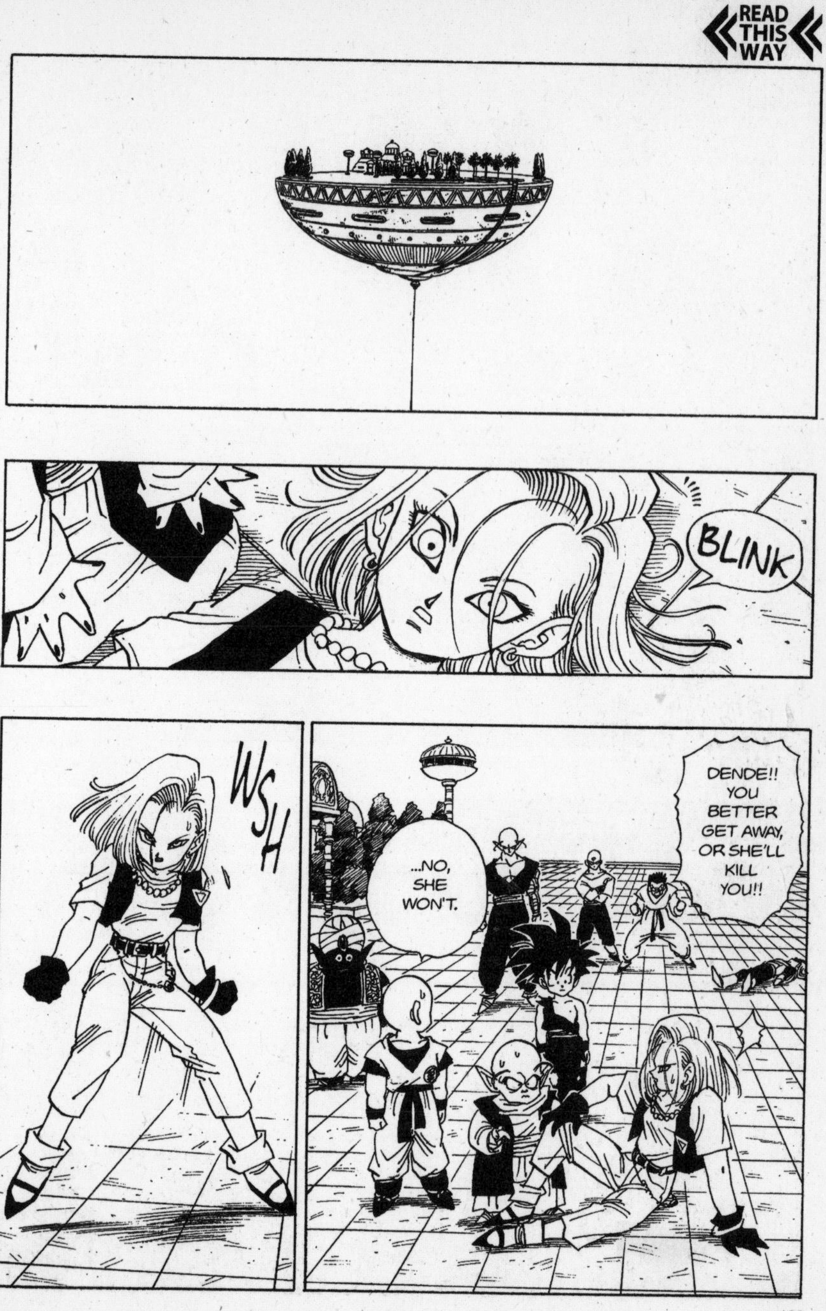

READ THIS WAY
BLINK
WSH
DENDE!! YOU BETTER GET AWAY, OR SHE'LL KILL YOU!!
...NO, SHE WON'T.

READ THIS WAY

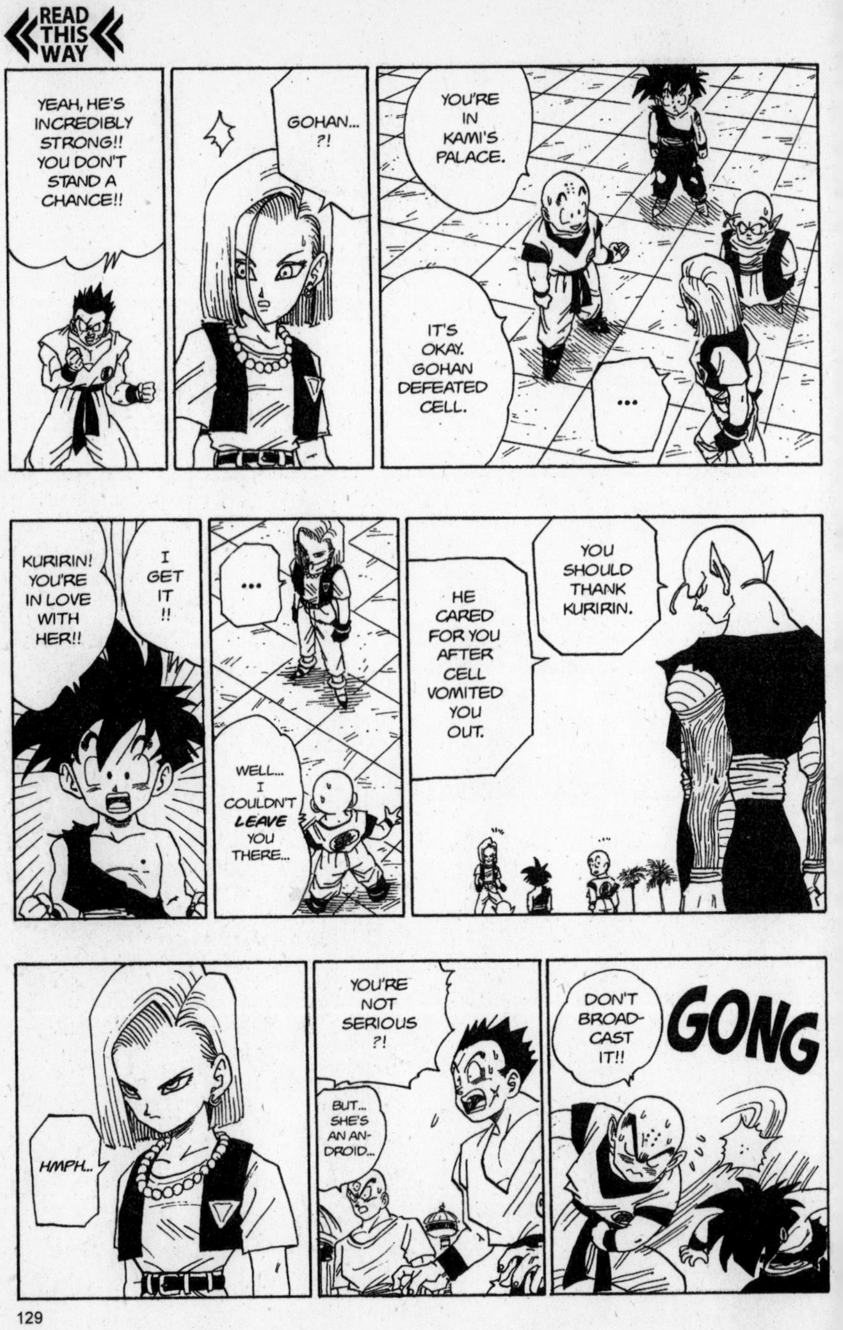
YOU'RE IN KAMI'S PALACE.
IT'S OKAY. GOHAN DEFEATED CELL.
...
GOHAN...?!
YEAH, HE'S INCREDIBLY STRONG!! YOU DON'T STAND A CHANCE!!
YOU SHOULD THANK KURIRIN.
HE CARED FOR YOU AFTER CELL VOMITED YOU OUT.
...
WELL... I COULDN'T *LEAVE* YOU THERE...
I GET IT!!
KURIRIN! YOU'RE IN LOVE WITH HER!!
GONG
DON'T BROAD-CAST IT!!
YOU'RE NOT SERIOUS?!
BUT... SHE'S AN AN-DROID...
HMPH...

READ THIS WAY

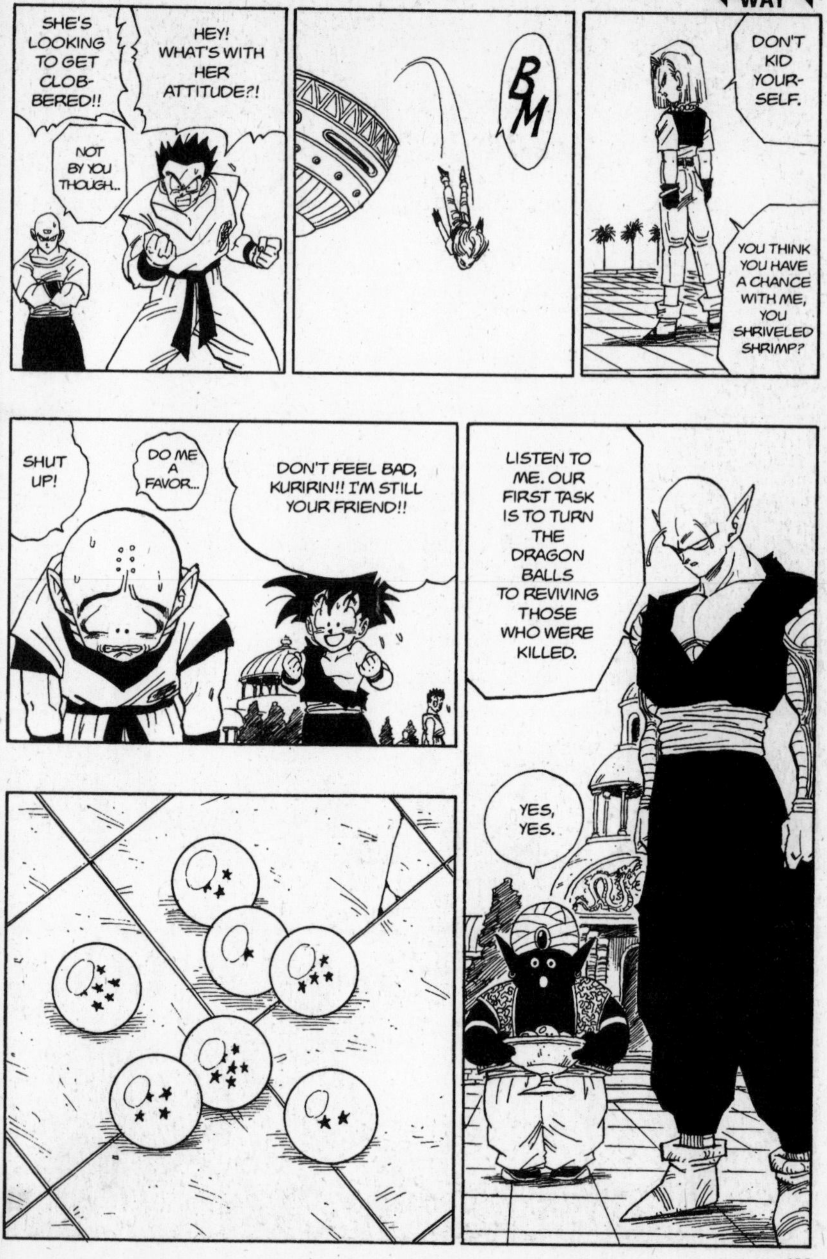
DON'T KID YOURSELF.
YOU THINK YOU HAVE A CHANCE WITH ME, YOU SHRIVELED SHRIMP?
BM
HEY! WHAT'S WITH HER ATTITUDE?!
SHE'S LOOKING TO GET CLOBBERED!!
NOT BY YOU THOUGH..
LISTEN TO ME. OUR FIRST TASK IS TO TURN THE DRAGON BALLS TO REVIVING THOSE WHO WERE KILLED.
YES, YES.
DON'T FEEL BAD, KURIRIN!! I'M STILL YOUR FRIEND!!
DO ME A FAVOR...
SHUT UP!

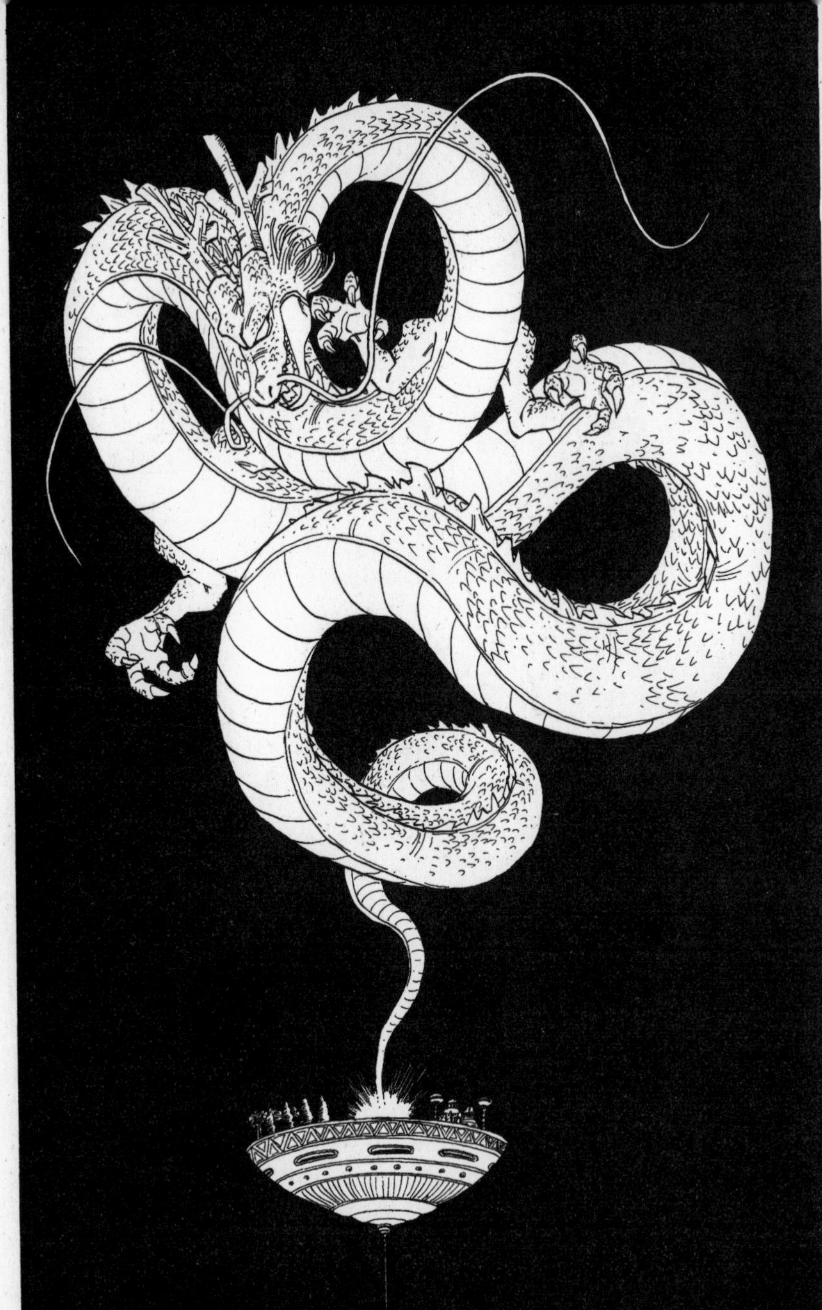

READ THIS WAY

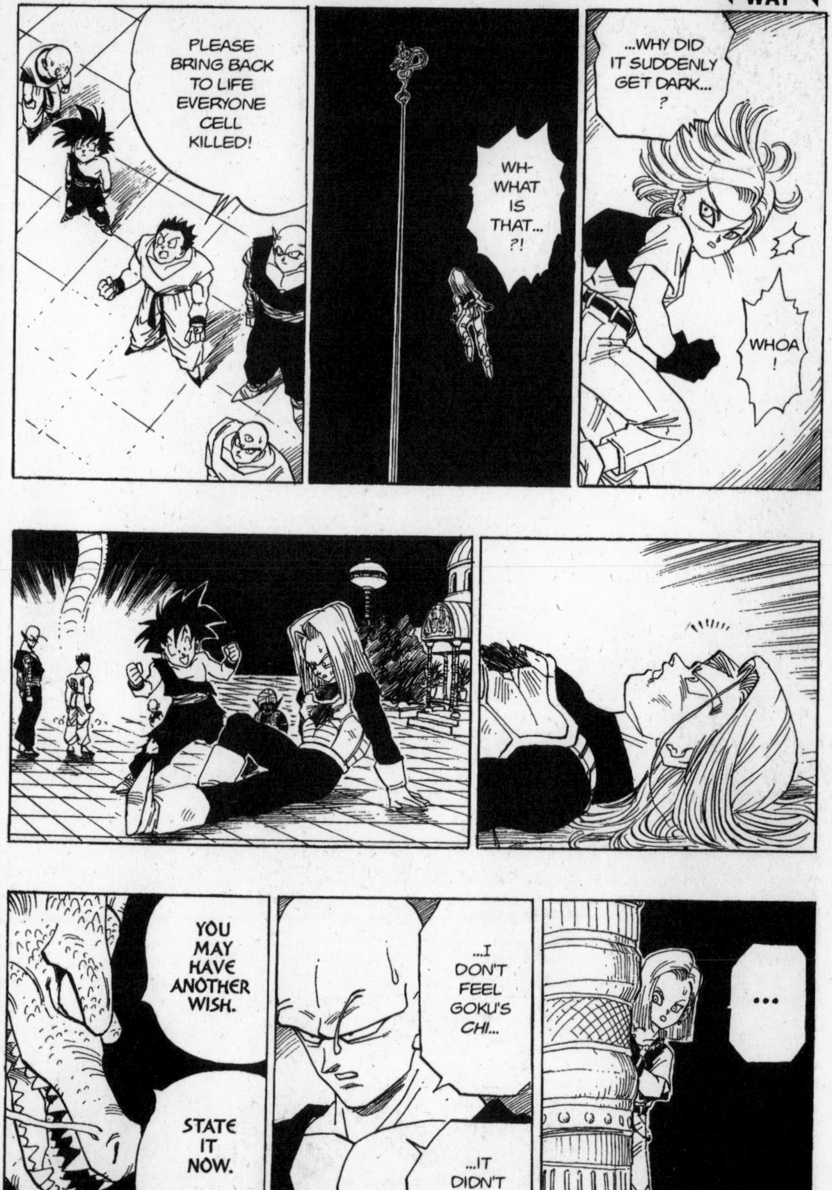
...WHY DID IT SUDDENLY GET DARK... ?
WHOA !
WH- WHAT IS THAT... ?!
PLEASE BRING BACK TO LIFE EVERYONE CELL KILLED!
...
...I DON'T FEEL GOKU'S CHI...
...IT DIDN'T WORK...
YOU MAY HAVE ANOTHER WISH.
STATE IT NOW.

READ THIS WAY

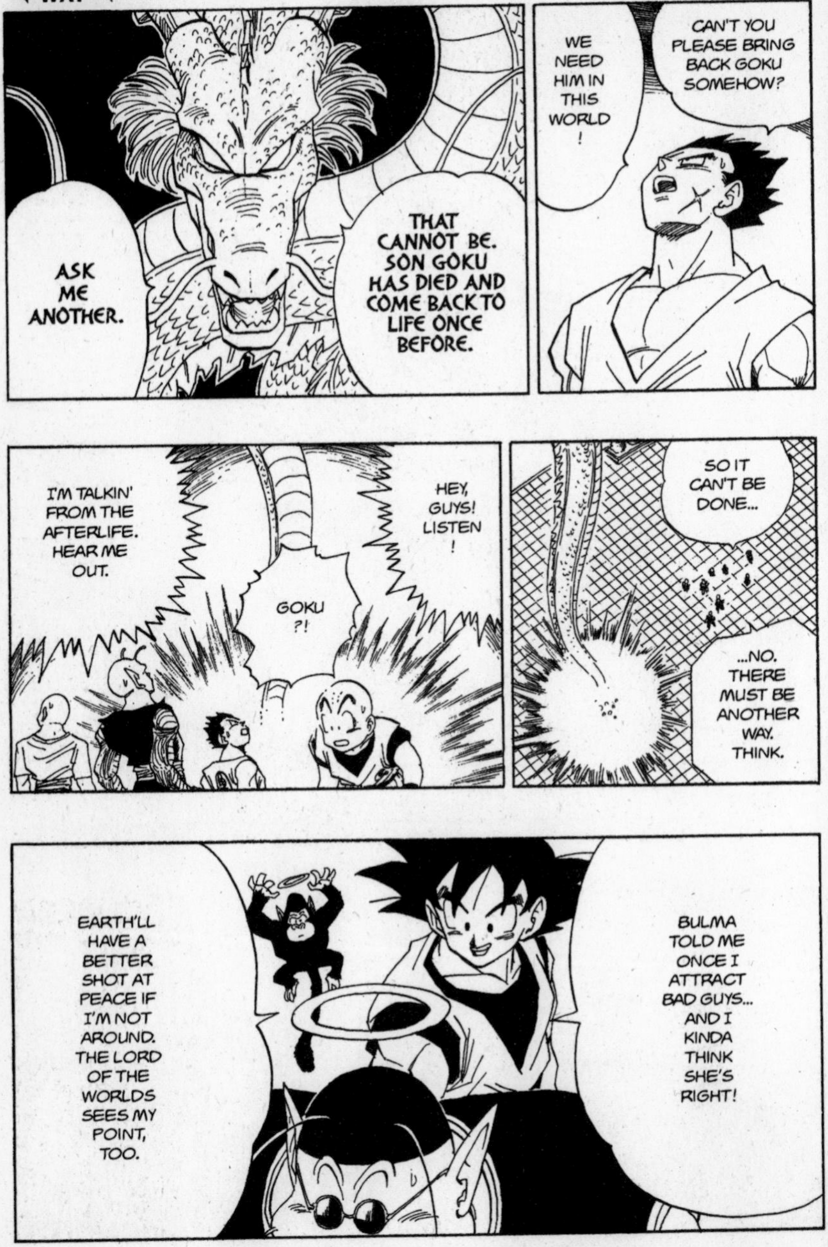
CAN'T YOU PLEASE BRING BACK GOKU SOMEHOW?
WE NEED HIM IN THIS WORLD!
THAT CANNOT BE. SON GOKU HAS DIED AND COME BACK TO LIFE ONCE BEFORE.
ASK ME ANOTHER.
SO IT CAN'T BE DONE...
...NO. THERE MUST BE ANOTHER WAY. THINK.
HEY, GUYS! LISTEN!
I'M TALKIN' FROM THE AFTERLIFE. HEAR ME OUT.
GOKU?!
BULMA TOLD ME ONCE I ATTRACT BAD GUYS... AND I KINDA THINK SHE'S RIGHT!
EARTH'LL HAVE A BETTER SHOT AT PEACE IF I'M NOT AROUND. THE LORD OF THE WORLDS SEES MY POINT, TOO.

READ THIS WAY

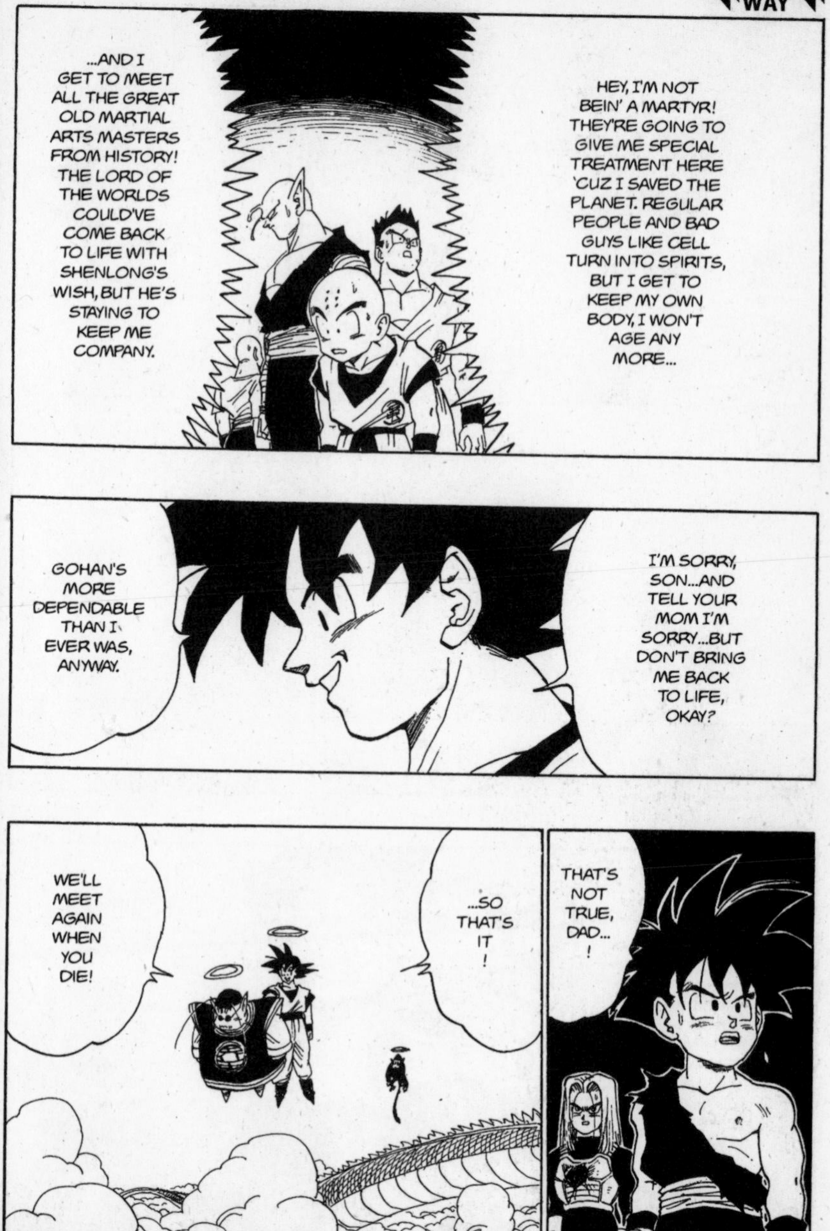
HEY, I'M NOT BEIN' A MARTYR! THEY'RE GOING TO GIVE ME SPECIAL TREATMENT HERE 'CUZ I SAVED THE PLANET. REGULAR PEOPLE AND BAD GUYS LIKE CELL TURN INTO SPIRITS, BUT I GET TO KEEP MY OWN BODY, I WON'T AGE ANY MORE...
...AND I GET TO MEET ALL THE GREAT OLD MARTIAL ARTS MASTERS FROM HISTORY! THE LORD OF THE WORLDS COULD'VE COME BACK TO LIFE WITH SHENLONG'S WISH, BUT HE'S STAYING TO KEEP ME COMPANY.
I'M SORRY, SON...AND TELL YOUR MOM I'M SORRY...BUT DON'T BRING ME BACK TO LIFE, OKAY?
GOHAN'S MORE DEPENDABLE THAN I EVER WAS, ANYWAY.
THAT'S NOT TRUE, DAD...!
...SO THAT'S IT!
WE'LL MEET AGAIN WHEN YOU DIE!

READ THIS WAY

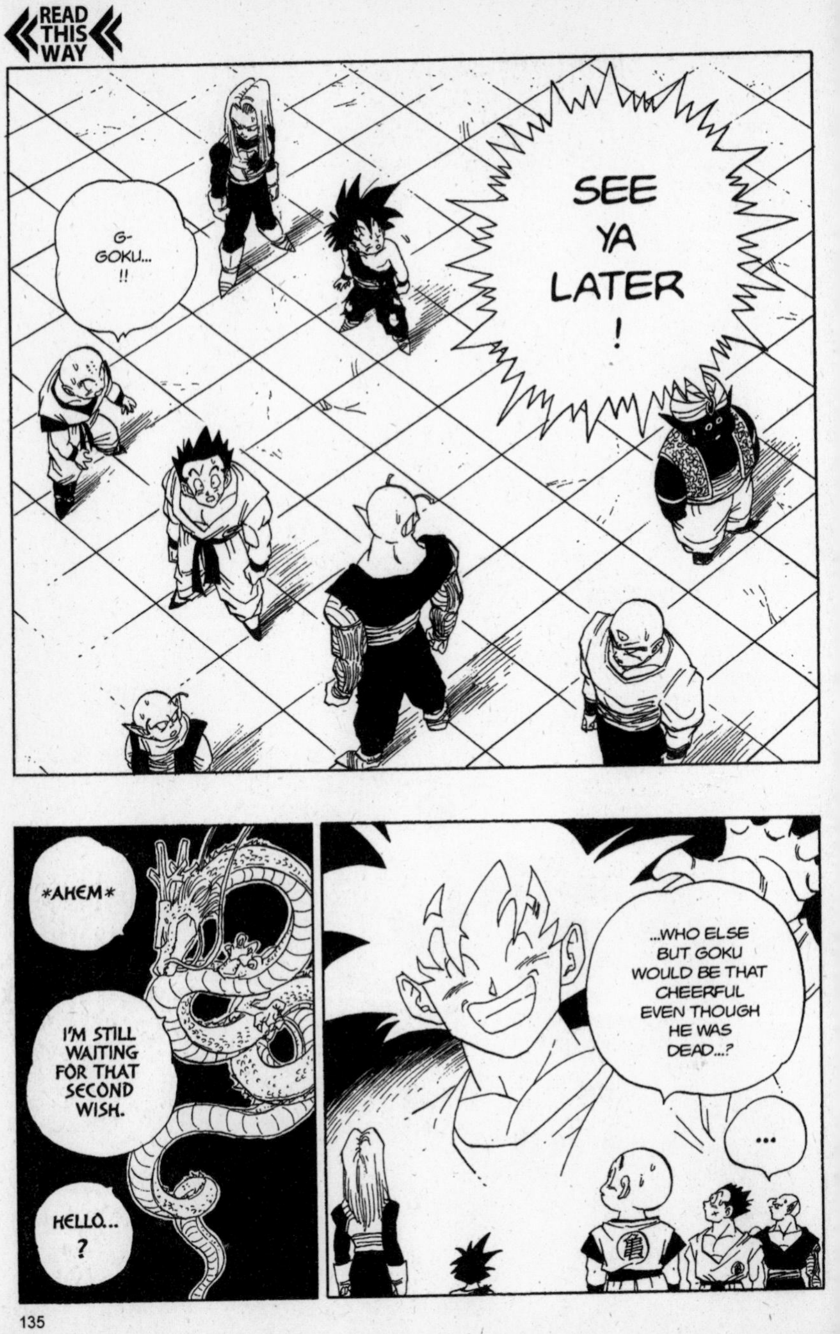

SEE YA LATER!
G-GOKU...!!
...WHO ELSE BUT GOKU WOULD BE THAT CHEERFUL EVEN THOUGH HE WAS DEAD...?
...
AHEM
I'M STILL WAITING FOR THAT SECOND WISH.
HELLO...?

DBZ:224
Farewell, Warriors

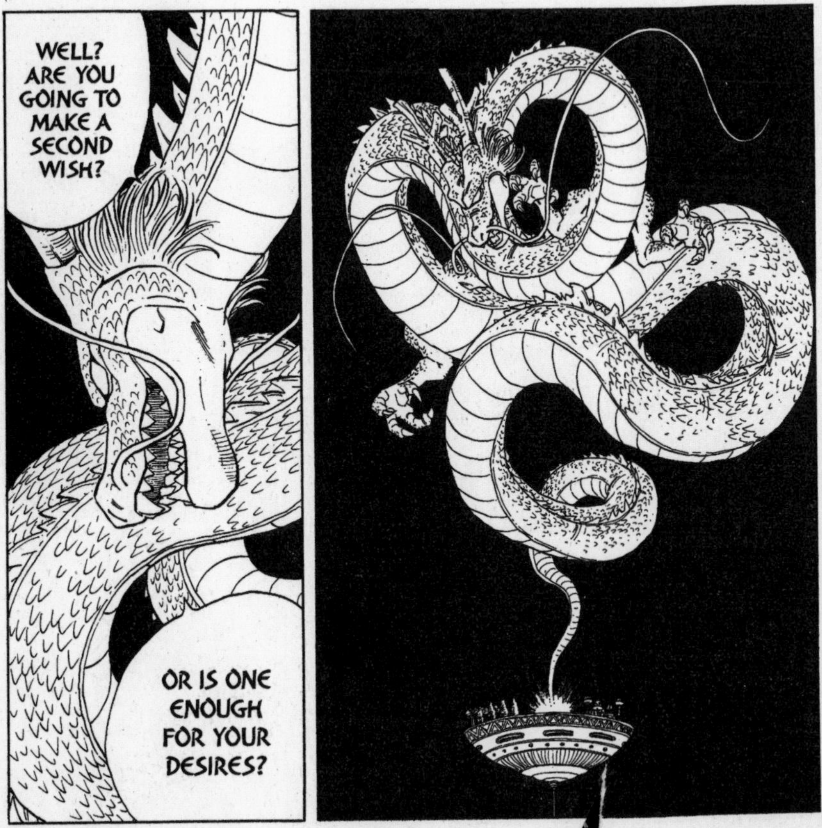
WELL? ARE YOU GOING TO MAKE A SECOND WISH?
OR IS ONE ENOUGH FOR YOUR DESIRES?

READ THIS WAY

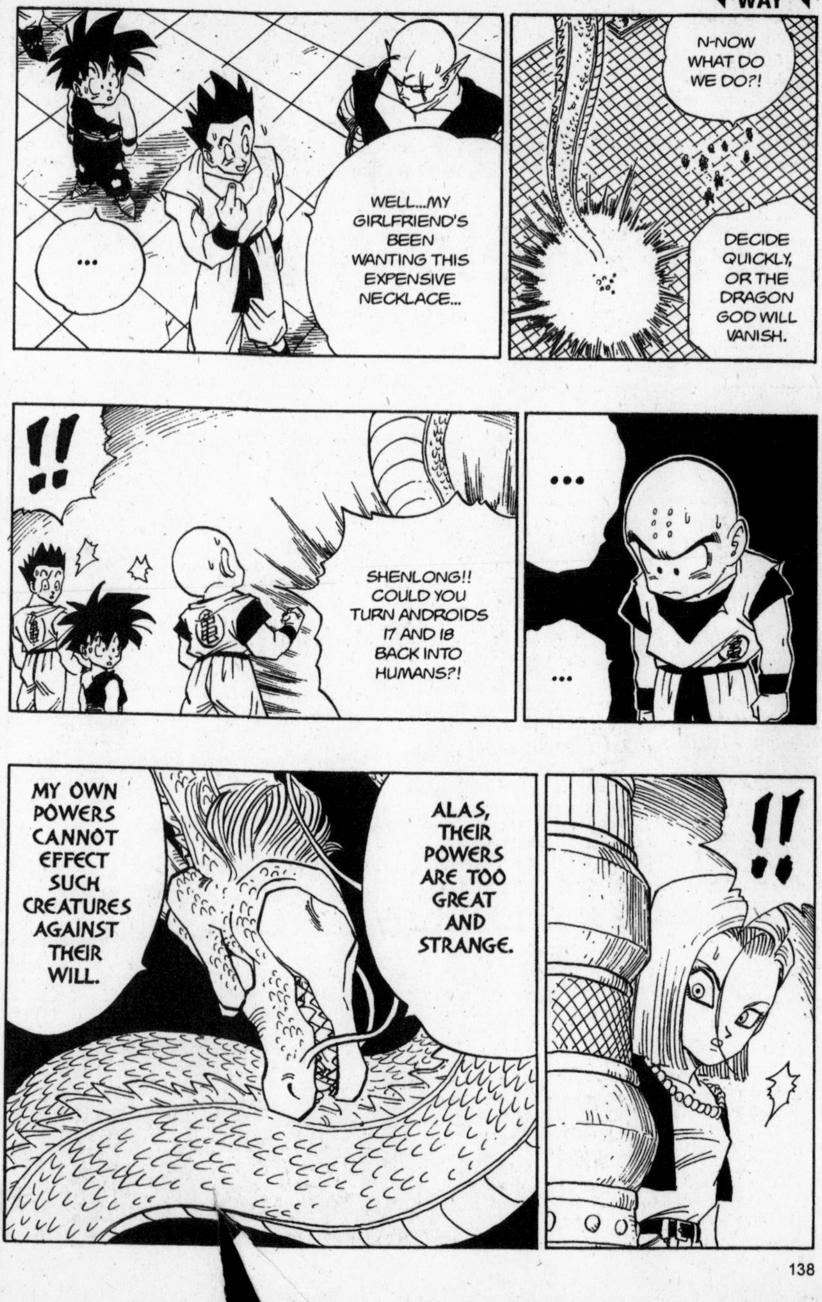
N-NOW WHAT DO WE DO?!
DECIDE QUICKLY, OR THE DRAGON GOD WILL VANISH.
WELL...MY GIRLFRIEND'S BEEN WANTING THIS EXPENSIVE NECKLACE...
...
...
...
SHENLONG!! COULD YOU TURN ANDROIDS 17 AND 18 BACK INTO HUMANS?!
!!
!!
ALAS, THEIR POWERS ARE TOO GREAT AND STRANGE.
MY OWN POWERS CANNOT EFFECT SUCH CREATURES AGAINST THEIR WILL.

READ THIS WAY

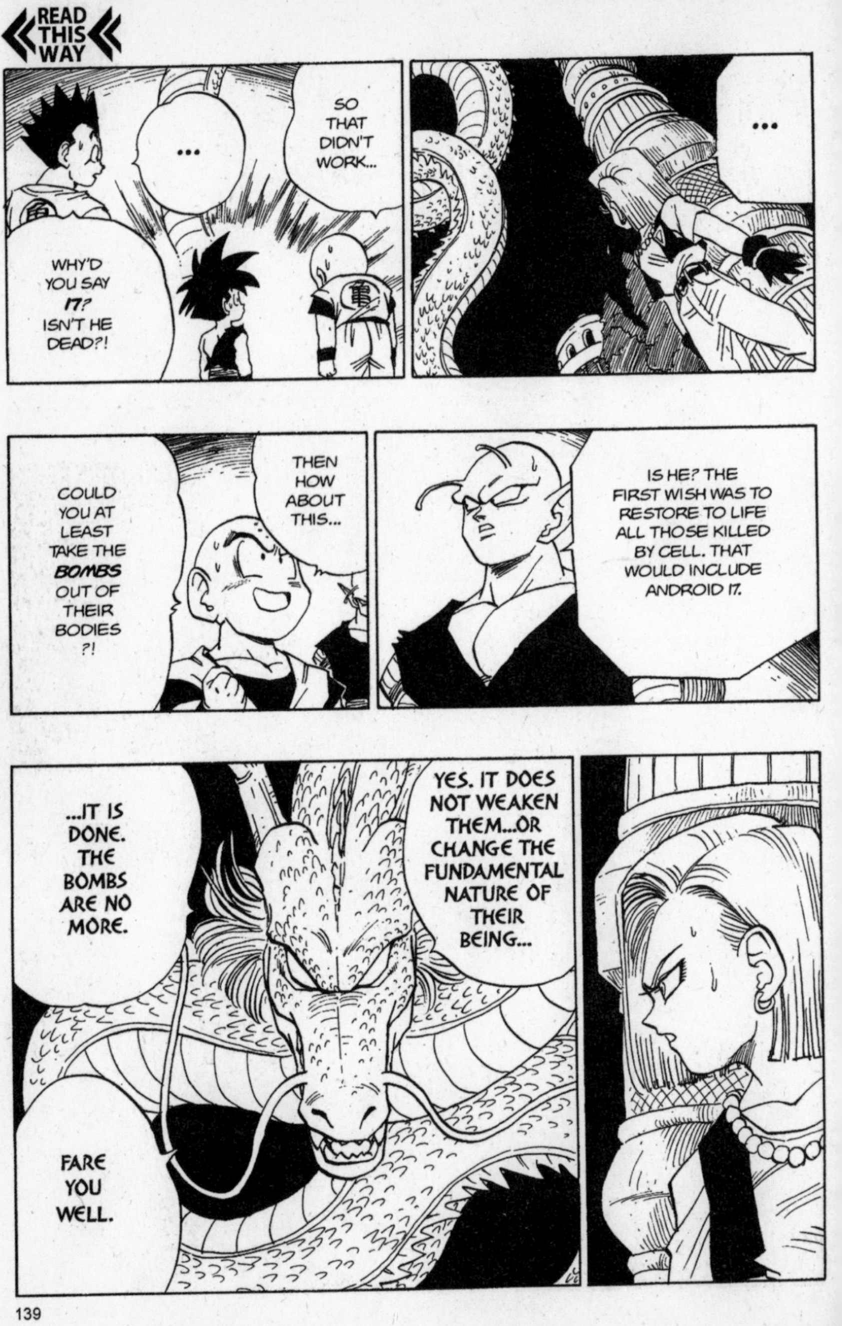
...
SO THAT DIDN'T WORK...
...
WHY'D YOU SAY *17?* ISN'T HE DEAD?!
IS HE? THE FIRST WISH WAS TO RESTORE TO LIFE ALL THOSE KILLED BY CELL. THAT WOULD INCLUDE ANDROID 17.
THEN HOW ABOUT THIS...
COULD YOU AT LEAST TAKE THE *BOMBS* OUT OF THEIR BODIES ?!
YES. IT DOES NOT WEAKEN THEM...OR CHANGE THE FUNDAMENTAL NATURE OF THEIR BEING...
...IT IS DONE. THE BOMBS ARE NO MORE.
FARE YOU WELL.

READ THIS WAY

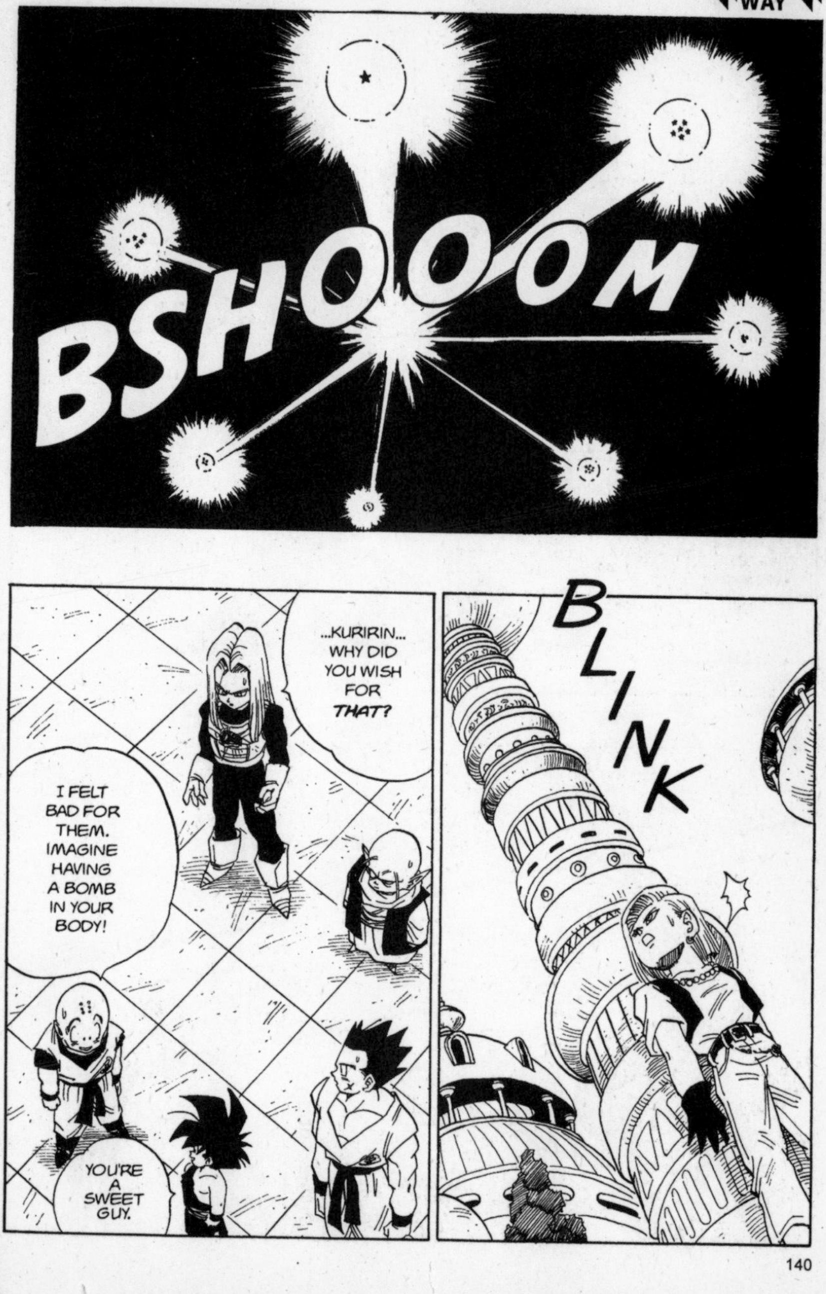
BSHOOOM
BLINK
...KURIRIN... WHY DID YOU WISH FOR *THAT?*
I FELT BAD FOR THEM. IMAGINE HAVING A BOMB IN YOUR BODY!
YOU'RE A SWEET GUY.

...

YOU THINK I'D USE SHENLONG FOR SOMETHING THAT STUPID?!

CAN'T YOU TELL A *JOKE* WHEN YOU HEAR ONE?!

THE—?

I'M SORRY YOU COULDN'T GET THE NECKLACE FOR YOUR GIRLFRIEND.

I DO NOT UNDERSTAND IT...

IS THIS WHAT IS KNOWN AS "LOVE"?

WELL, YEAH.... I *DID* LIKE HER... AND I KNOW 17 IS THE PERFECT GUY FOR HER.

SO WHY REMOVE THE BOMB FROM #17?

KURIRIN... I THOUGHT YOU LIKED #18.

READ THIS WAY

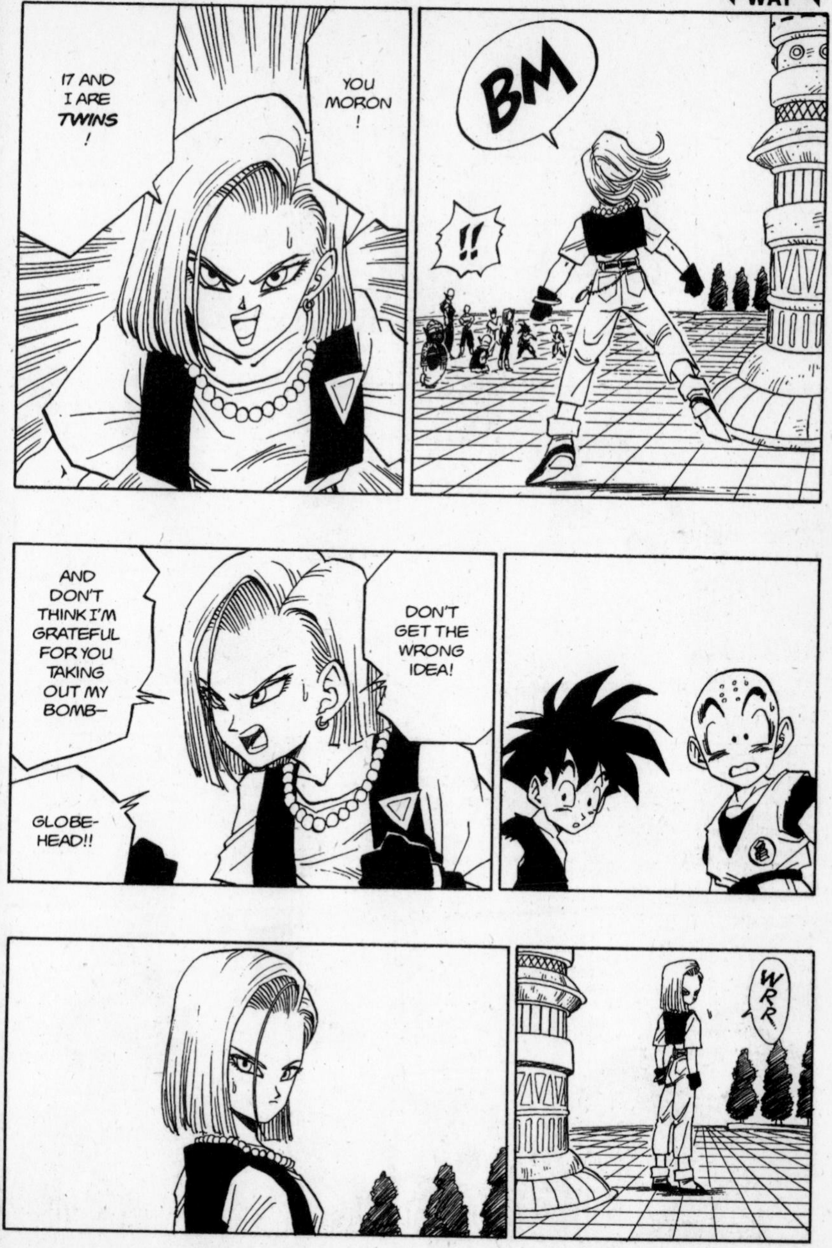
BM
!!
YOU MORON!
17 AND I ARE TWINS!
DON'T GET THE WRONG IDEA!
AND DON'T THINK I'M GRATEFUL FOR YOU TAKING OUT MY BOMB—
GLOBE-HEAD!!
WRR

READ THIS WAY

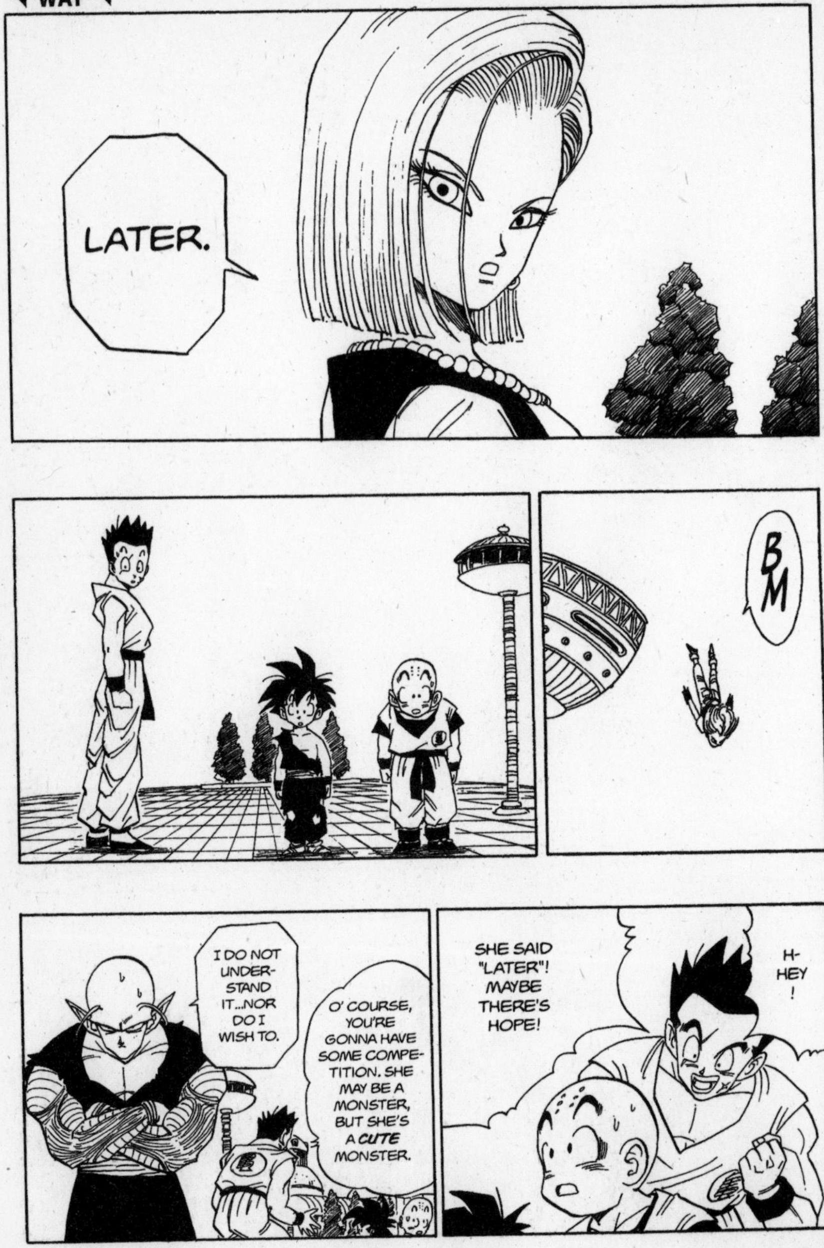

LATER.
BM
H-HEY!
SHE SAID "LATER"! MAYBE THERE'S HOPE!
O' COURSE, YOU'RE GONNA HAVE SOME COMPETITION. SHE MAY BE A MONSTER, BUT SHE'S A *CUTE* MONSTER.
I DO NOT UNDERSTAND IT...NOR DO I WISH TO.

READ THIS WAY

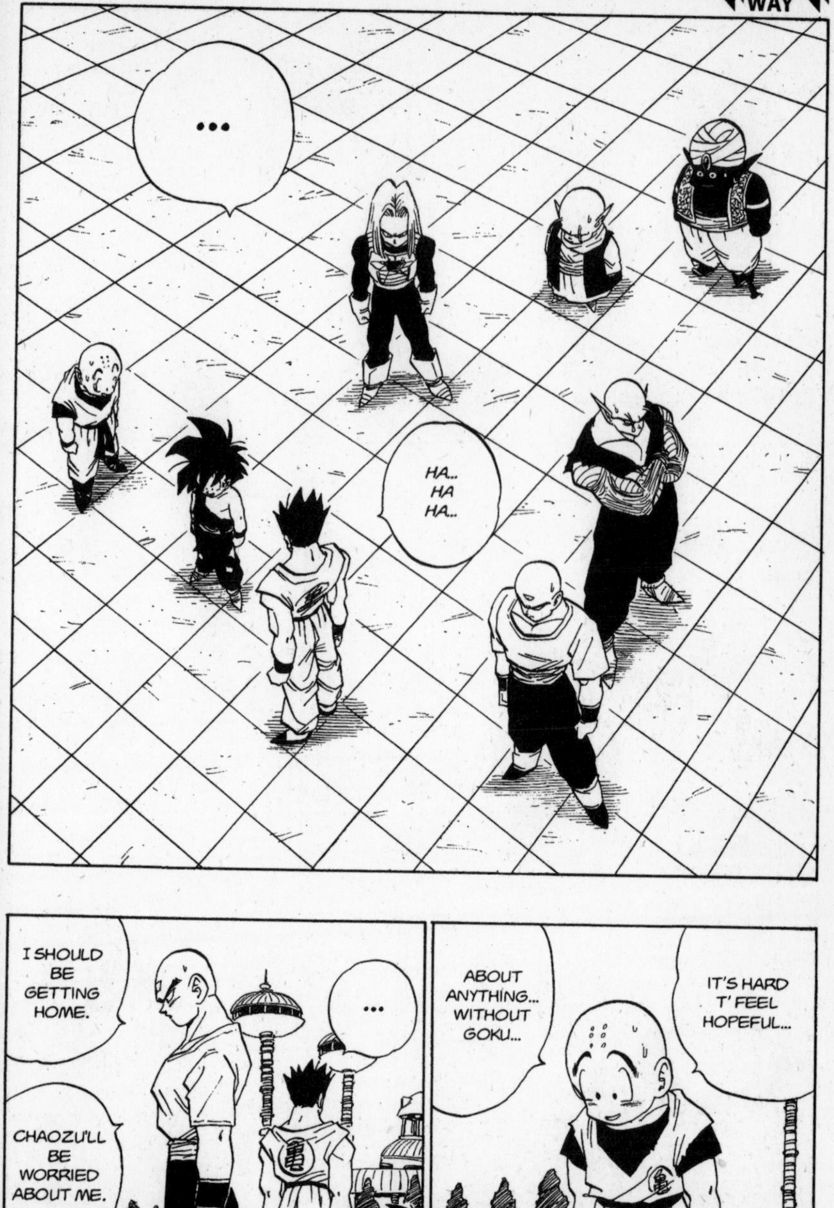

...
HA... HA HA...
IT'S HARD T' FEEL HOPEFUL...
ABOUT ANYTHING... WITHOUT GOKU...
I SHOULD BE GETTING HOME.
CHAOZU'LL BE WORRIED ABOUT ME.
...

READ THIS WAY

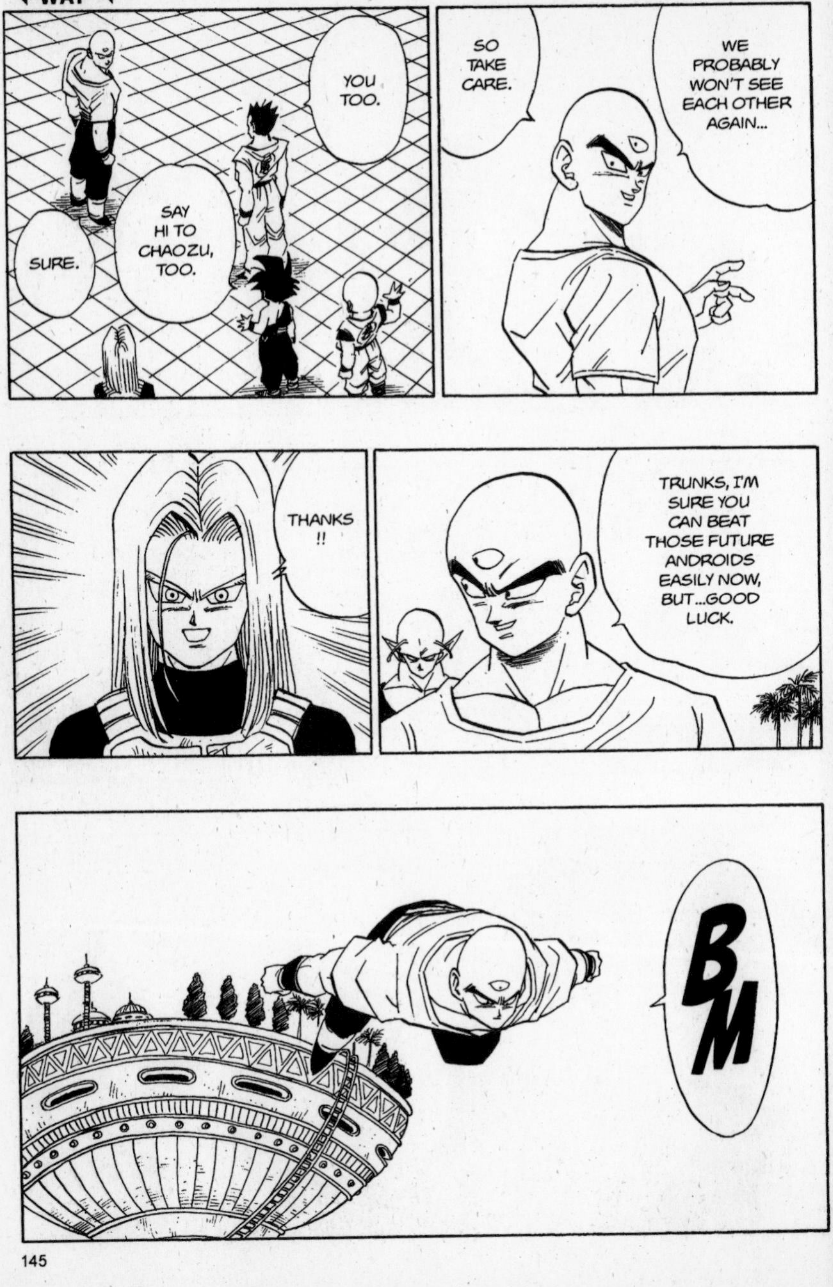
WE PROBABLY WON'T SEE EACH OTHER AGAIN...
SO TAKE CARE.
YOU TOO.
SAY HI TO CHAOZU, TOO.
SURE.
TRUNKS, I'M SURE YOU CAN BEAT THOSE FUTURE ANDROIDS EASILY NOW, BUT...GOOD LUCK.
THANKS !!
BM

READ THIS WAY

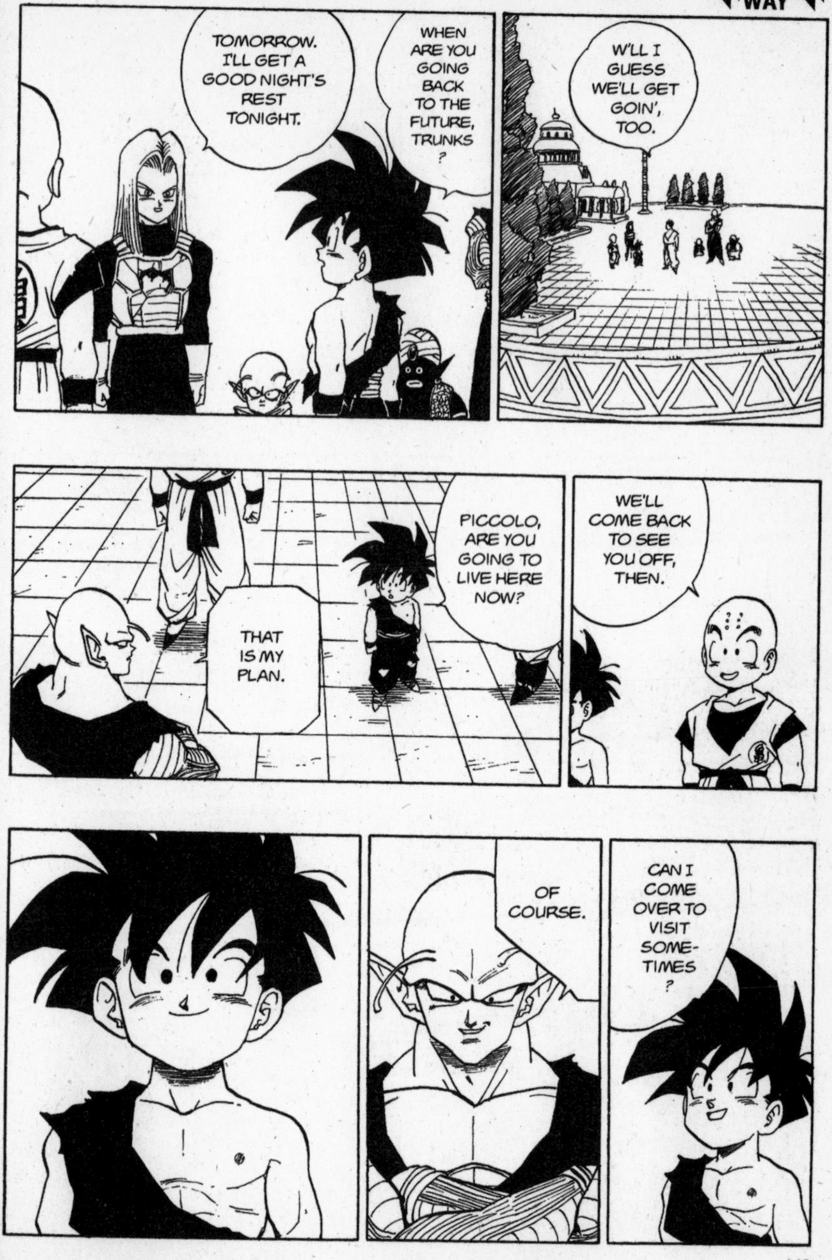
W'LL I GUESS WE'LL GET GOIN', TOO.
WHEN ARE YOU GOING BACK TO THE FUTURE, TRUNKS?
TOMORROW. I'LL GET A GOOD NIGHT'S REST TONIGHT.
WE'LL COME BACK TO SEE YOU OFF, THEN.
PICCOLO, ARE YOU GOING TO LIVE HERE NOW?
THAT IS MY PLAN.
CAN I COME OVER TO VISIT SOME-TIMES?
OF COURSE.

READ THIS WAY

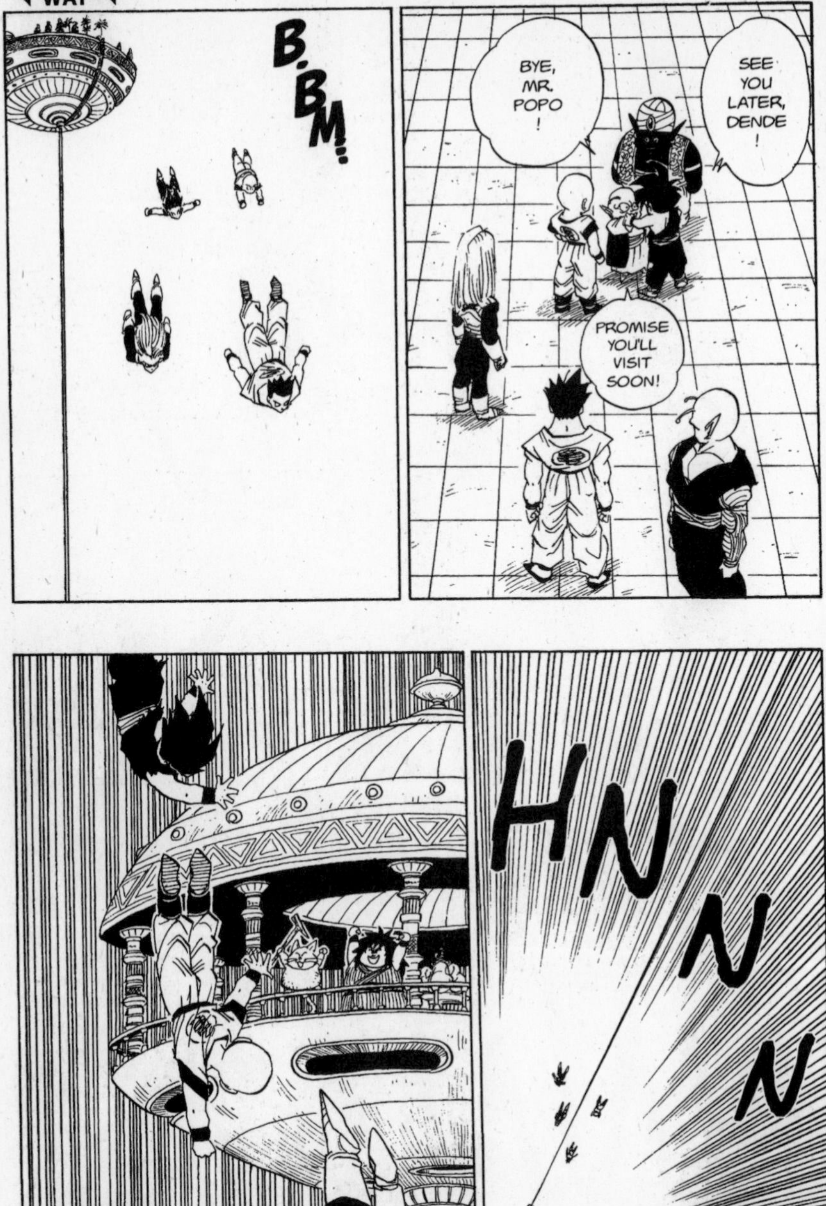
SEE YOU LATER, DENDE!
BYE, MR. POPO!
PROMISE YOU'LL VISIT SOON!
B.BM!!
HNNN

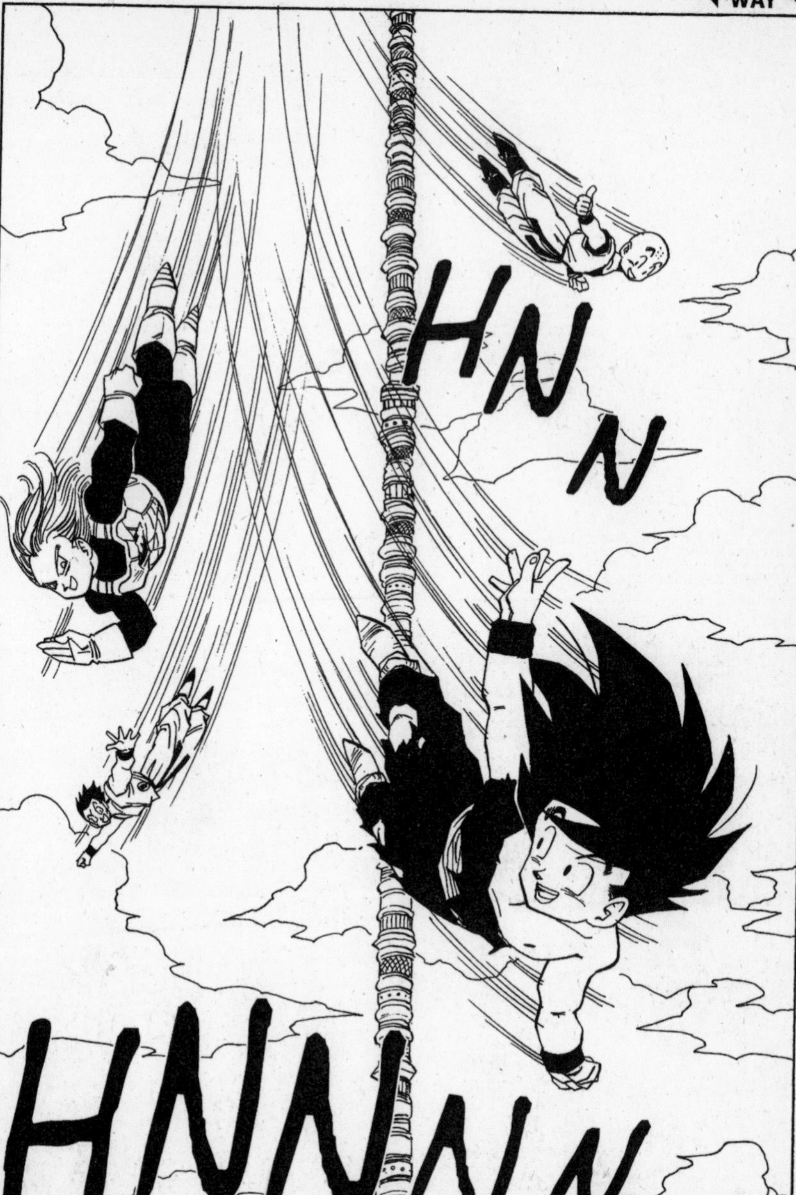
HNN
HNNNNN

READ THIS WAY

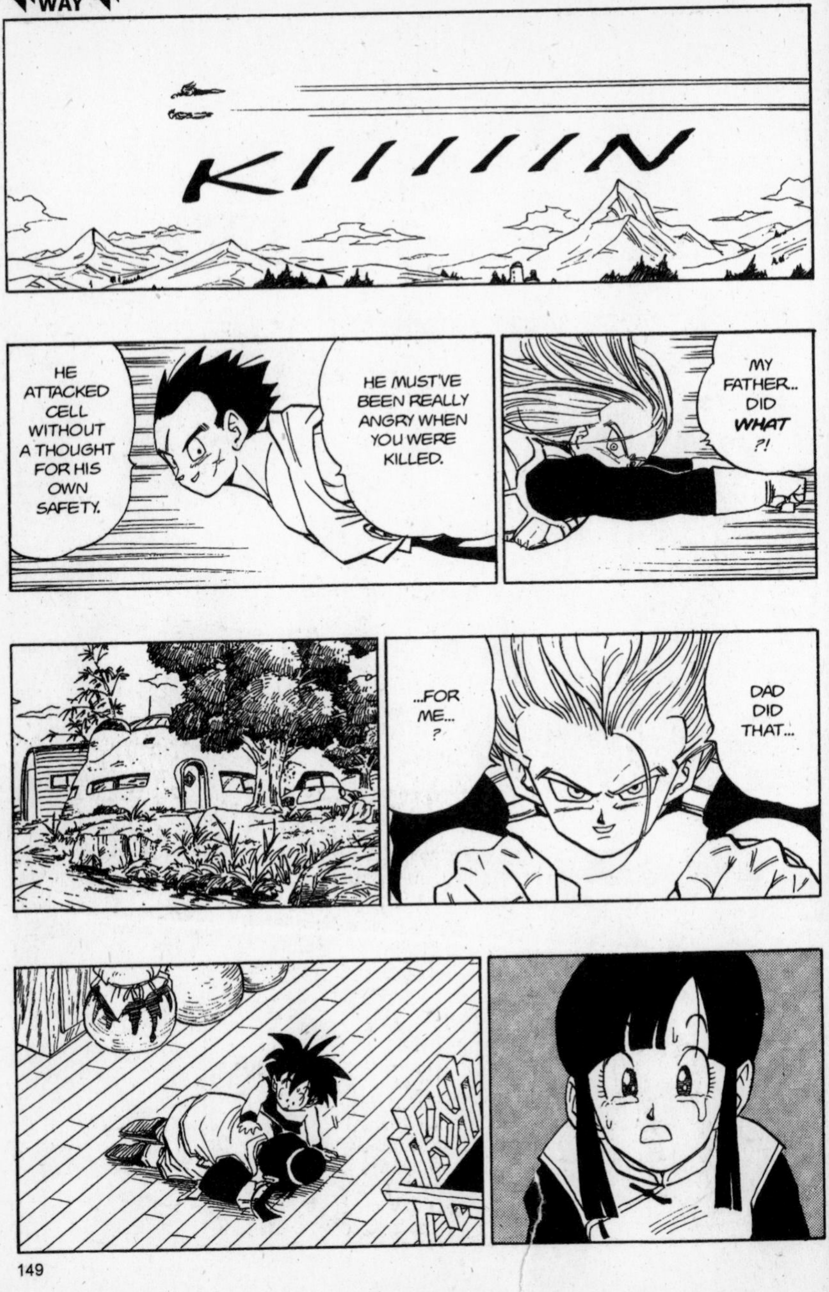
KIIIIN
MY FATHER.. DID WHAT ?!
HE MUST'VE BEEN REALLY ANGRY WHEN YOU WERE KILLED.
HE ATTACKED CELL WITHOUT A THOUGHT FOR HIS OWN SAFETY.
DAD DID THAT...
...FOR ME... ?

READ THIS WAY

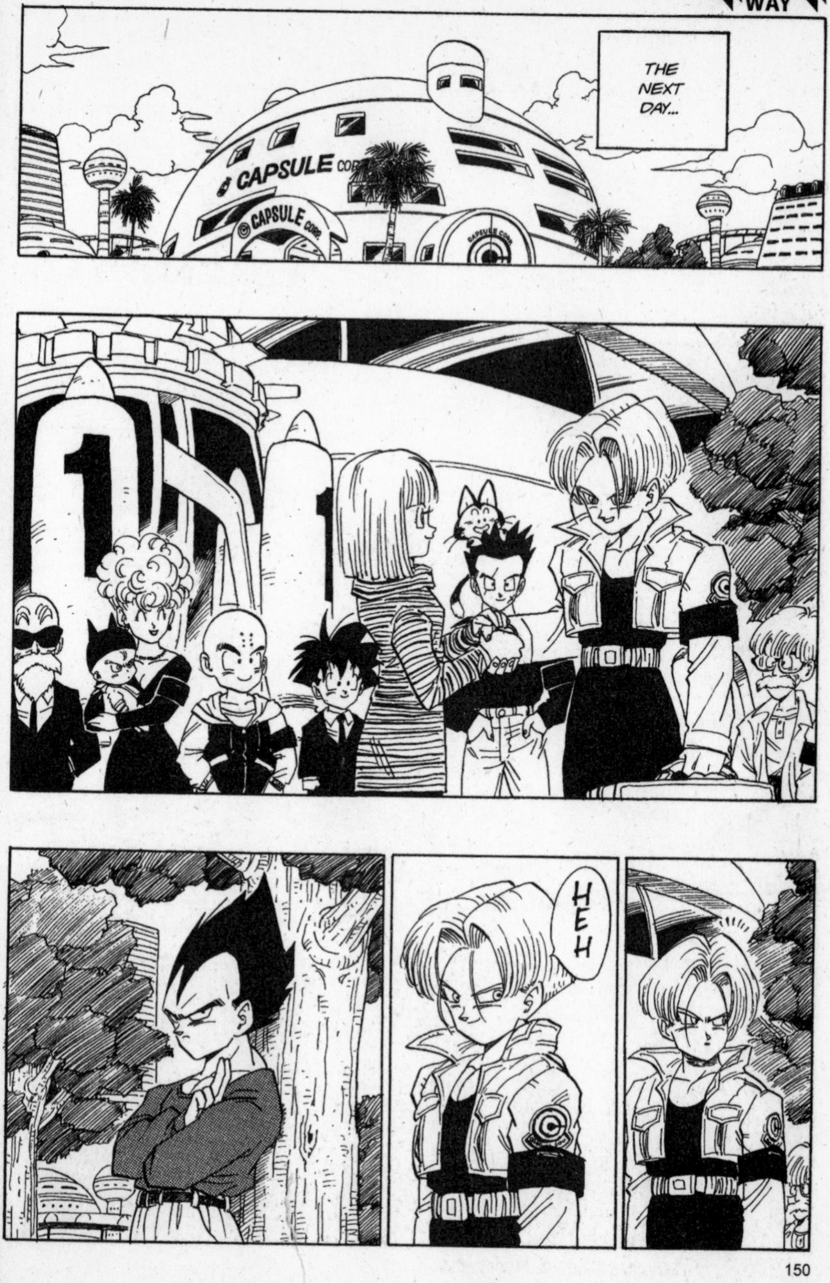
THE NEXT DAY...
CAPSULE CORP
CAPSULE CORP
HEH

READ THIS WAY

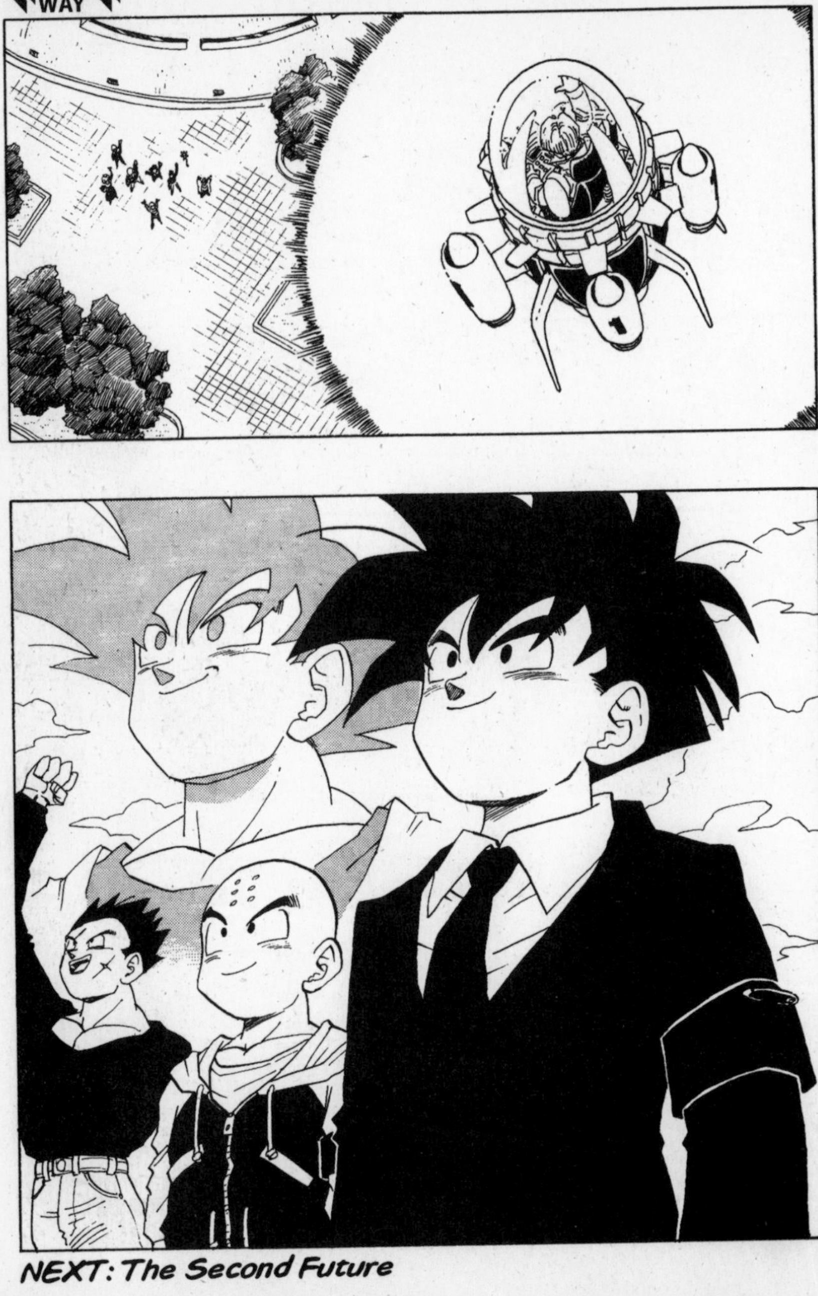

NEXT: The Second Future

DBZ:225 • The Other Outcome

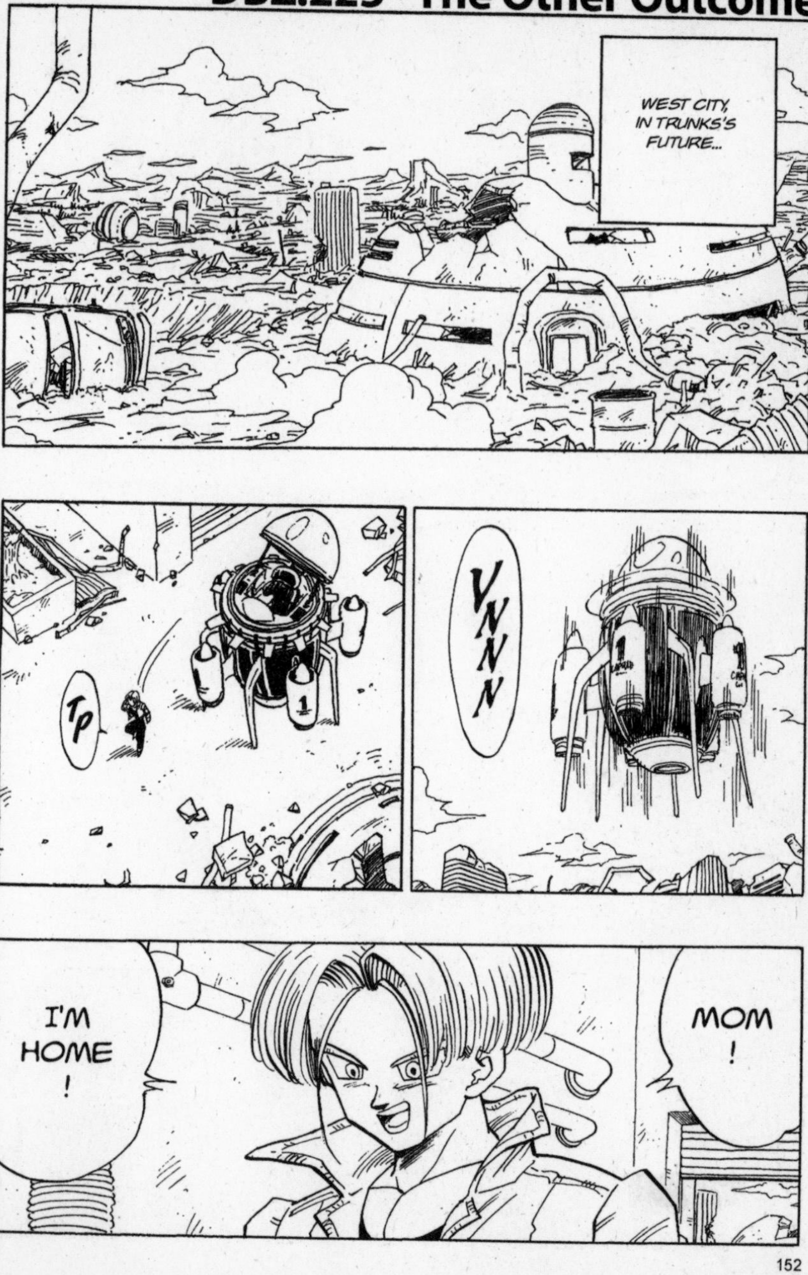
WEST CITY, IN TRUNKS'S FUTURE...
VNNN
TP
MOM!
I'M HOME!

READ THIS WAY

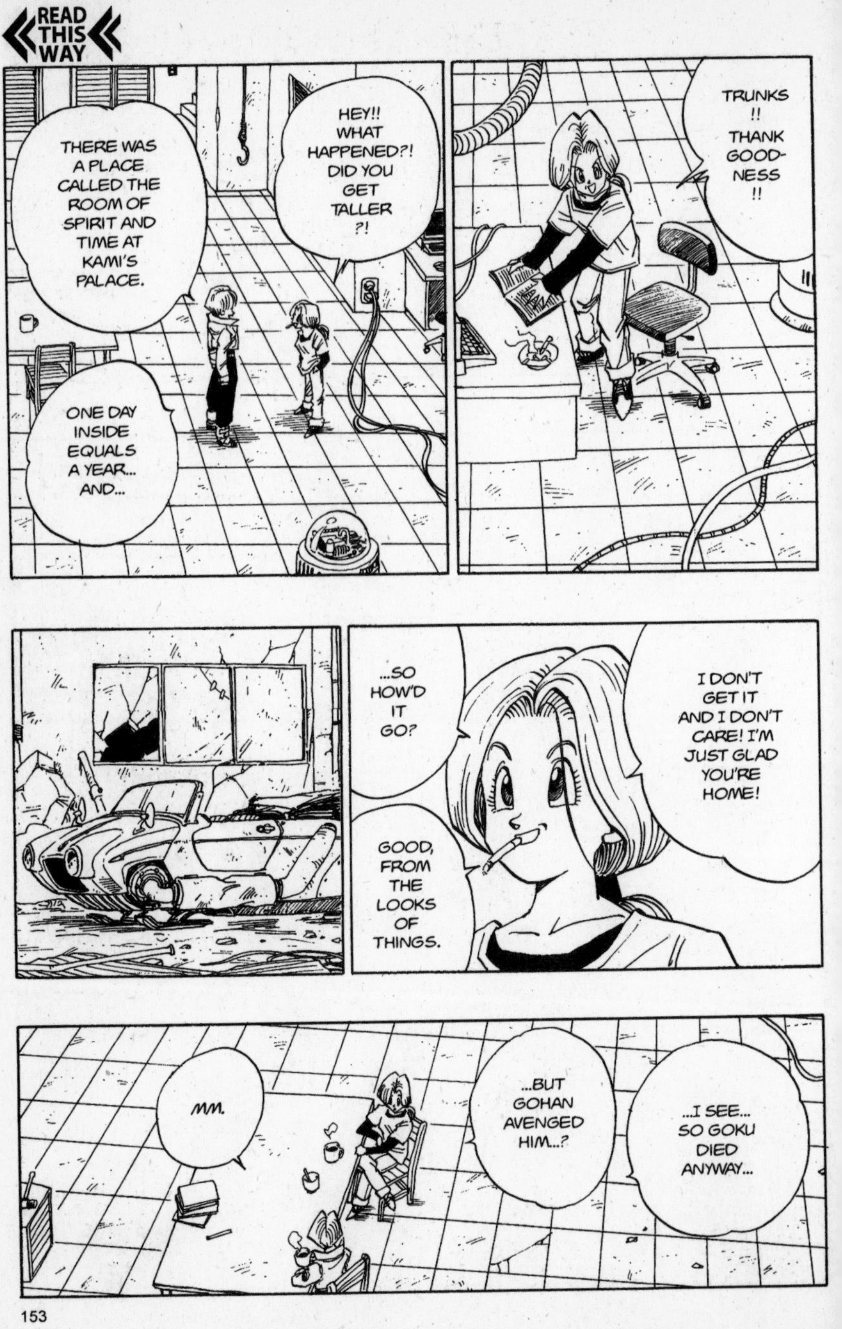
TRUNKS!! THANK GOODNESS!!
HEY!! WHAT HAPPENED?! DID YOU GET TALLER?!
THERE WAS A PLACE CALLED THE ROOM OF SPIRIT AND TIME AT KAMI'S PALACE.
ONE DAY INSIDE EQUALS A YEAR... AND...
I DON'T GET IT AND I DON'T CARE! I'M JUST GLAD YOU'RE HOME!
...SO HOW'D IT GO?
GOOD, FROM THE LOOKS OF THINGS.
...I SEE... SO GOKU DIED ANYWAY...
...BUT GOHAN AVENGED HIM...?
MM.

READ THIS WAY

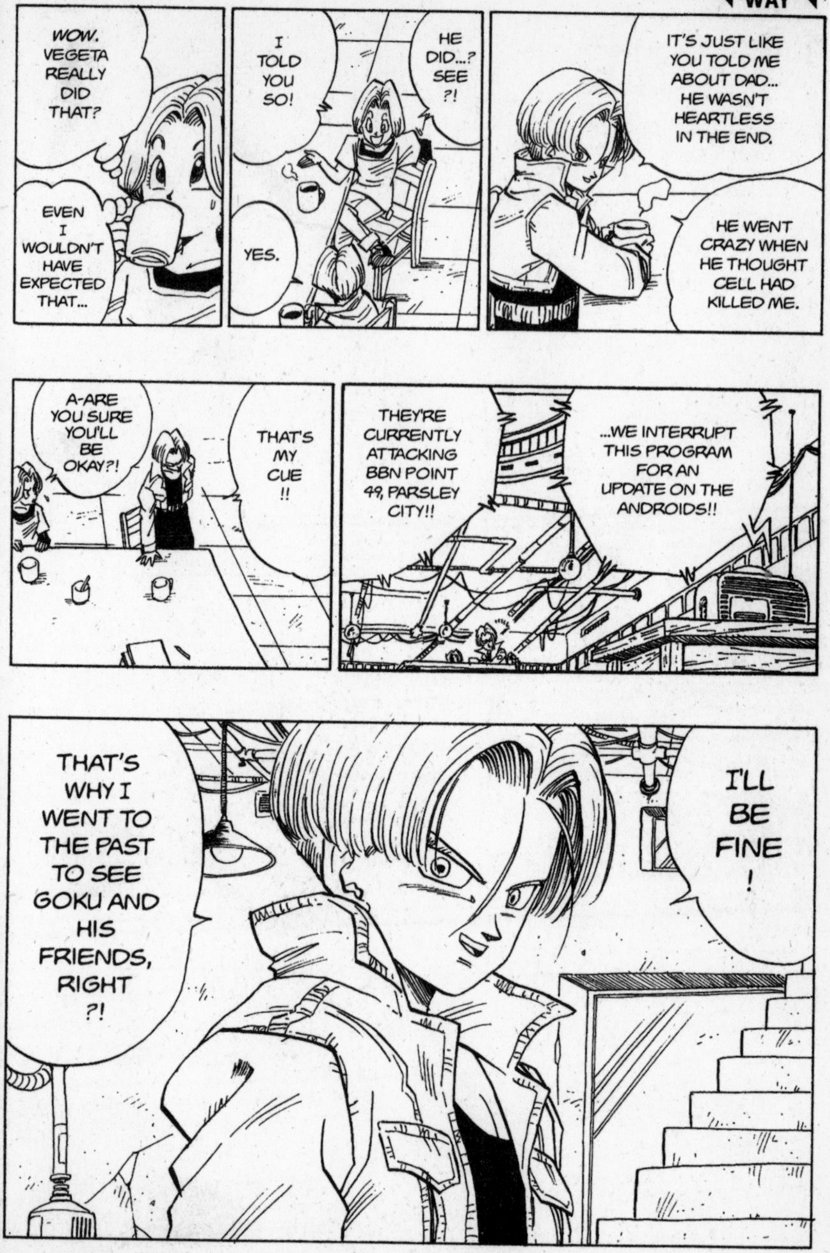
IT'S JUST LIKE YOU TOLD ME ABOUT DAD... HE WASN'T HEARTLESS IN THE END.
HE WENT CRAZY WHEN HE THOUGHT CELL HAD KILLED ME.
HE DID...? SEE ?!
I TOLD YOU SO!
YES.
WOW. VEGETA REALLY DID THAT?
EVEN I WOULDN'T HAVE EXPECTED THAT...
...WE INTERRUPT THIS PROGRAM FOR AN UPDATE ON THE ANDROIDS!!
THEY'RE CURRENTLY ATTACKING BBN POINT 49, PARSLEY CITY!!
THAT'S MY CUE !!
A-ARE YOU SURE YOU'LL BE OKAY?!
I'LL BE FINE !
THAT'S WHY I WENT TO THE PAST TO SEE GOKU AND HIS FRIENDS, RIGHT ?!

READ THIS WAY

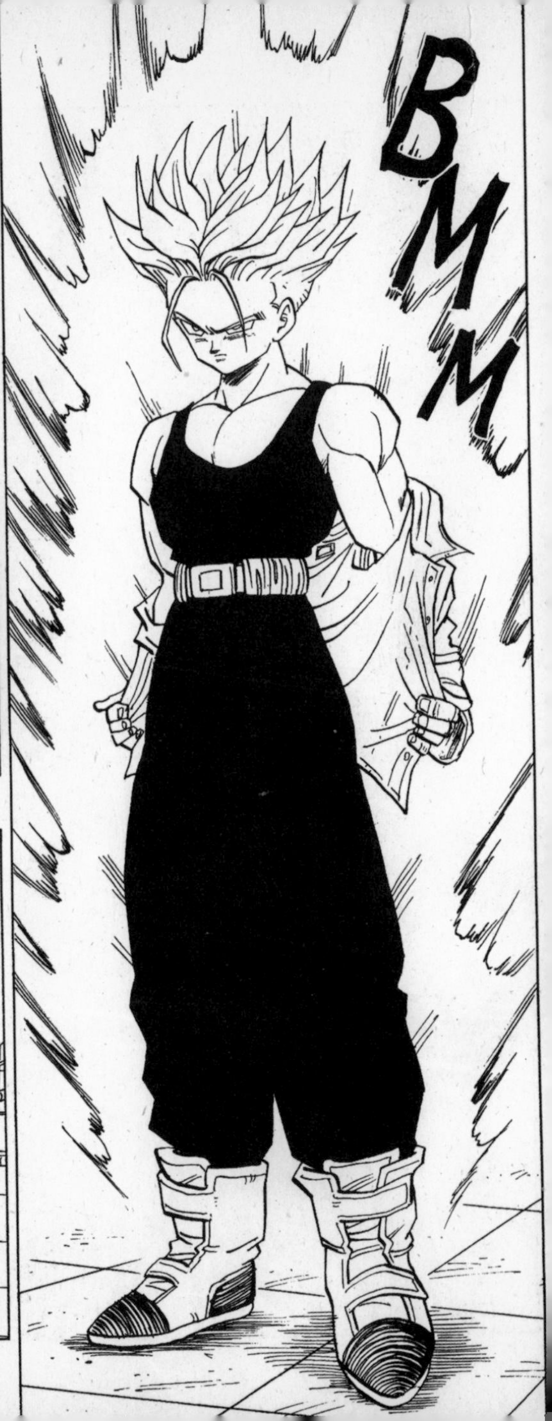
BMM

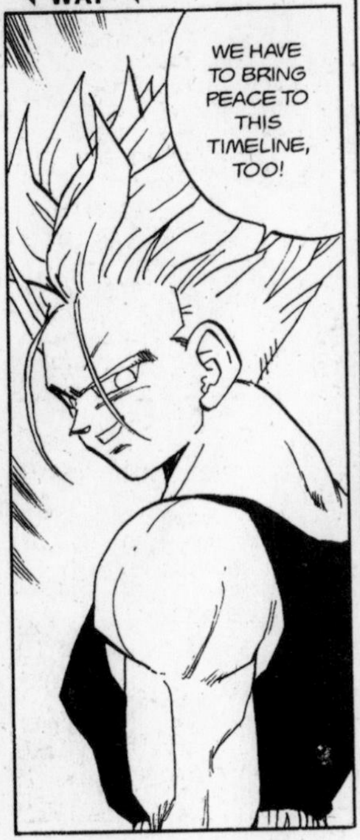
WE HAVE TO BRING PEACE TO THIS TIMELINE, TOO!

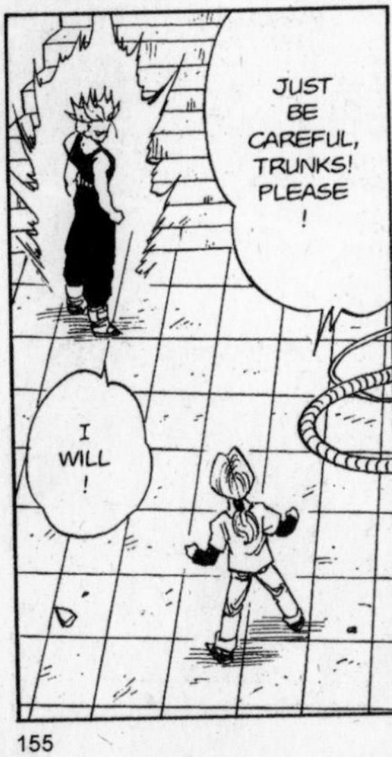
JUST BE CAREFUL, TRUNKS! PLEASE !
I WILL !

READ THIS WAY

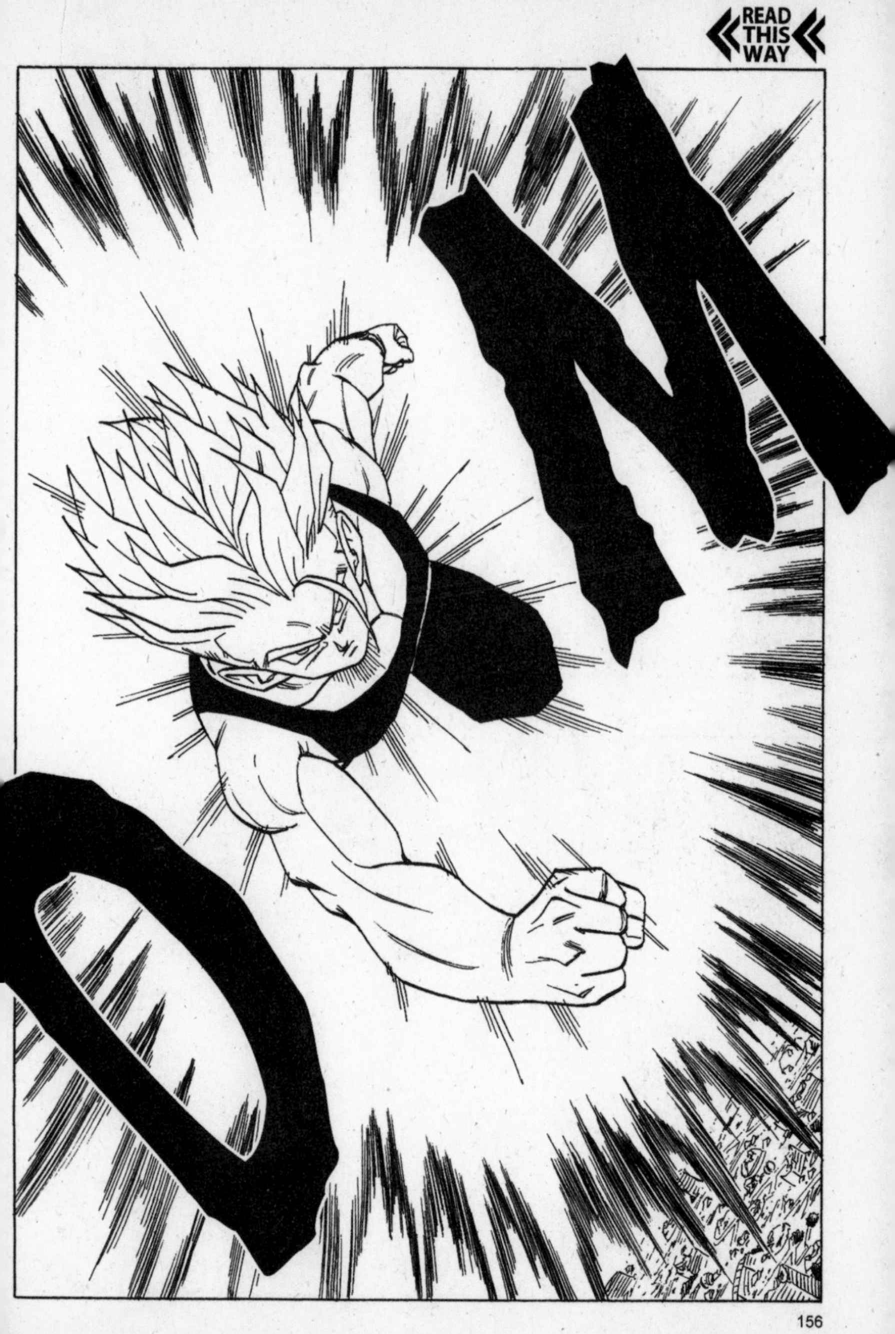

READ THIS WAY

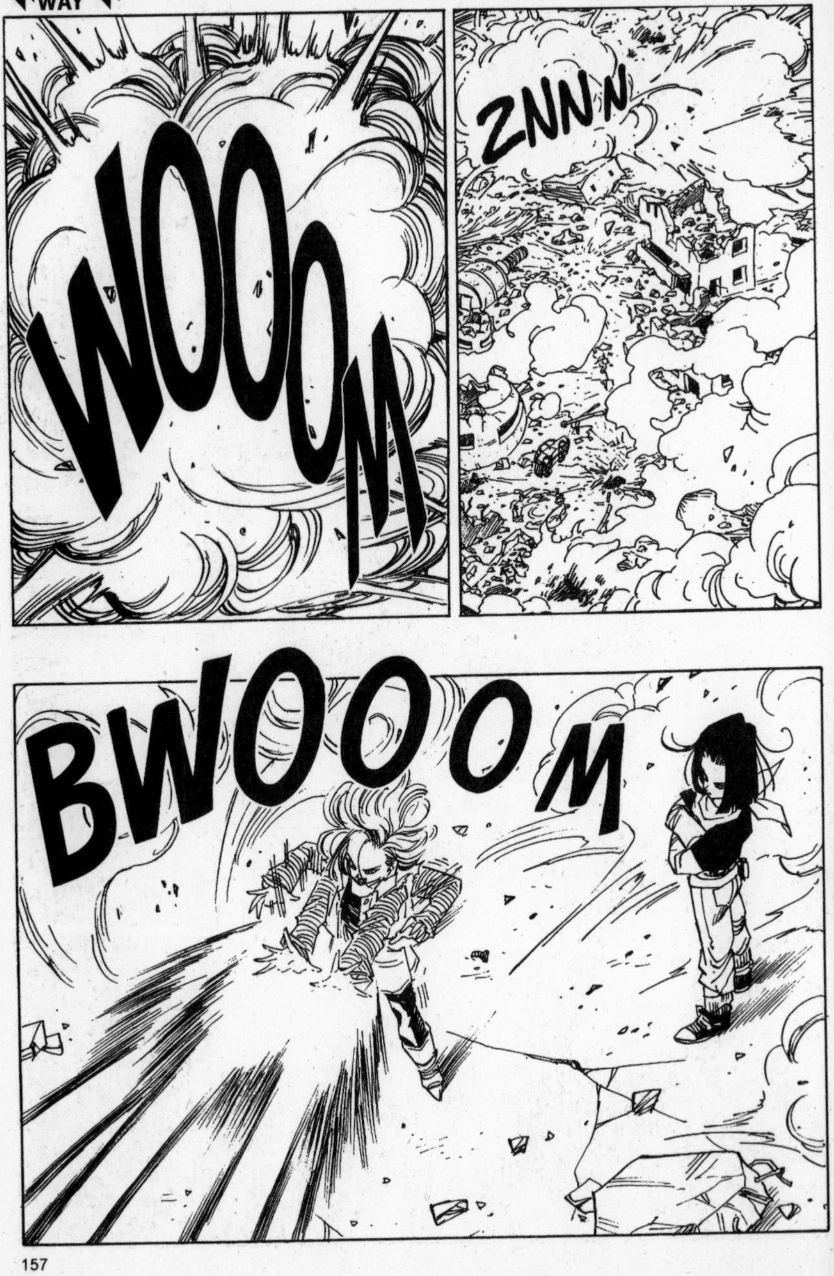
ZNNN
WOOOM
BWOOOM

READ THIS WAY

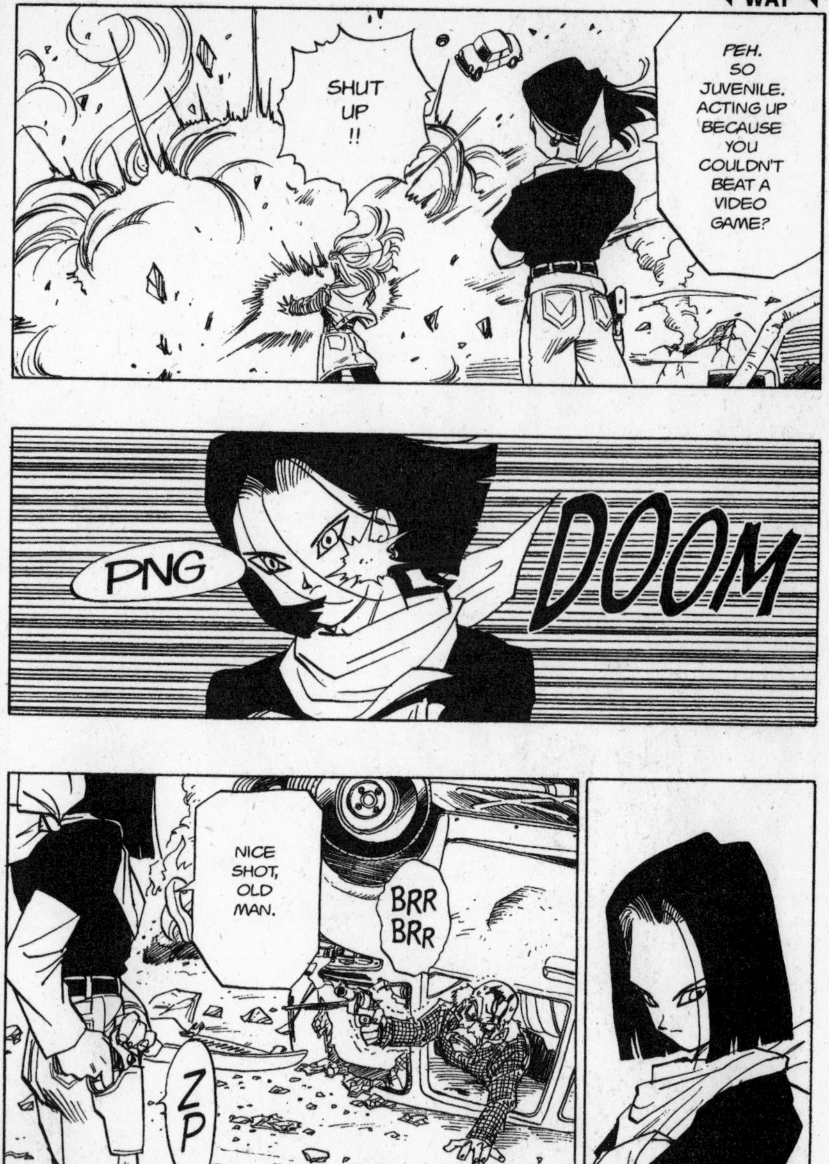
PEH. SO JUVENILE. ACTING UP BECAUSE YOU COULDN'T BEAT A VIDEO GAME?
SHUT UP !!
DOOM
PNG
NICE SHOT, OLD MAN.
BRR BRR
ZP

READ THIS WAY

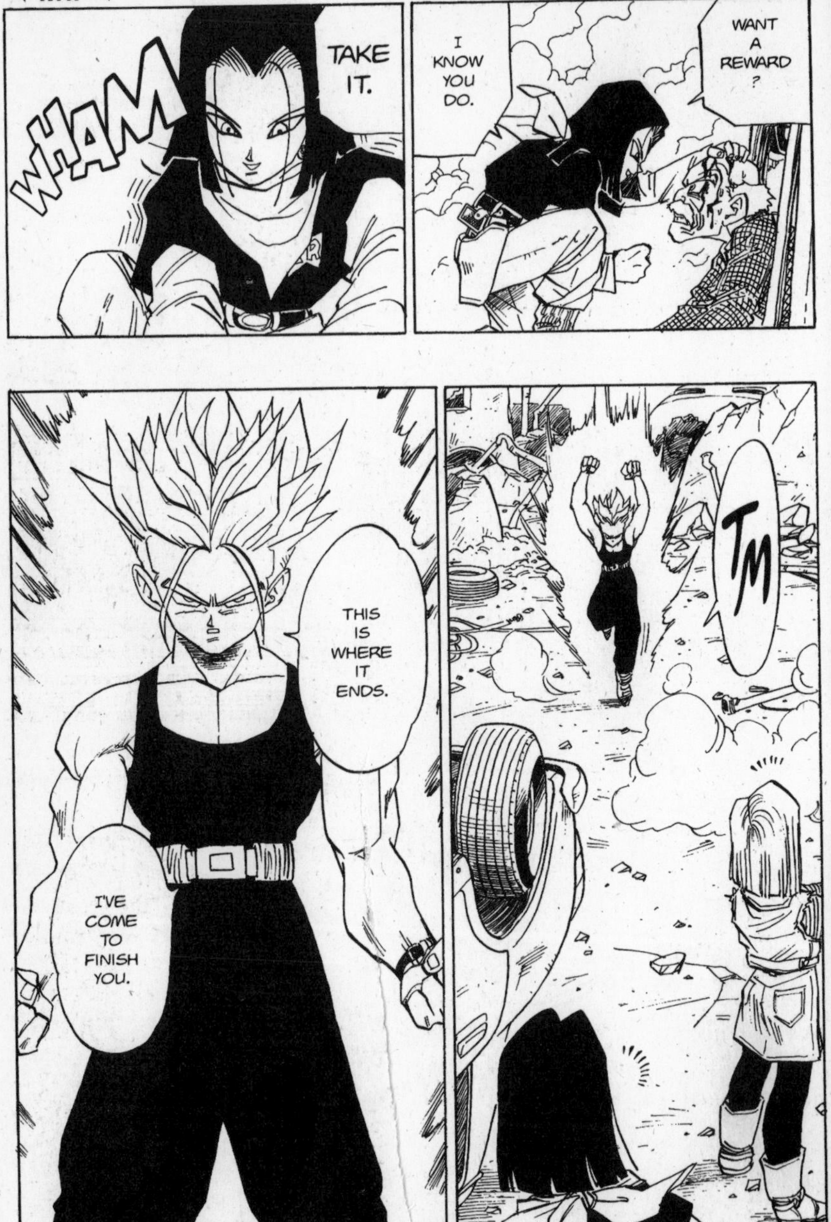
WANT A REWARD ?
I KNOW YOU DO.
TAKE IT.
WHAM
TM
THIS IS WHERE IT ENDS.
I'VE COME TO FINISH YOU.

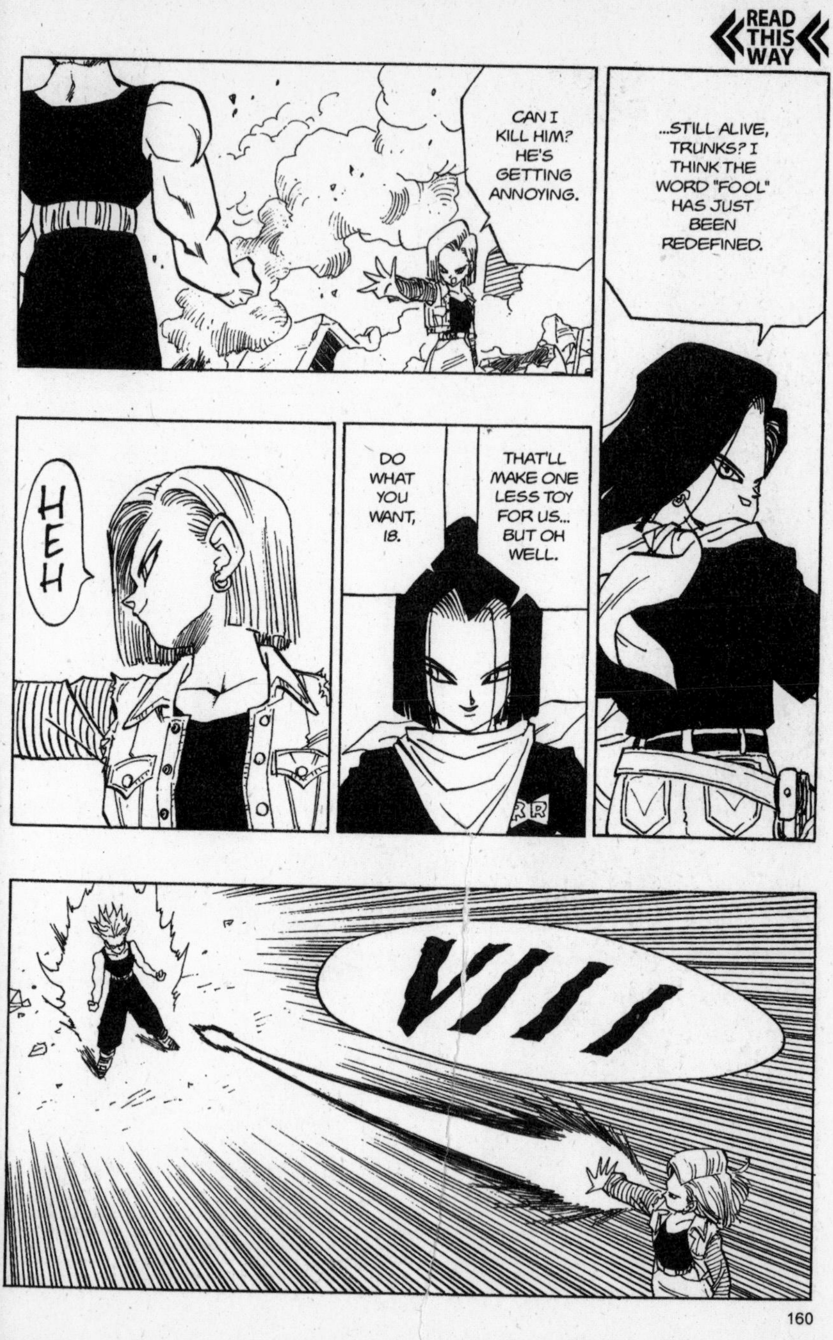
READ THIS WAY
...STILL ALIVE, TRUNKS? I THINK THE WORD "FOOL" HAS JUST BEEN REDEFINED.
CAN I KILL HIM? HE'S GETTING ANNOYING.
THAT'LL MAKE ONE LESS TOY FOR US... BUT OH WELL.
DO WHAT YOU WANT, 18.
HEH
VIII

READ THIS WAY

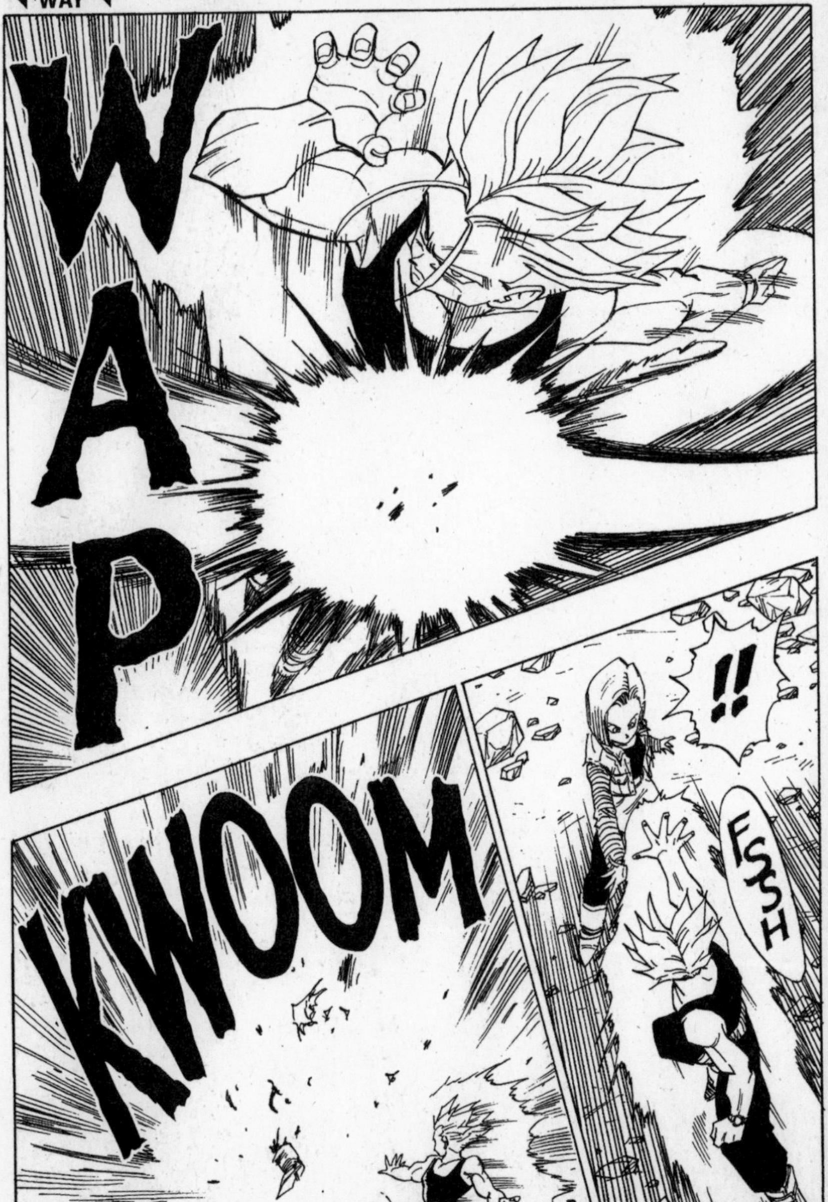
WAP
!!
FSSH
KWOOM

READ THIS WAY

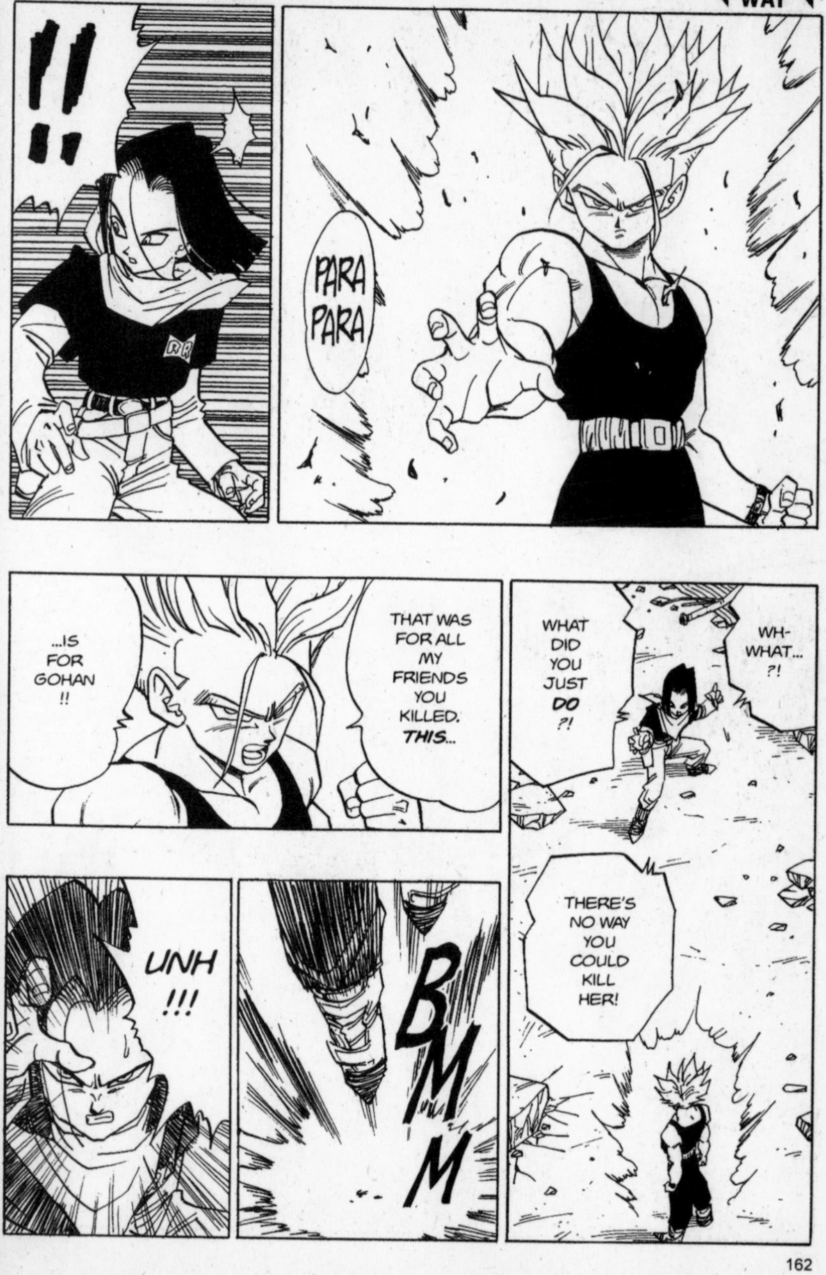

PARA PARA
!!
WH- WHAT...?!
WHAT DID YOU JUST DO?!
THERE'S NO WAY YOU COULD KILL HER!
THAT WAS FOR ALL MY FRIENDS YOU KILLED. THIS...
...IS FOR GOHAN!!
BMM
UNH!!!

READ THIS WAY

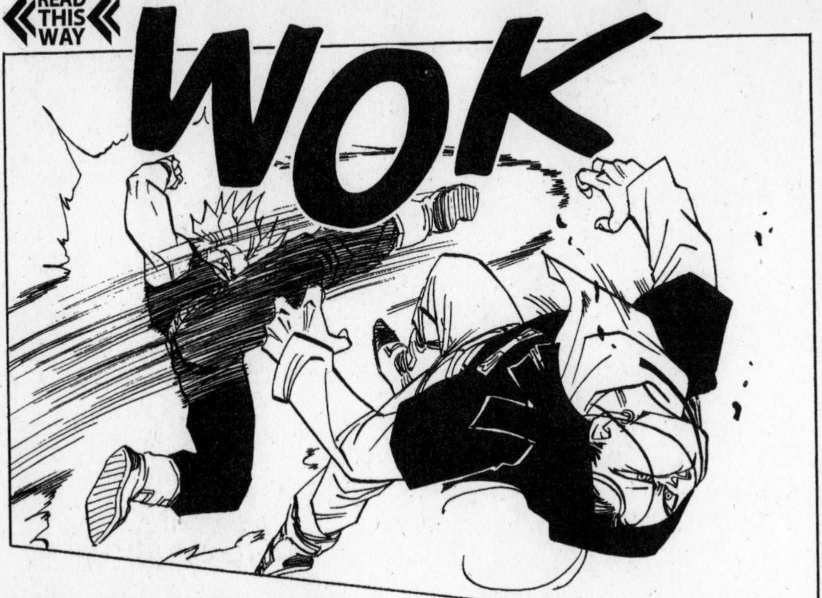
WOK

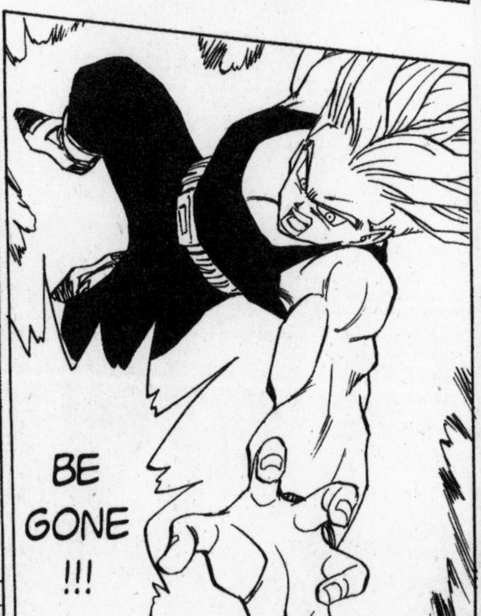
BE GONE !!!

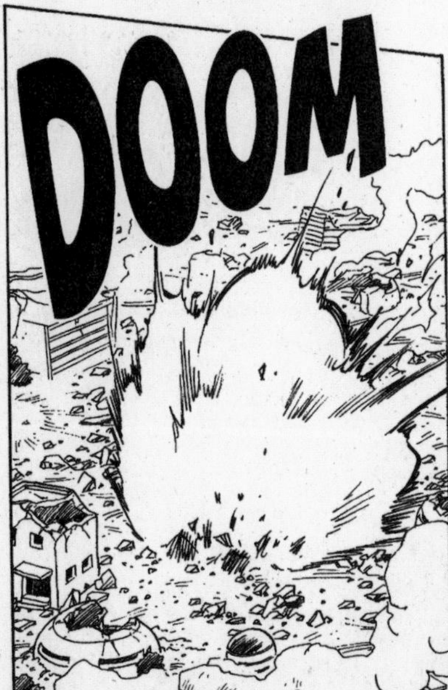
DOOM

READ THIS WAY

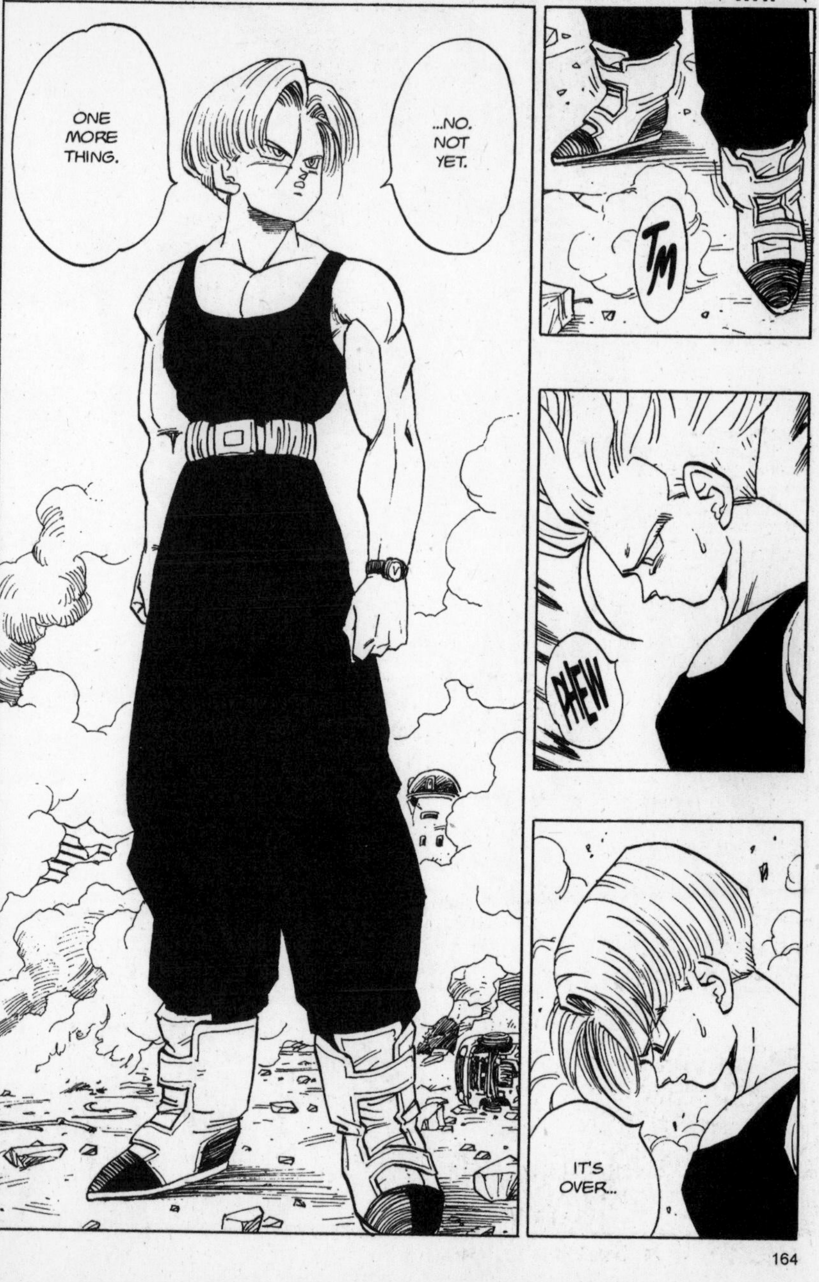

TM
PHEW
IT'S OVER...
...NO. NOT YET.
ONE MORE THING.

READ THIS WAY

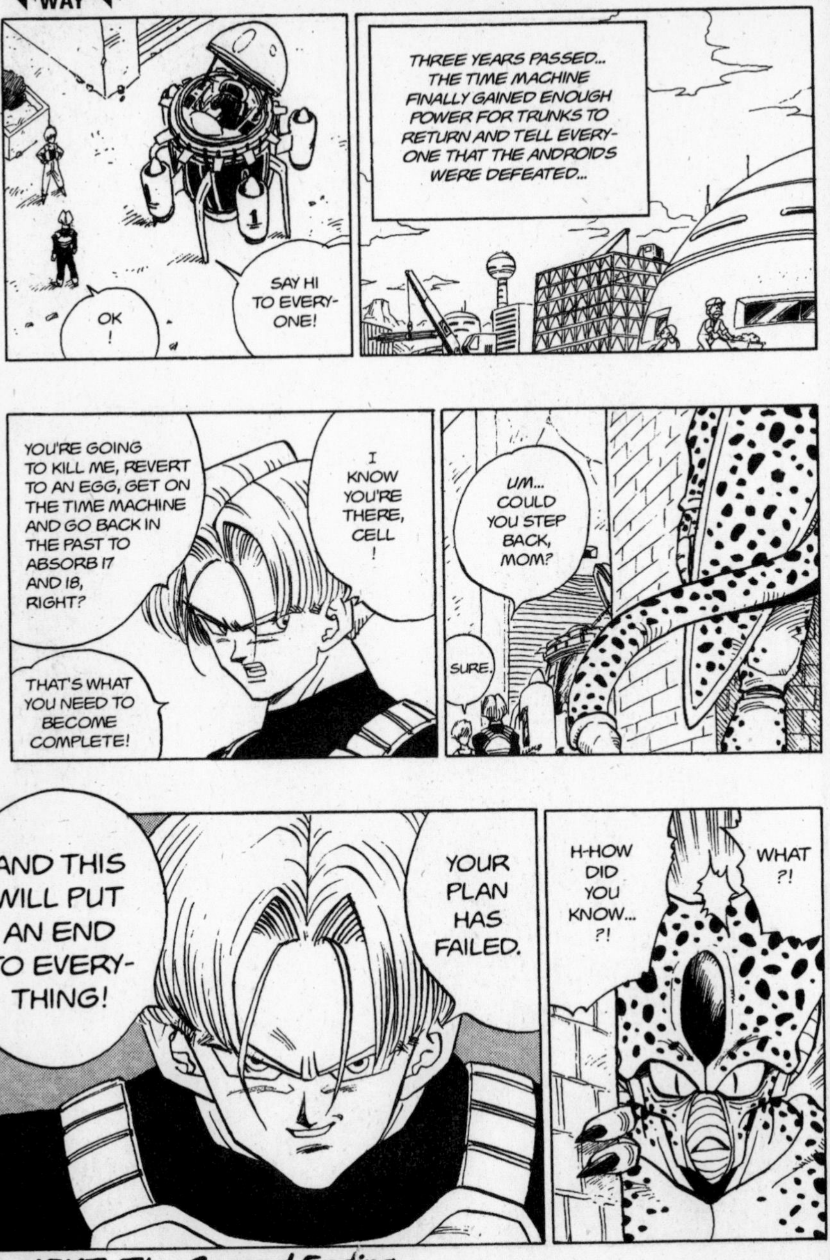
THREE YEARS PASSED... THE TIME MACHINE FINALLY GAINED ENOUGH POWER FOR TRUNKS TO RETURN AND TELL EVERY-ONE THAT THE ANDROIDS WERE DEFEATED...
SAY HI TO EVERY-ONE!
OK!
UM... COULD YOU STEP BACK, MOM?
SURE.
I KNOW YOU'RE THERE, CELL!
YOU'RE GOING TO KILL ME, REVERT TO AN EGG, GET ON THE TIME MACHINE AND GO BACK IN THE PAST TO ABSORB 17 AND 18, RIGHT?
THAT'S WHAT YOU NEED TO BECOME COMPLETE!
WHAT?!
H-HOW DID YOU KNOW...?!
YOUR PLAN HAS FAILED.
AND THIS WILL PUT AN END TO EVERY-THING!

NEXT: The Second Ending

DBZ:226 • Peace to the Future

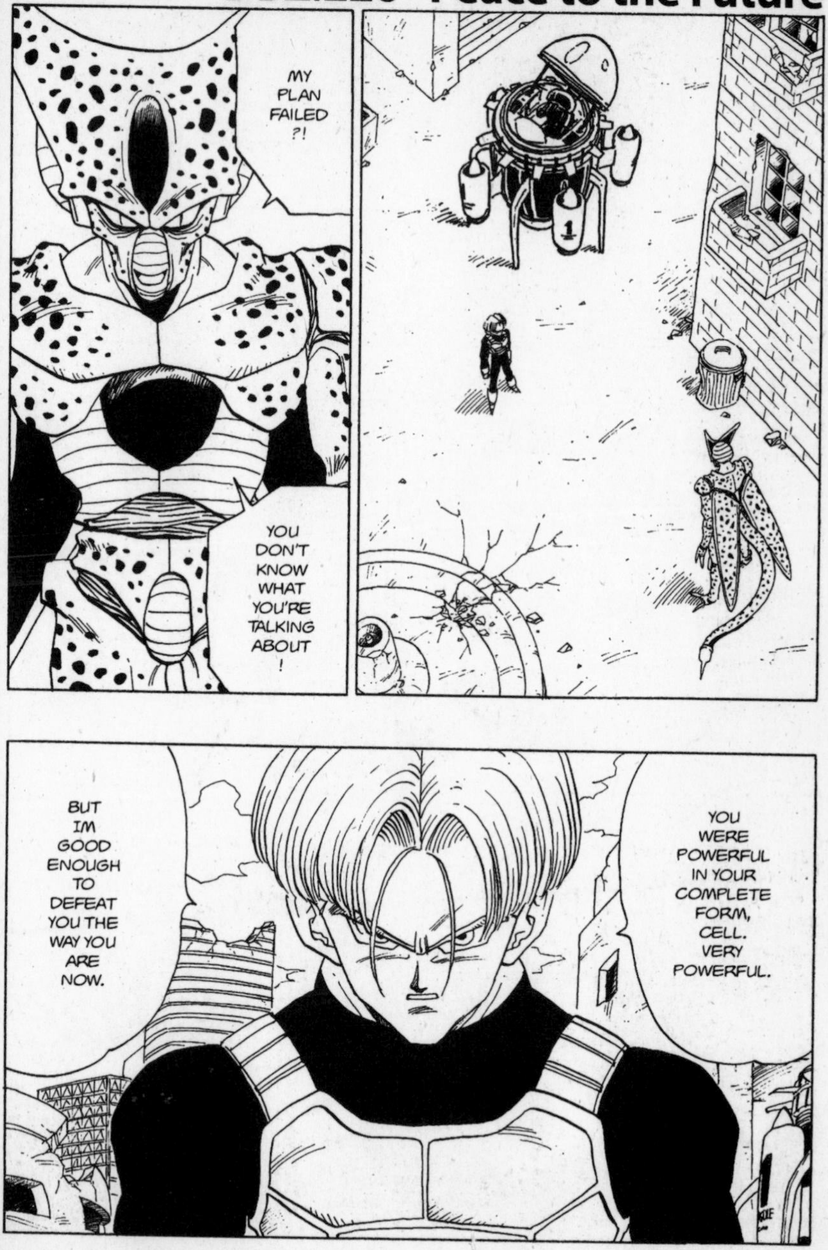
MY PLAN FAILED?!
YOU DON'T KNOW WHAT YOU'RE TALKING ABOUT!
YOU WERE POWERFUL IN YOUR COMPLETE FORM, CELL. VERY POWERFUL.
BUT I'M GOOD ENOUGH TO DEFEAT YOU THE WAY YOU ARE NOW.

READ THIS WAY

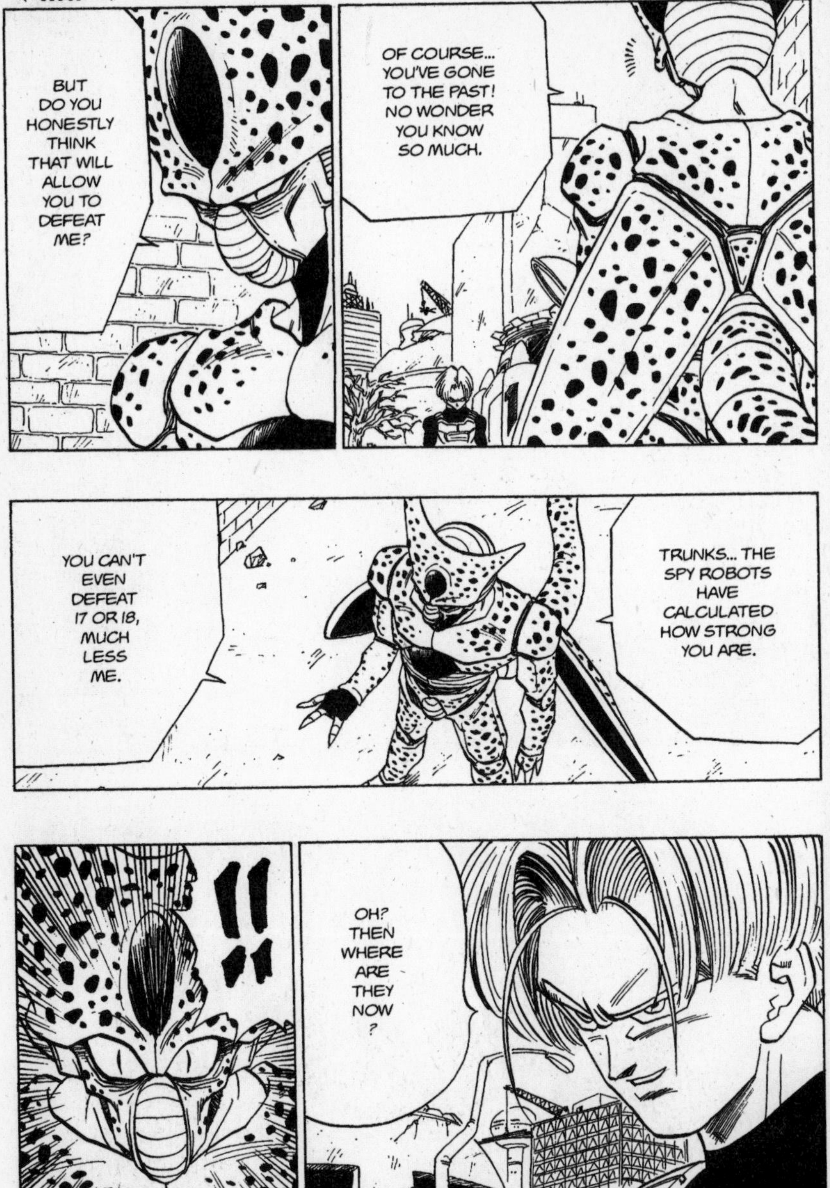
OF COURSE... YOU'VE GONE TO THE PAST! NO WONDER YOU KNOW SO MUCH.
BUT DO YOU HONESTLY THINK THAT WILL ALLOW YOU TO DEFEAT ME?
TRUNKS... THE SPY ROBOTS HAVE CALCULATED HOW STRONG YOU ARE.
YOU CAN'T EVEN DEFEAT 17 OR 18, MUCH LESS ME.
OH? THEN WHERE ARE THEY NOW?
!!

READ THIS WAY

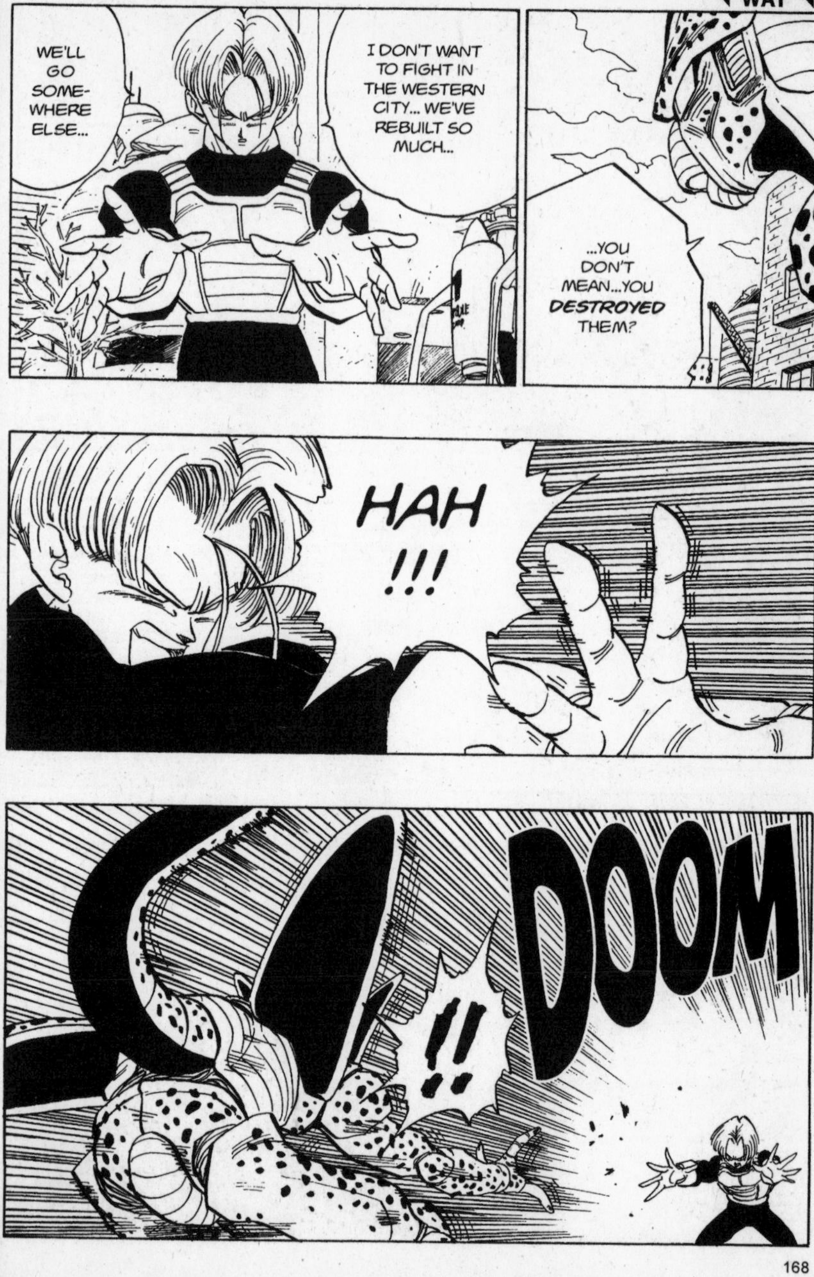
...YOU DON'T MEAN...YOU **DESTROYED** THEM?
I DON'T WANT TO FIGHT IN THE WESTERN CITY... WE'VE REBUILT SO MUCH...
WE'LL GO SOME-WHERE ELSE...
HAH !!!
DOOM !!

READ THIS WAY

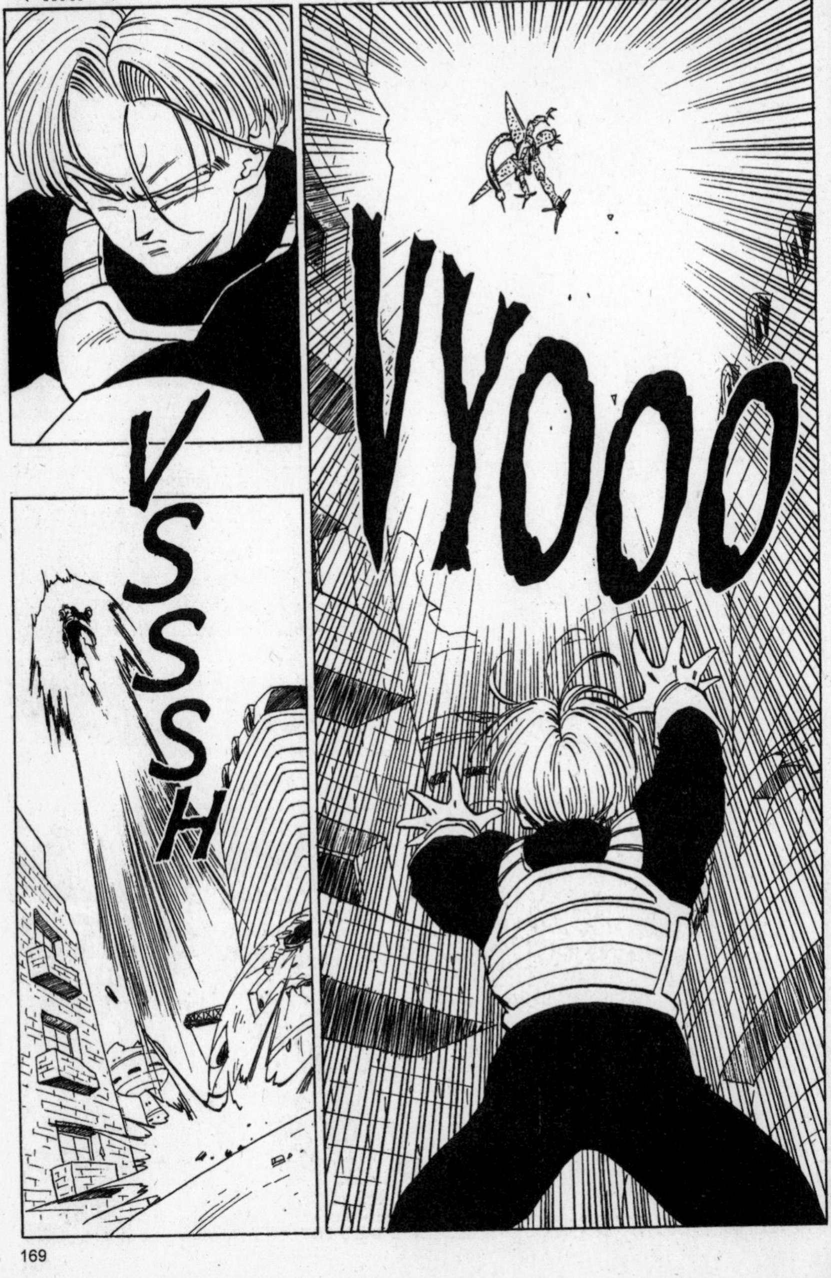
VYOOO
VSSSH

READ THIS WAY

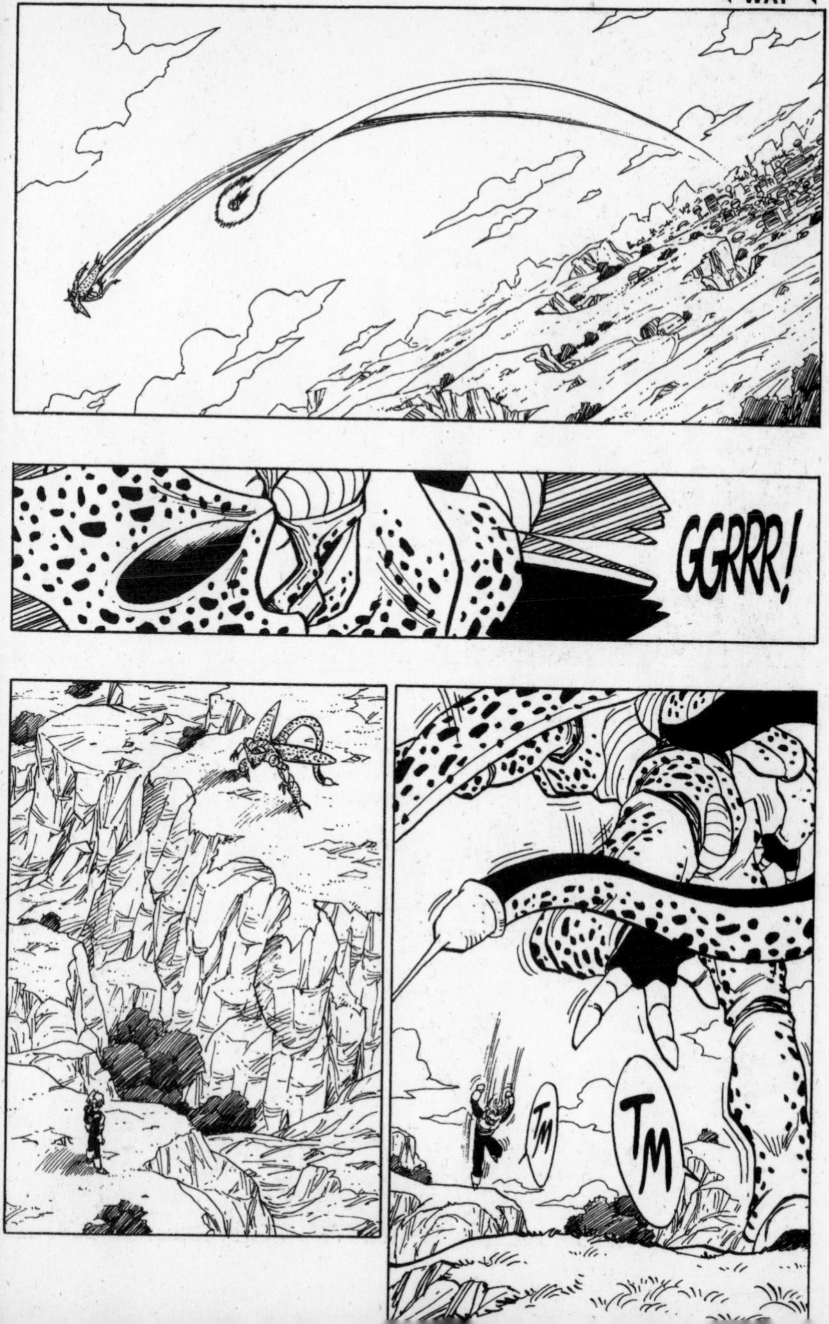
GGRRR!
TM
TM

READ THIS WAY

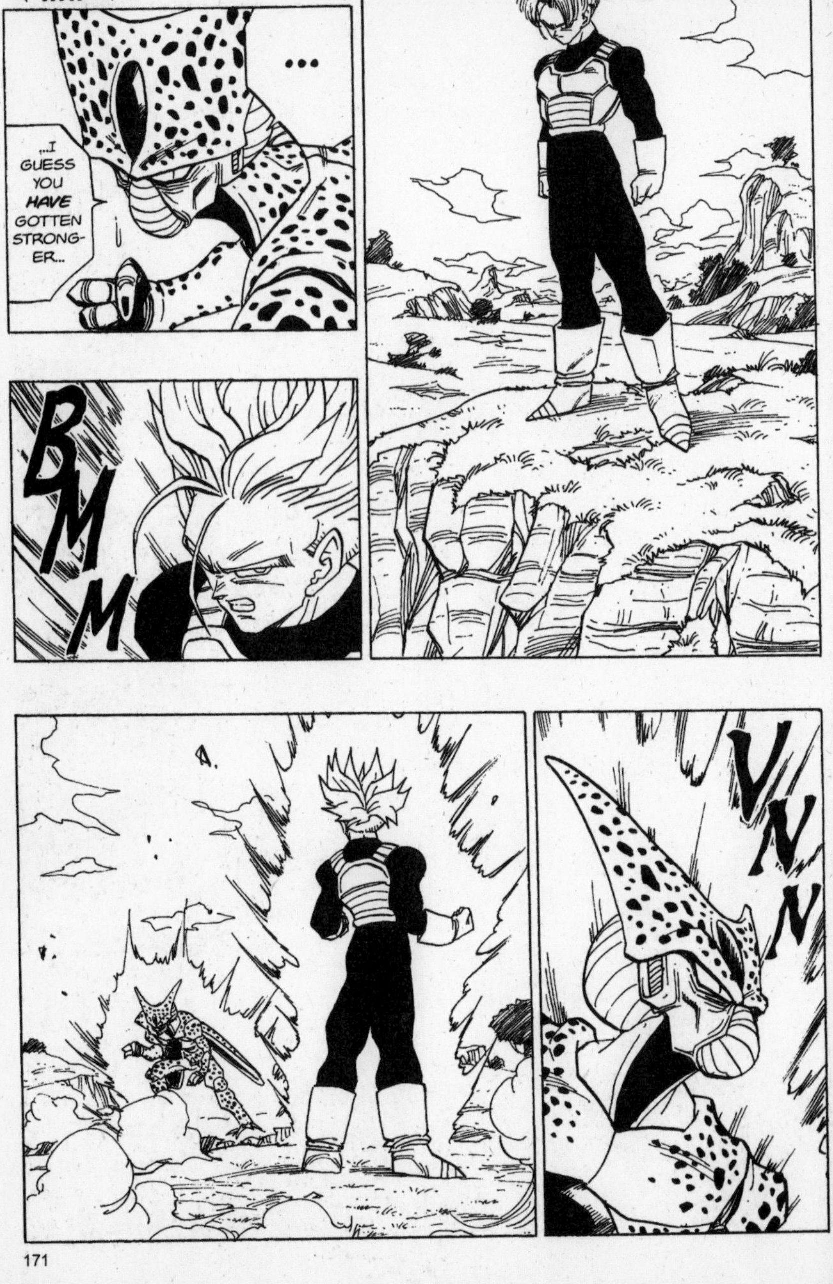
...
...I GUESS YOU *HAVE* GOTTEN STRONGER...
BMM
VNN

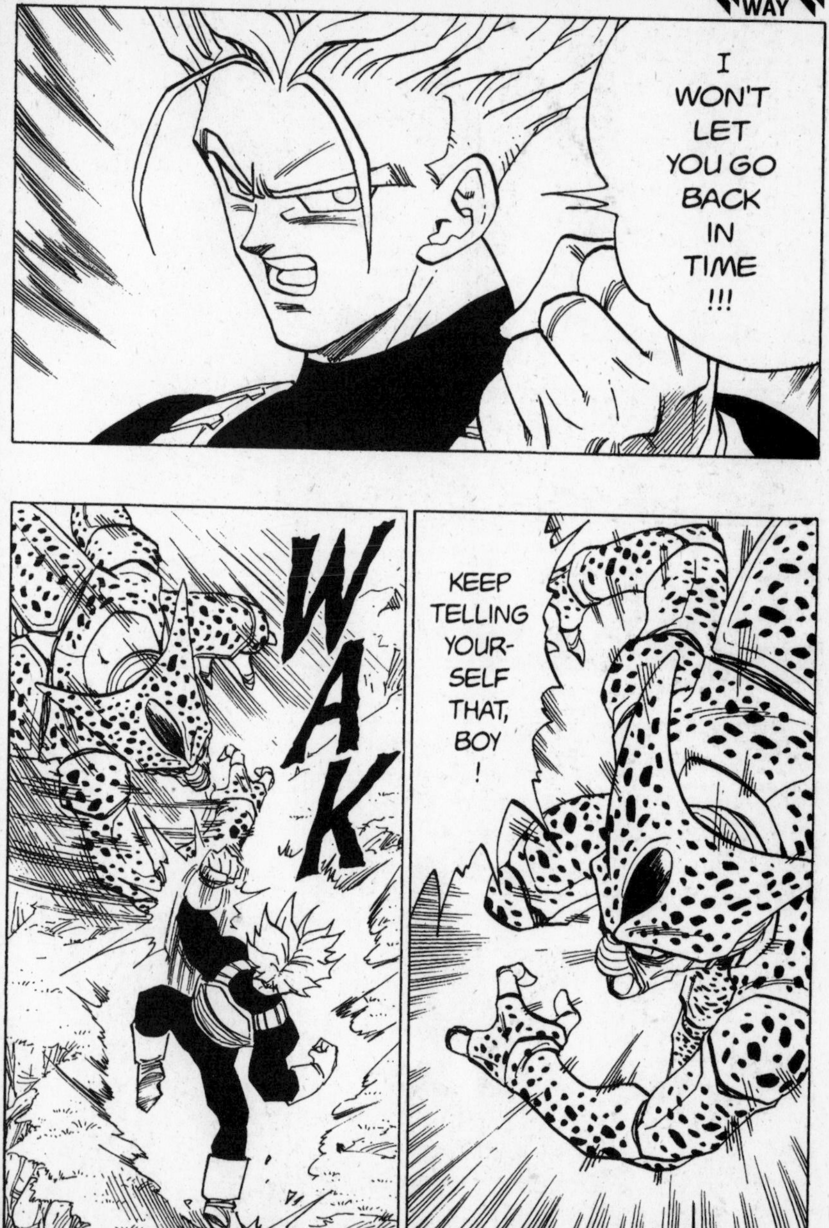
I WON'T LET YOU GO BACK IN TIME !!!
KEEP TELLING YOURSELF THAT, BOY !
WAK

READ THIS WAY

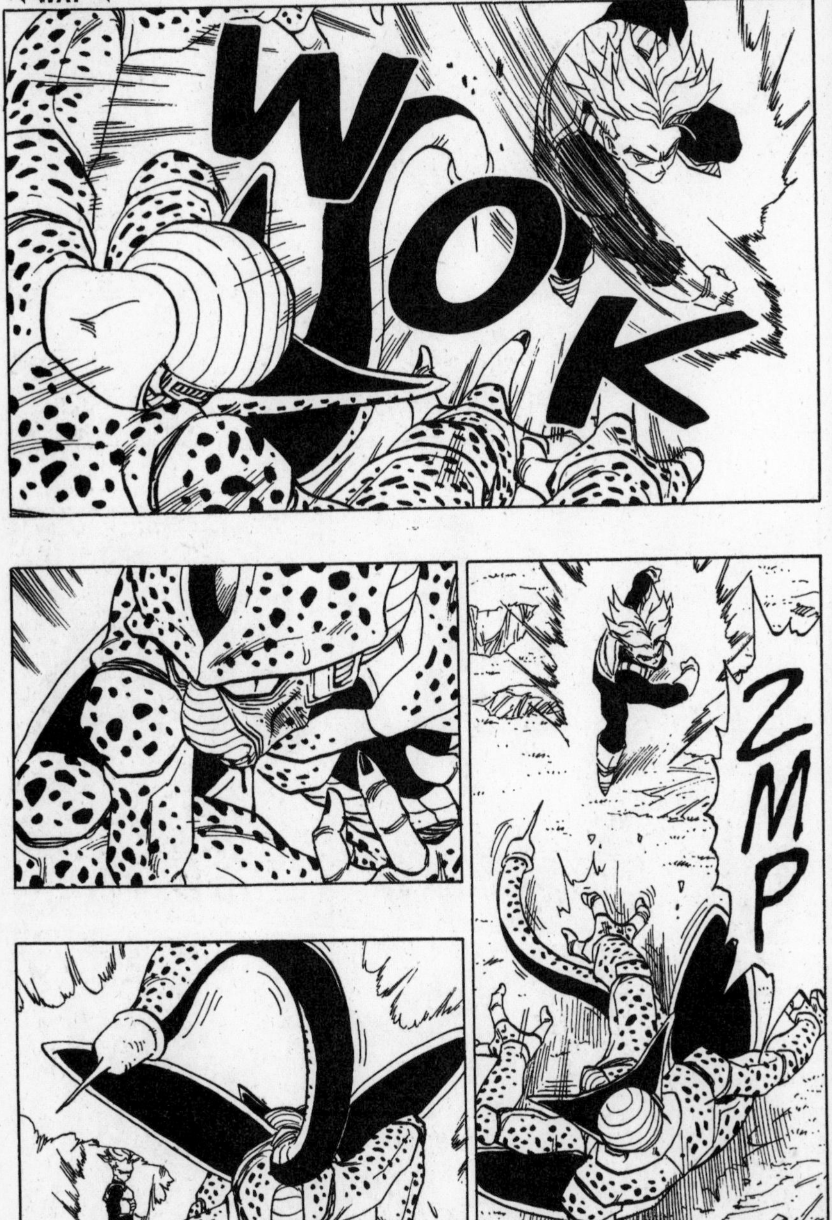
WOK
ZMP

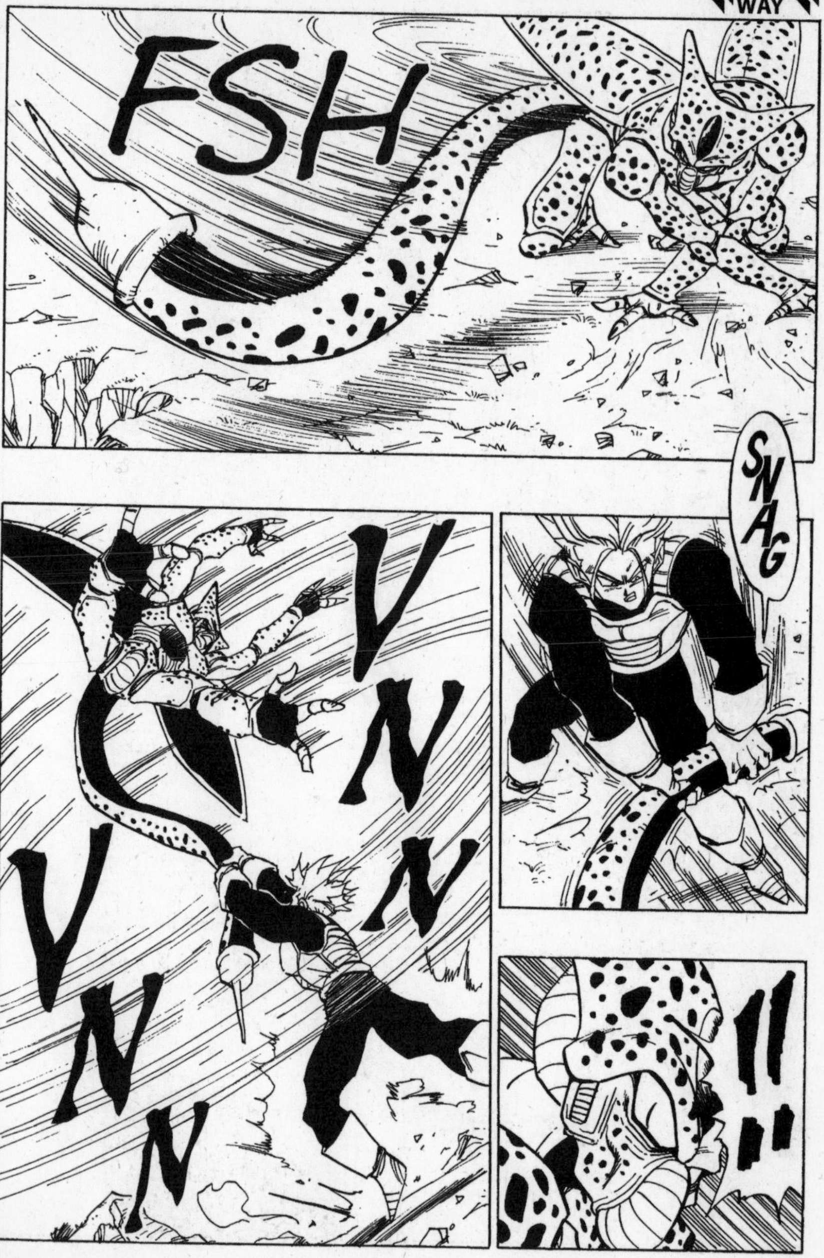
FSH
SNAG
VNNN
VNNN
!!

READ THIS WAY

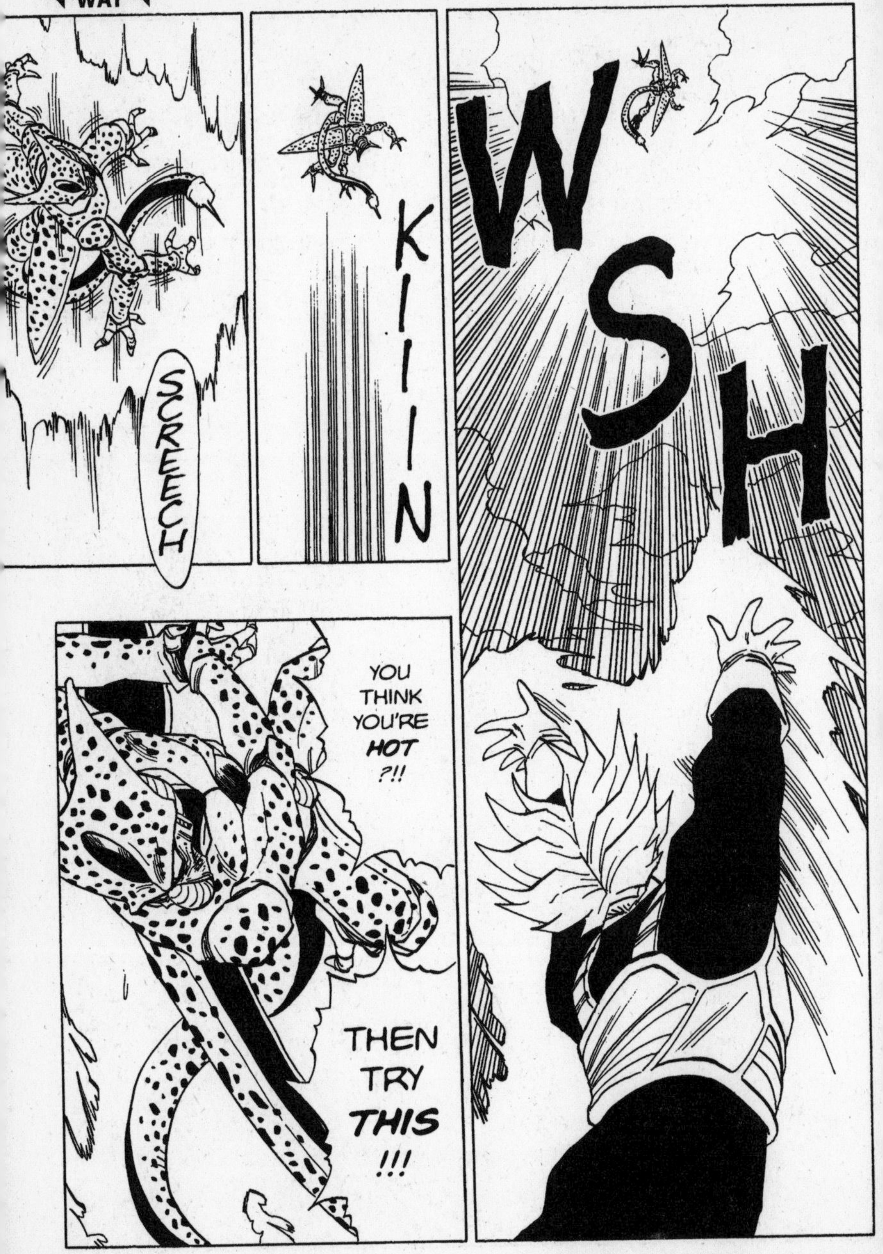
WSH
KIIN
SCREECH
YOU THINK YOU'RE ***HOT*** ?!!
THEN TRY ***THIS*** !!!

READ THIS WAY

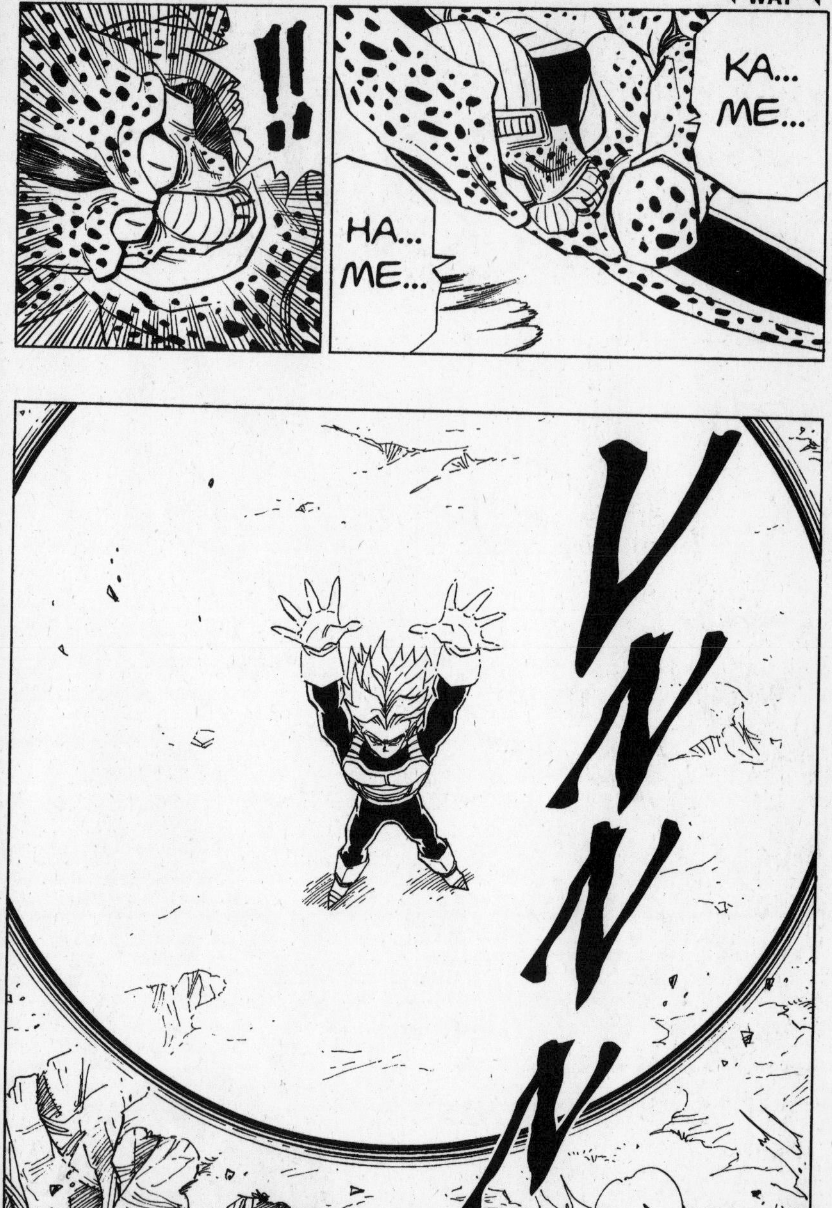
KA... ME...
HA... ME...
!!
VNNN

READ THIS WAY

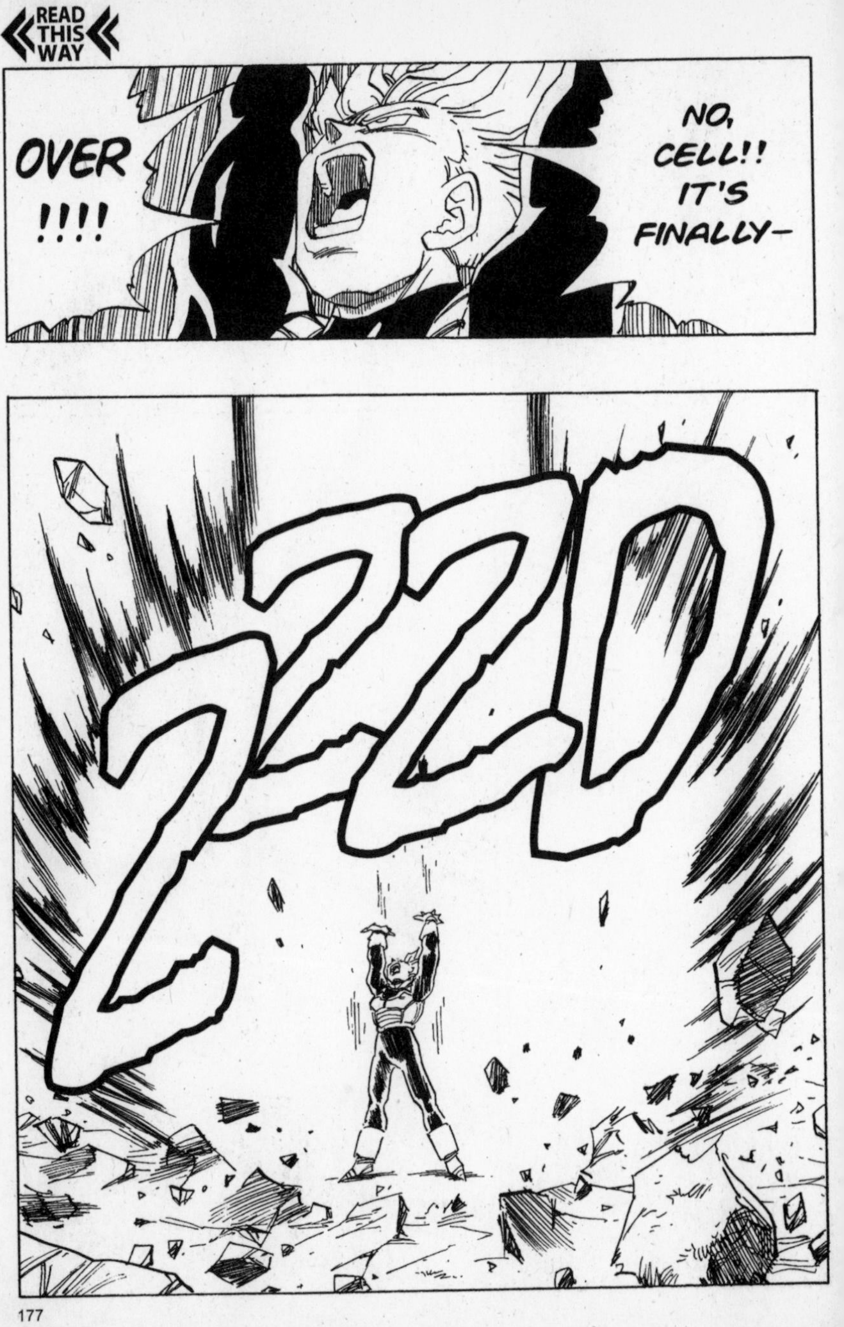
NO, CELL!! IT'S FINALLY—
OVER!!!!
ZZD

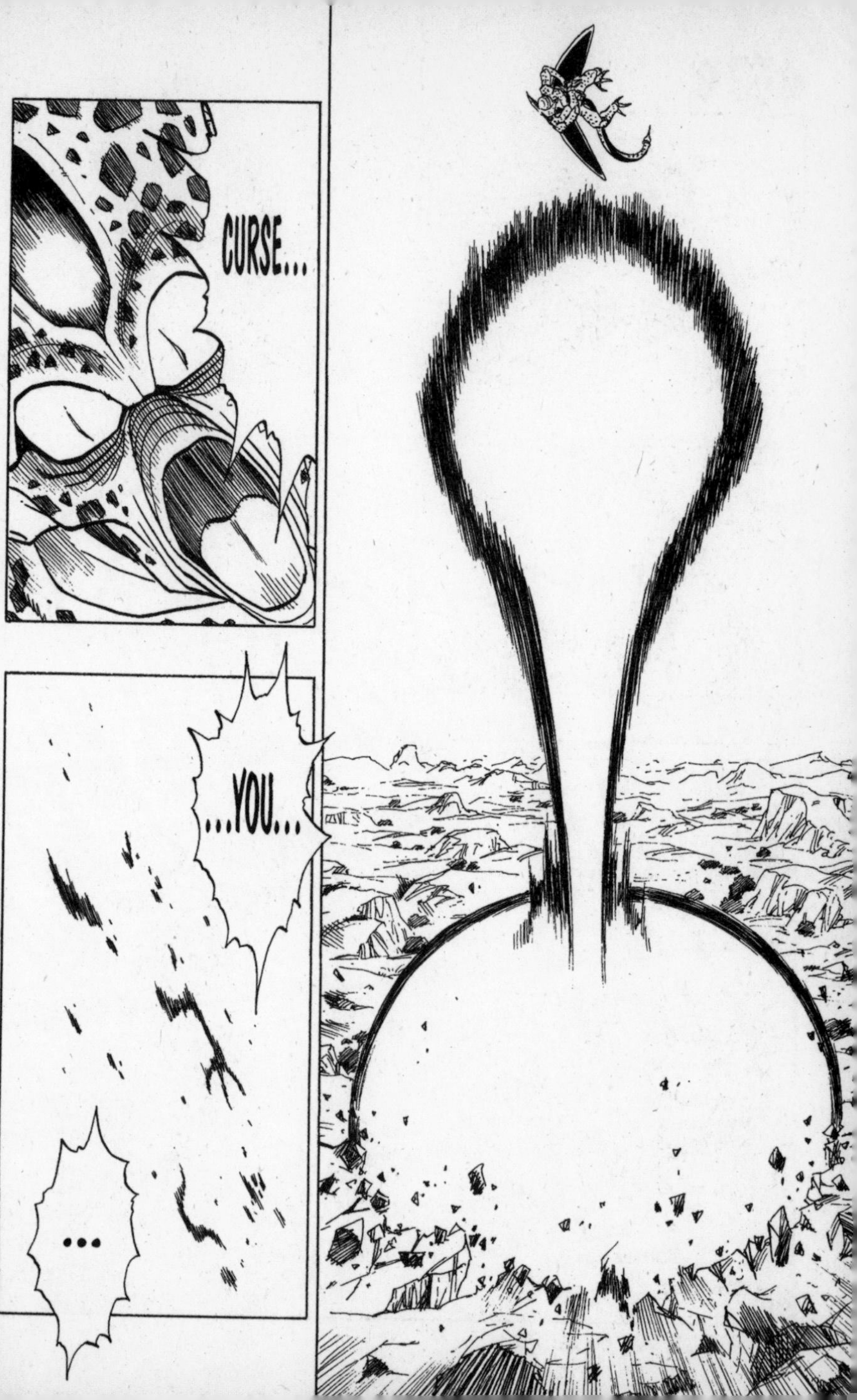
CURSE...
...YOU...
...

AT LAST.

THANKS, GOKU... EVERY- ONE...

IT'S FINISHED.

TRUNKS AND BULMA HAD LIVED A HARD LIFE...BUT TRUE PEACE HAD COME AT LAST. A PEACE THAT WOULD BE ENJOYED AS LONG AS TRUNKS WAS THERE TO DEFEND IT!

TO BE CONTINUED...!

TITLE PAGE GALLERY

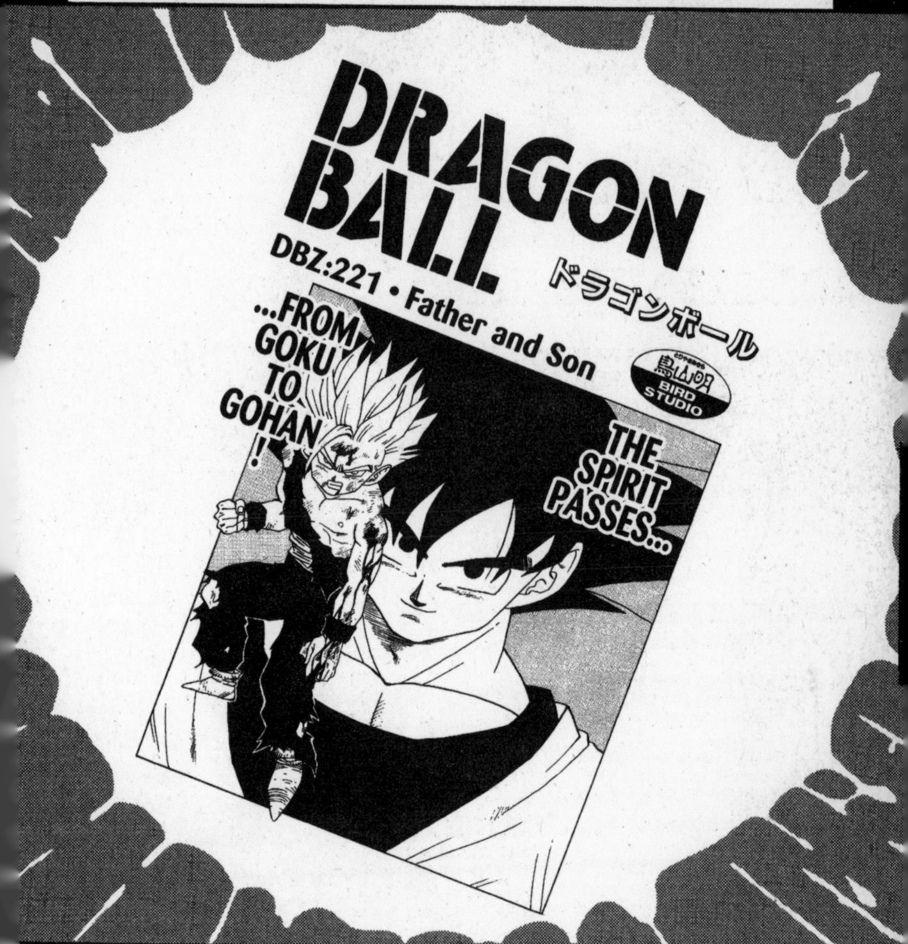
DRAGON BALL
ドラゴンボール
DBZ:221 • Father and Son
鳥山明
BIRD STUDIO
...FROM GOKU TO GOHAN!
THE SPIRIT PASSES...

These title pages were used when these chapters of **Dragon Ball Z** were originally published in Japan in 1993 in **Weekly Shonen Jump** magazine.

DRAGON BALL
ドラゴンボール

DBZ:225 • The Other Outcome

WHEN I GIVE THE THUMBS UP...

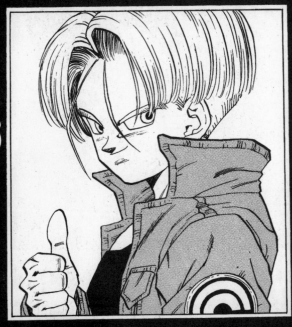

...I'M GOING TO SET THINGS RIGHT!

鳥山明 とりやまあきら

BIRD STUDIO

DRAGON BALL

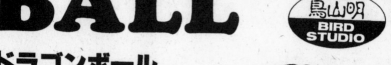

とりやまあきら
鳥山明
BIRD STUDIO

ドラゴンボール

DBZ:226
Peace to the Future

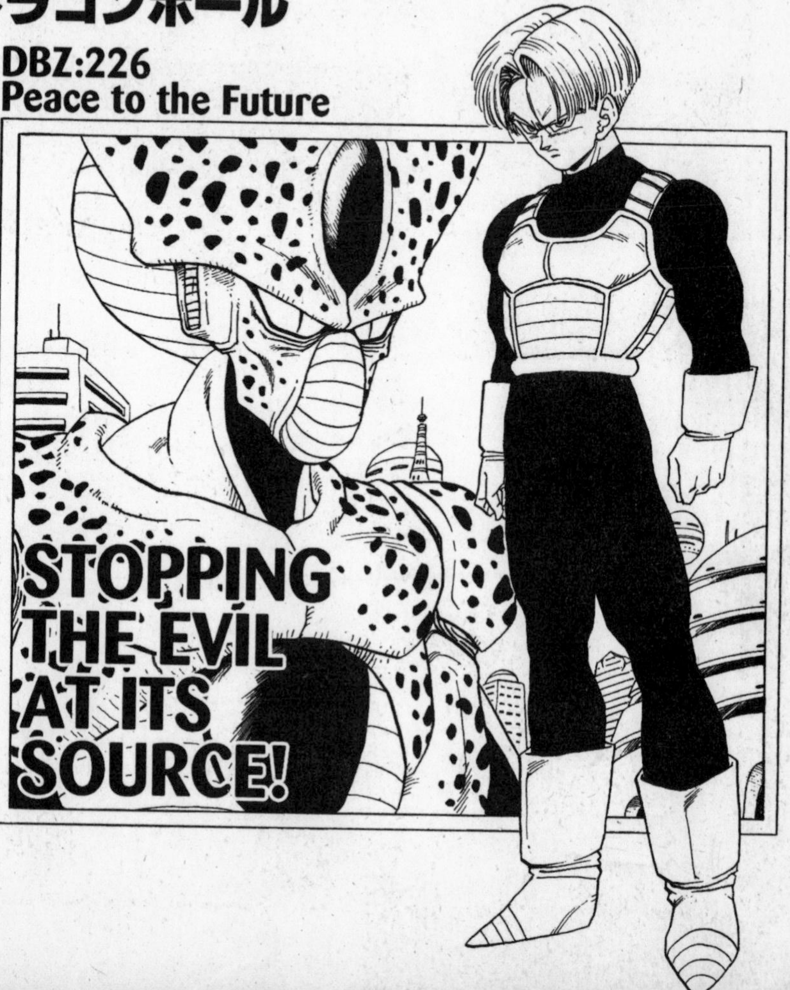
STOPPING THE EVIL AT ITS SOURCE!

IN THE NEXT VOLUME...

Fast-forward into the future! Years after the battle with Cell, Earth is at peace, and Gohan is living the life of a mild-mannered high school student. Mild-mannered, that is, until evil strikes...and the world needs the power of the Great Saiyaman! As Gohan's high school classmates ponder the similarity between their classmate and the masked crime-fighter, two even stronger warriors prepare to make their names known. Their names are Goten and Trunks, the toughest—and youngest—fighters the world has ever seen...

AVAILABLE NOW!

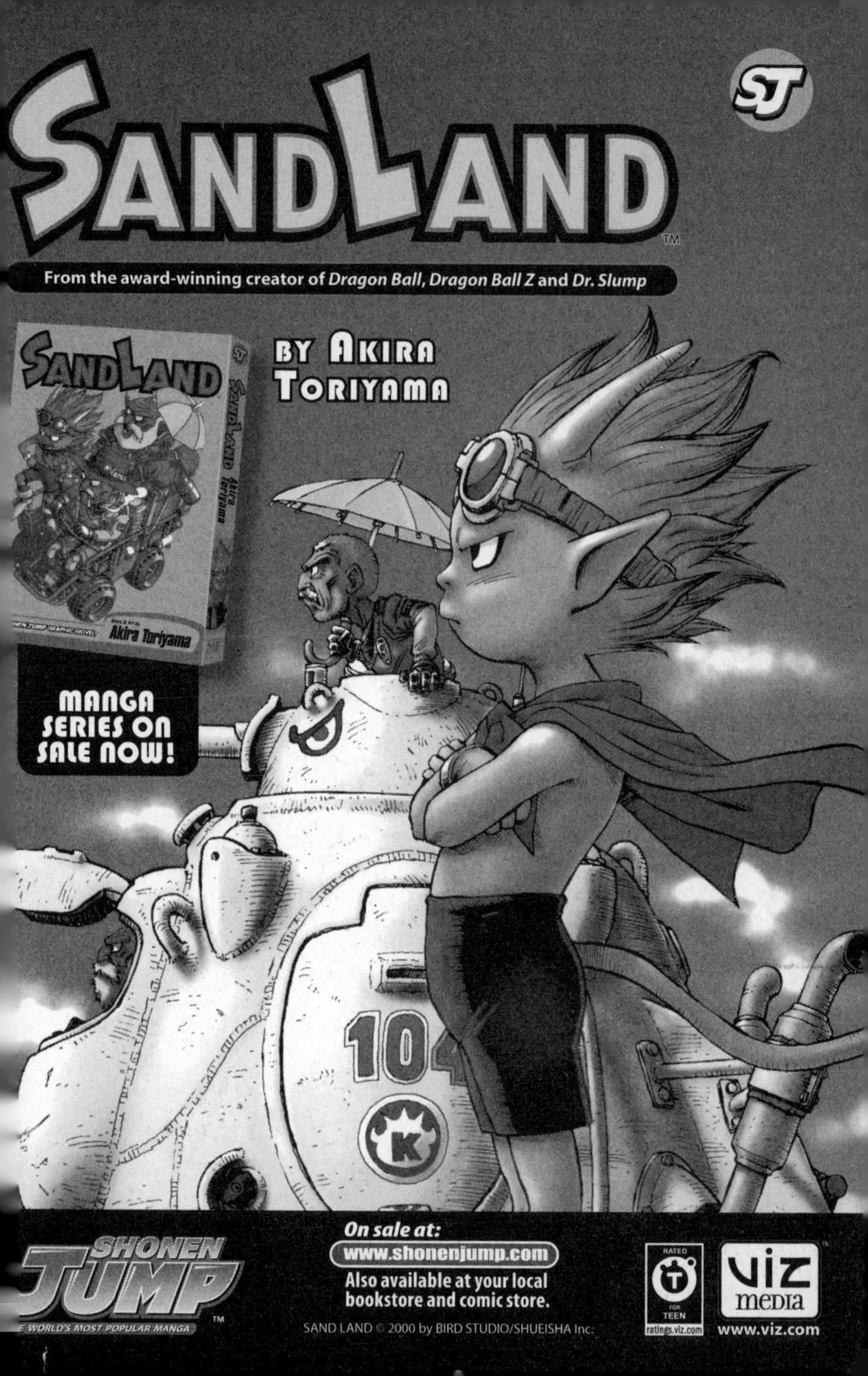
SJ
SANDLAND™
From the award-winning creator of Dragon Ball, Dragon Ball Z and Dr. Slump
SANDLAND
Akira Toriyama
BY AKIRA TORIYAMA
MANGA SERIES ON SALE NOW!
104
SHONEN JUMP™
THE WORLD'S MOST POPULAR MANGA
On sale at:
www.shonenjump.com
Also available at your local bookstore and comic store.
SAND LAND © 2000 by BIRD STUDIO/SHUEISHA Inc.
RATED T FOR TEEN
ratings.viz.com
viz media™
www.viz.com

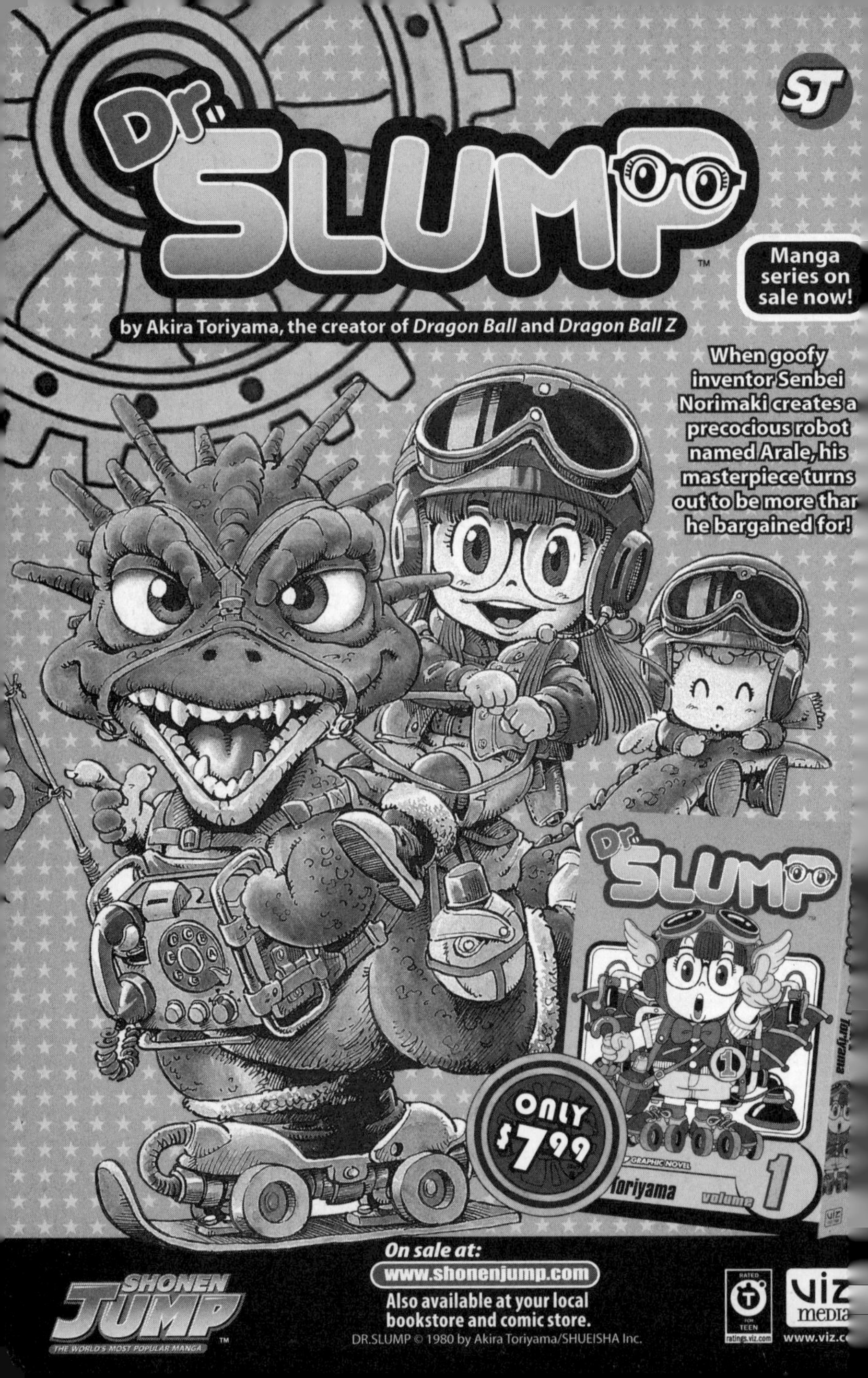
SJ
Dr. SLUMP™
Manga series on sale now!
by Akira Toriyama, the creator of *Dragon Ball* and *Dragon Ball Z*
When goofy inventor Senbei Norimaki creates a precocious robot named Arale, his masterpiece turns out to be more than he bargained for!
Dr. SLUMP™
Toriyama
GRAPHIC NOVEL
Toriyama volume 1
ONLY $7.99
On sale at:
www.shonenjump.com
Also available at your local bookstore and comic store.
DR.SLUMP © 1980 by Akira Toriyama/SHUEISHA Inc.
SHONEN JUMP™
THE WORLD'S MOST POPULAR MANGA
RATED T FOR TEEN
ratings.viz.com
VIZ media
www.viz.c

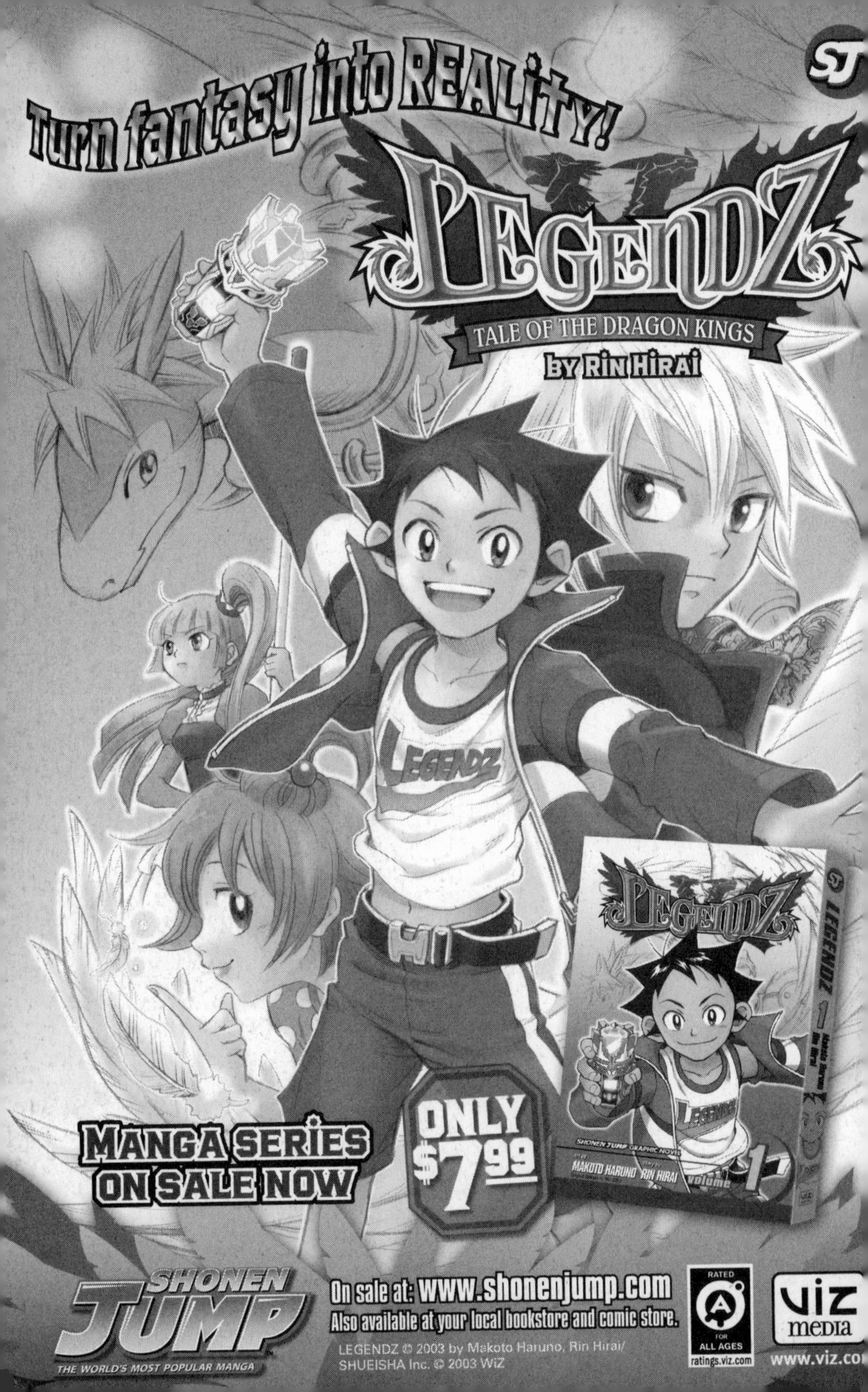

SJ
Turn fantasy into REALity!
LEGENDZ
TALE OF THE DRAGON KINGS
BY RIN HIRAI
LEGENDZ
LEGENDZ
SHONEN JUMP GRAPHIC NOVEL
MAKOTO HARUNO
RIN HIRAI
volume 1
MANGA SERIES ON SALE NOW
ONLY $7.99
SHONEN JUMP
THE WORLD'S MOST POPULAR MANGA
On sale at: www.shonenjump.com
Also available at your local bookstore and comic store.
LEGENDZ © 2003 by Makoto Haruno, Rin Hirai/ SHUEISHA Inc. © 2003 WiZ
RATED A FOR ALL AGES
ratings.viz.com
VIZ media
www.viz.co

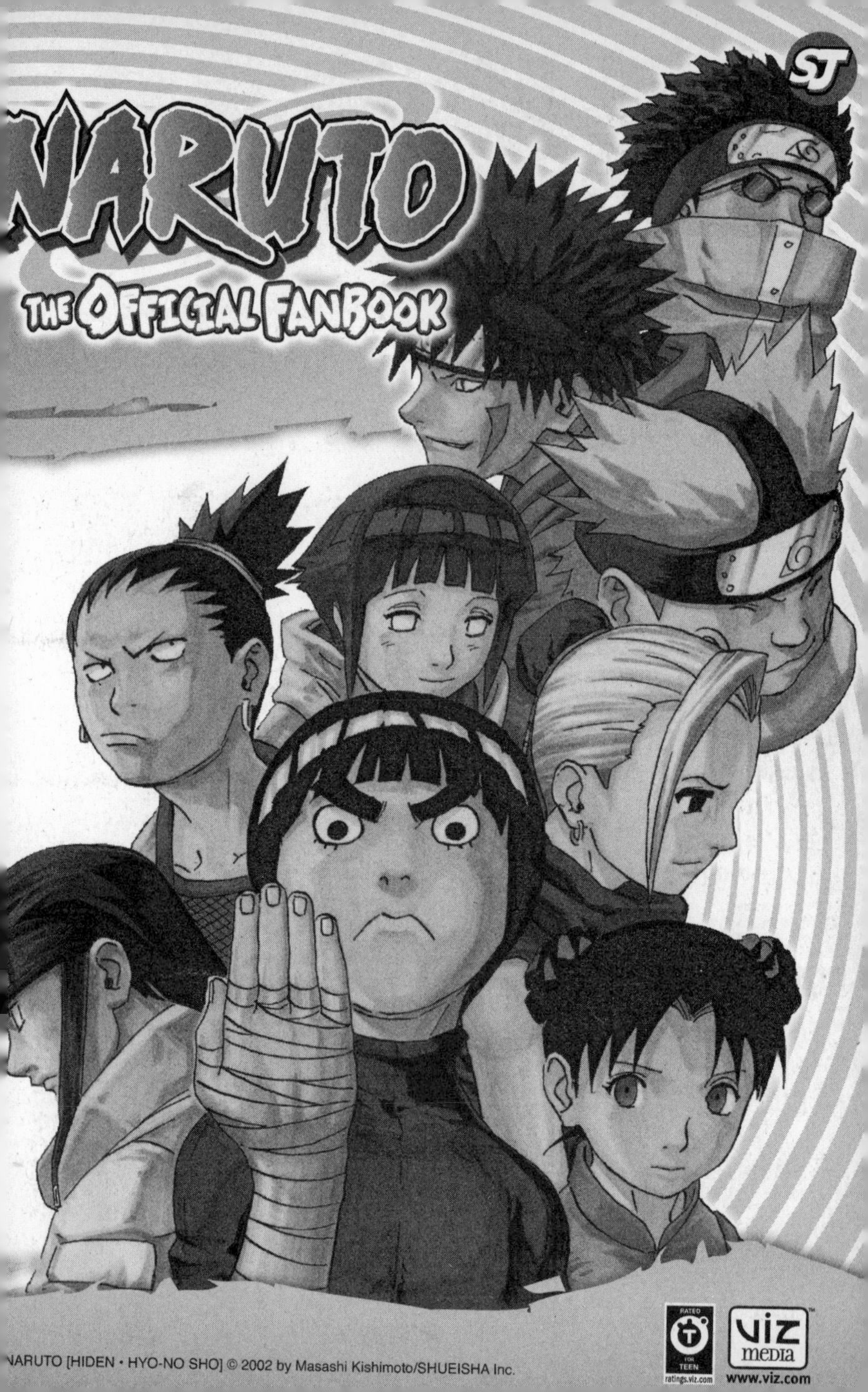
SJ
NARUTO
THE OFFICIAL FANBOOK
RATED T TEEN
ratings.viz.com
VIZ media
www.viz.com

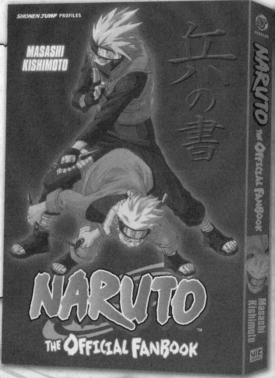

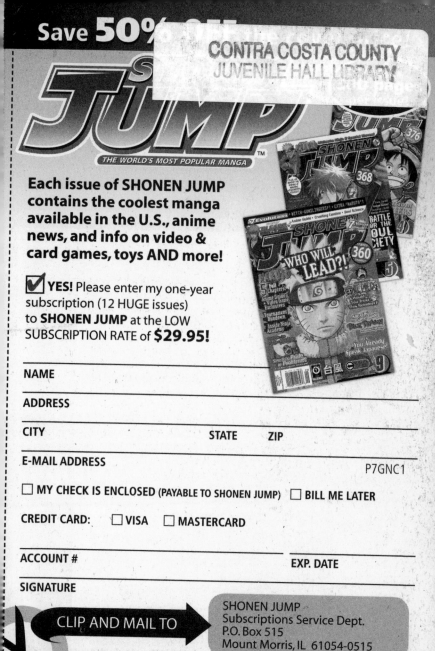

Save **50%** OFF

S JUMP

THE WORLD'S MOST POPULAR MANGA

Each issue of SHONEN JUMP contains the coolest manga available in the U.S., anime news, and info on video & card games, toys AND more!

☑ **YES!** Please enter my one-year subscription (12 HUGE issues) to **SHONEN JUMP** at the LOW SUBSCRIPTION RATE of **$29.95!**

NAME

ADDRESS

CITY   STATE   ZIP

E-MAIL ADDRESS   P7GNC1

☐ MY CHECK IS ENCLOSED (PAYABLE TO SHONEN JUMP)   ☐ BILL ME LATER

CREDIT CARD: ☐ VISA   ☐ MASTERCARD

ACCOUNT #   EXP. DATE

SIGNATURE

CLIP AND MAIL TO ➤

SHONEN JUMP
Subscriptions Service Dept.
P.O. Box 515
Mount Morris, IL 61054-0515

Make checks payable to: **SHONEN JUMP**. Canada price for 12 issues: $41.95 USD, including GST, HST and QST. US/CAN orders only. Allow 6-8 weeks for delivery.

BLEACH © 2001 by Tite Kubo/SHUEISHA Inc. NARUTO © 1999 by Masashi Kishimoto/SHUEISHA Inc.
ONE PIECE © 1997 by Eiichiro Oda/SHUEISHA Inc.

RATED
T
FOR
TEEN
ratings.viz.com